D0779798

SHADOWS OF DECEIT . . .

Near Appeldoorn a large bridge was blown sky high. The incident was highly publicized, but no mention was made that it was an old, abandoned structure—or that the perpetrators were German soldiers disguised as resistance men. At Arnhem and elsewhere around The Netherlands, railroad sidetracks no longer in use were destroyed by explosives, and worn-out boxcars were blown to smithereens. The "resistance" received full "credit" in Dutch newspapers. Hermann Giskes saw to that. To unknowing observers it appeared that organized underground groups were raising merry hell with the German war effort all over Holland . . .

WITHDRAWN

Jove Books by William B. Breuer

DROP ZONE SICILY
DEVIL BOATS: THE PT WAR AGAINST JAPAN
OPERATION DRAGOON
THE SECRET WAR WITH GERMANY

THE SECRET WAR WITH GERMANY

DECEPTION, ESPIONAGE, AND DIRTY TRICKS 1939–1945

WILLIAM B. BREUER

CALVIN T. RYAN LIBRARY
U. OF NEBRASKA AT KEARNEY

JOVE BOOKS, NEW YORK

This Jove book contains the complete
text of the original hardcover edition.
It has been completely reset in a typeface
designed for easy reading, and was printed
from new film.

THE SECRET WAR WITH GERMANY

A Jove Book / published by arrangement with
Presidio Press

PRINTING HISTORY
Presidio Press edition published 1988
Jove edition / May 1989

All rights reserved.
Copyright © 1988 by William B. Breuer.
This book may not be reproduced in whole
or in part, by mimeograph or any other means,
without permission. For information address:
Presidio Press, 31 Pamaron Way,
Novato, California 94947.

ISBN: 0-515-10013-7

Jove Books are published by The Berkley Publishing Group,
200 Madison Avenue, New York, New York 10016.
The name "JOVE" and the "J" logo
are trademarks belonging to Jove Publications, Inc.

PRINTED IN THE UNITED STATES OF AMERICA

10 9 8 7 6 5 4 3 2 1

Dedicated to the memory of
SIR WINSTON LEONARD SPENCER CHURCHILL
the British bulldog whose
courage, resolve and vision
served as a beacon in the darkness
for his countrymen and for the free
world when England stood alone and
defiant against the mightiest war
machine that history had known

There are many kinds of maneuvres in war, some only of which take place on the battlefield. There are maneuvres on the flank or rear. There are maneuvres in time, in diplomacy, in mechanics, in psychology; all of which are removed from the battlefield, but react often decisively upon it, and the object of all is to find easier ways, other than sheer slaughter, of achieving the main purpose.

—WINSTON CHURCHILL

The English Channel No-Man's-Sea (U.S. Navy)

CONTENTS

ACKNOWLEDGMENTS

It is accurate to state that *The Secret War With Germany* has been evolving over four decades. Since the conclusion of World War II, I have studied informally the undercover war-within-a-war. During that period, I have collected a mass of pertinent information from books by qualified authors, from official histories and documents, from newspapers and magazines, from interviews with many military and civilian participants, through conversations and exchange of correspondence with historians on both sides of the Atlantic, and from visits to the locales in Europe where many of the events in this book had taken place.

If anyone were to try to tell the entire fascinating story of the shadow war with Adolf Hitler's regime, he would have to write a carload of books. Even then the story would be incomplete, for countless tales of intrigue, hoaxes, and secret machinations have been lost in the fog of war or they will forever remain secret because of a wide spectrum of complex reasons.

Among those who have been of significant help in piecing together this book (by no means is the list all-inclusive) are British radar wizard Professor Reginald V. Jones, General John D. Frost (Ret.), Major Keith H. M. O'Kelly (Ret.), Airborne Forces Museum curator Major G. G. Norton (Ret.) and Mrs. Hilary Roberts and her dedicated associates at the Imperial War Museum, London.

Most helpful also were a number of United States military officers who had special knowledge of and/or were involved in the secret war: Colonel Aaron Bank (Ret.), Lieutenant General William P. Yarborough (Ret.), Lieutenant General James M.

Gavin (Ret.), and Rear Admiral John D. Bulkeley. Thanks are also expressed to the staff of the United States Army Military History Institute, Carlisle Barracks, Pennsylvania.

The author is indebted to Jack Nissenthall (now Nissen), of Toronto, Canada, "The Mad Scientist of Dieppe," for his insights into that intriguing operation; to military buff Keith Rose of Dayton, Ohio, and to Jim Phillips of Phillips Publications.

A special vote of gratitude is given to the energetic and talented ladies at Willowbrook (Illinois) Library, particularly those in the reference department, who literally scoured sources nationwide to locate crucial information: Debbie Wordinger, Mary Nordstrom, Jane Bykowski, Karen Merritt, Bayneeta Freeland, Lenore Schacht and Paras Patel.

The author was fortunate to have available the consummate professionalism and talents of Mrs. Adele Horwitz, editor-in-chief, and her associates at Presidio Press.

Finally appreciation goes to those on both sides of the Atlantic (in the United States, in Great Britain, in West Germany, and in Holland) who must remain anonymous but who contributed heavily to the creation of this book.

WILLIAM B.BREUER
Willowbrook, Illinois
January 1987

INTRODUCTION

Force and fraud have been recognized as the two cardinal virtues of war since the Chinese conqueror Sun Tzu recorded his military theories in 550 B.C.: "Undermine the enemy first, then his army will fall to you. Subvert him, attack his morale, strike at his economy, corrupt him. Sow internal discord among his leaders, destroy him without fighting him."

During World War II, both the Western Allies (particularly the British, later the Americans) and the Germans blended these ancient precepts with modern technology to fight a secret war of devious machinations, as each side sought the slight edge that could mean the difference between victory and defeat.

Tens of thousands of shadow warriors on both sides were involved in what Winston Churchill called the sinister touches of legerdemain. Their principal weapons were intrigue, deceit, fakery, stealth, skullduggery, and periodic mayhem. No holds were barred. No scheme was too brutal or immoral. The survival of nations was at stake.

Operation Himmler

On the morning of August 22, 1939, inhabitants of the picturesque sixteenth-century Bavarian village of Berchtesgaden watched with apprehension and curiosity as a stream of staff cars carrying top generals and admirals of the *Wehrmacht* (armed forces) rolled along the cobblestone streets and onto a road climbing sharply up towering Kehlstein Mountain. The villagers knew that a momentous event was brewing, for in recent months, war clouds, black and ominous, had been gathering over Europe.

Halfway up Kehlstein Mountain the procession halted at two massive metal doors guarded by black-uniformed, heavily armed men of the elite *Schutzstaffel* (SS). The doors swung open, and the cars drove through a tunnel to an underground garage where the brass alighted and strolled a short distance to an elevator whose shaft had been blasted out of solid rock. Spacious, with a gold-plated gate, telephones, expensive leather chairs, and plush red carpeting, the elevator whisked the generals and admirals upward, and when the doors opened they were in Berghof, Fuehrer Adolf Hitler's rustic retreat on the Obersalzberg, 6,208 feet above Berchtesgaden.

As was his custom, the 50-year-old, black-haired fuehrer, absolute master of eighty million Germans, kept his military chiefs cooling their heels in an anteroom. In guarded tones they speculated over their being summoned to Berghof. Was Hitler planning another strong-arm venture? In 1938 the fuehrer, against the advice of his generals, had sent his booted legions to take over Austria, and in March 1939 the Wehrmacht overran defenseless Czechoslovakia. Both takeovers had been achieved with hardly a shot being fired.

A few days after the plunder of Czechoslovakia, England and France had announced that they would spring to the aid of Poland should she be attacked. Undaunted, Adolf Hitler, at a gigantic rally of Nazi Party faithful in Berlin in April 1939, had thundered to the wildly cheering audience: "Conquest is not only a right but a duty."

Thirty minutes after their arrival, the generals and admirals were ushered into Berghof's 50-by-60-foot living room, where each was greeted warmly by Hitler. During World War I, the fuehrer had served for four years as an infantry corporal in the muddy trenches of France, where he had been wounded and decorated for gallantry. Just over two decades later, without benefit of university or military-staff training, he was supreme commander of German armed forces.

As the Wehrmacht officers sank into the plush, oversized chairs surrounded by large oil paintings, ornate tapestries, and classic statuary, a hushed air of expectancy fell over the room as the fuehrer prepared to speak. Unbeknownst to Hitler, in his audience were five generals and an admiral who were active in the *Schwarze Kapelle* (Black Orchestra), a small, tightly knit group of German military officers, government officials, and civic leaders who for several years had been conspiring to overthrow (or assassinate) the fuehrer and destroy his Nazi regime. Hitler, the conspirators were convinced, was taking Germany hell-bent down the road to destruction.

The fuehrer got right to the point. "There probably will never again be a man with more authority than I have," he declared. "My existence is therefore a factor of great value. But I can be eliminated at any time by a criminal or lunatic." Hitler paused briefly, then added: "There is no time to lose. *War must come in my lifetime!*"[1]

Then the fuehrer shocked his listeners: he had signed a Treaty of Friendship with the Soviet Union, a communist nation and, as such, a sworn archenemy of Adolf Hitler. It would be but a brief marriage of convenience. "We can now strike at the heart of Poland," Hitler stated, "as Great Britain and France will not dare to come to Poland's rescue without the aid of Russia."[2]

Now Hitler's face turned red with anger as he lashed out at the leaders of England, France, and Poland. "Our enemies are little worms," he bellowed. "I saw them at Munich. I am only afraid that at the last minute some *schweinhund* will produce a plan of mediation."[3]

The conference adjourned to the dining room for lunch. General Hermann Goering, the flabby-jowled, bombastic commander of the Luftwaffe, was in an ecstatic mood. He leaped onto a table and as the others watched disapprovingly began dancing about.

When the conference—meaning an Adolf Hitler monologue—resumed, the fuehrer dropped yet another bombshell: Poland would be invaded by 1.5 million troops and hundreds of panzers that were already massed at the frontier. Y day would be August 26 (later to be postponed to September 1). Zero hour: 4:30 A.M. Objective: the total destruction of Poland.

Hitler concluded his all-day presentation with a ringing admonition: "Have no pity! Have a brutal attitude! Eighty million [German] people must get what is their right!"[4]

The Schwarze Kapelle conspirators were shaken. The European war that they had long risked their lives and those of their families to prevent was about to erupt. As soon as he could withdraw, 53-year-old Admiral Wilhelm Canaris, a leader of the conspiracy, leaped into his car and raced for Munich. Canaris, one of the kaiser's most successful spies in World War I, was now chief of the *Abwehr*, the Third Reich's secret service, a huge apparatus with three thousand agents around the world.

For many months the admiral, a small, nervous man with an intense disposition, had been feeding a stream of reports on the military and political situation in Germany to MI-6, Great Britain's secret service. He had been trying to frighten Prime Minister Neville Chamberlain and his cabinet into taking overt action that would cause Hitler to back off from his plans for conquest.

Reaching the Hotel of the Four Seasons in Munich, the

Abwehr chief rushed to his room and scribbled on several sheets of paper a digest of Hitler's Berghof presentation. He handed the notes to Colonel Hans Oster, his Abwehr deputy and fellow conspirator, with orders to hurry the message to The Netherlands Embassy in Berlin. Reaching the Reich capital, Oster turned over the notes to the Dutch attaché, Major Gijsbertus Sas, with whom the colonel had long been friends. By noon of the next day, August 23, heads of governments in France, England, and Belgium had copies on their desks.

It was not just the Schwarze Kapelle that wanted peace. So did most of the German civilian population. In late August William L. Shirer, an American correspondent for CBS-radio, strolled the streets of Berlin and talked to scores of ordinary citizens. That night he wrote in his diary: "Everybody here is against the war. People talking openly. How can a country go into a major war with a population so dead against it?"[5]

Adolf Hitler had already pondered that question. At Berghof, he had told his military chiefs: "I shall give a propaganda cause for starting the war. Never mind if it is plausible or not. The victor will not be asked afterward if he told the truth. In starting and waging a war, it is not right that matters, but victory."[6]

Now, only hours before striking Poland, the fuehrer was ready to spring a hoax code-named Operation Himmler. It would be the most bizarre of all Nazi hoaxes and provide, at least in Hitler's mind, the needed "cold-blooded provocation" to prove to the German people (and to the world) that Poland had attacked first and that the fuehrer was unleashing his Wehrmacht in order to avenge the wrongdoing.

The idea for Operation Himmler had been provided a few weeks earlier by Major General Erich von Mannstein, the chief of staff of Army Group South, who had been supervising planning for Case White, the invasion of Poland. Mannstein suggested that the war be kicked off by a carefully orchestrated scenario. Three battalions of SS troops, all wearing Polish army uniforms, would shoot up the German countryside near the border of Poland, then vanish, permitting Hitler to announce that he was launching a counterattack against Poland. Perhaps a few dead bodies of bogus Poles could be scattered about, Mannstein's staff officers suggested.

General Mannstein's proposal was received with enthusiasm by the fuehrer, who ordered the project to be turned over to the Abwehr. Now the harried Admiral Canaris found himself walking an even slimmer tightrope, on the one hand trying to prevent war by keeping the British informed of Germany's plans and on the other, masterminding a devious and macabre charade to kick off the violence.

Canaris had to obey orders. Underlings picked 372 men from the Abwehr's own combat unit, the Brandenburg Training Company, to conduct the operation. Then the fuehrer took away the fake-provocation mission from Canaris and turned it over to Heinrich Himmler, a one-time chicken farmer who headed the SS, along with Heinrich Mueller, chief of the *Geheime Staatspolizei* (Secret State Police, or Gestapo). Himmler would carry out the scheme. Himmler and Mueller were ideally suited for the chicanery as both were proven masters of intrigue.

Because of a lack of Polish uniforms, Operation Himmler had to be reduced in size. One of Himmler's SS ruffians, Alfred Naujocks, was designated to lead the operation. Naujocks was a good choice for the job. In early 1939, shortly before Hitler's legions overran Czechoslovakia, Naujocks had been busy sneaking explosives into that country, where they were used by pro-Nazis and fifth-columnists to "create incidents." These "incidents" were designed to prove to the world that tiny Slovakia was a threat to the security of the Third Reich.

Naujocks was typical of the strange breed often attracted to the SS—a combination intellectual and gangster. He had studied at the University of Kiel, where he had hoped to obtain an engineering degree, but instead spent much of his time in brawls with communist groups. Joining the SS in 1934, Naujocks quickly came to the attention of Heinrich Himmler, who regarded the tough, resourceful young officer as one who could be entrusted to carry out unsavory projects conceived by the SS chief. Now, in late August 1939, Naujocks was preparing to implement the greatest hoax of all.

For six days Naujocks had been holed up in the town of Opeln, the staging post for launching a raid by "Polish soldiers" on the radio station at nearby Gleiwitz, a small German town near the frontier of Poland. At noon on August 31, Berlin flashed word to Naujocks to launch Operation Himmler that night.

Twelve German criminals (who were code-named Canned Goods) were taken from prison, dressed in Polish army uniforms, and given drug injections by an SS doctor sworn to secrecy. Naujocks and a few of his men also donned Polish uniforms. At 8:00 P.M. the attack party arrived at the radio station where the drugged criminals were scattered about the premises and shot to death. Naujocks and his SS men dashed into the station, fired shots into the ceiling, and a Polish-speaking German shouted defiant slogans into the radio transmitter. Then the SS men departed.[7]

Early the following morning German newspaper photographers and reporters were rushed to the Gleiwitz radio station, and hours later publications throughout the Third Reich carried gruesome pictures of the "Polish soldiers" killed by "German soldiers defending the station."

At dawn on September 1, 1939, nine hours after Hitler's "cold-blooded provocation" at Gleiwitz, five German armies, paced by swarms of shrieking Stuka dive-bombers, poured over the Polish frontier, plunged forward, and began converging on Warsaw from three sides. Unleashed was a mechanized juggernaut bristling with guns. Its speed and power and finesse would create a new word in the languages of many nations: *Blitzkrieg* (lightning war).

When Adolf Hitler curtly rejected a British ultimatum to withdraw, England and France, on September 3, declared war. That night German submarine U-30, commanded by Oberleutnant Fritz Julius Lemp, was cruising two hundred miles west of the Hebrides when, through his periscope, the skipper sighted the 13,000-ton British luxury liner *Athenia*, bound for Montreal with 1,408 passengers. The U-boat fired a torpedo into the ship, and it began sinking immediately. Among the 112 passengers who drowned, were 28 Americans.

News of the sinking of the *Athenia* reached Hitler on his plush private train taking him to Poland. The fuehrer needed a villain to blame, so he ordered Reich newspapers to identify the heinous culprit: the "devious British warmonger [Winston]

Churchill" (First Lord of the Admiralty), who had arranged to hide a powerful time bomb in the bowels of the *Athenia* in a desperate effort to discredit the Third Reich in the eyes of the world.[8]

Rounding Up the Spies

Within hours of the declaration of war, agents of MI-5 (Britain's counterespionage agency) and Scotland Yard men began fanning out over the British Isles in a mammoth roundup of German spies. The spybusters would have their hands full: there were 356 names on their Class A espionage list, plus hundreds of others suspected of spying for Hitler.

Actually, the Abwehr had 256 spies in Great Britain, many of whom had been working in deep undercover for years. Creating such a large network had been a long and tedious task. Largely responsible for the extensive espionage apparatus in Britain was Navy Captain Joachim Burghardt, who had been chief of an Abwehr outpost in Hamburg. Burly, unkempt, seemingly lethargic, Burghardt was hardly the stereotype of a spy master. But he had a keen mind, was innovative, and had an unfailing knack for attracting able and zealous officers to his staff.

Captain Burghardt had four deputies to carry out his covert plans. Captain Hilmar "Hans" Dierks, a one-time insurance salesman, was in charge of naval intelligence. Captain Wolfgang Lips, an army career officer, was responsible for ground intelligence. An expert in economic matters, Major Karl Praetorius, was charged with collecting technological data, and Captain Nikolaus Ritter who headed air intelligence. These four key operatives had been with Captain Burghardt since 1937 when the mission of establishing a spy network in Great Britain had begun in earnest.

The Abwehr espionage apparatus had been organized into two networks. One was called the R-chain, consisting of mobile agents who (before the war) moved in and out of Britain collecting intelligence on what seemed to be legitimate business. The other network was the S-chain of "silent" or "sleeper" agents—Germans, citizens of neutral nations, and British traitors who had blended into the population and everyday life. There were at least ten women in S-chain, including a pair in their fifties who worked as maids in the homes of two British admirals.

Despite his success in creating a widespread espionage ring in Great Britain, Captain Burghardt had been bounced from his Hamburg post in 1938 after having been caught in the middle of an Abwehr internal power struggle. He was replaced by Captain Herbert Wichmann, also a low-key, dedicated, and clever operative. Like Burghardt before him, Wichmann possessed a key trait for success as a spy master: an intense passion for anonymity.

As a result of the big German spy roundup in Great Britain during the first ten days of war, the espionage apparatus the Abwehr had painstakingly built up over the years was in shambles. Most Abwehr spies (or suspected spies) were hauled from their homes or places of work, but a few, seeing the handwriting on the wall and hoping to save their necks (literally), turned themselves in to authorities. One of the latter was Alfred G. Owens, a Canadian who operated his own business in London, the Owens Battery Equipment Company.

Owens, bright, devious, and energetic, was known to his Abwehr masters in Hamburg by the code-name Johnny. Captain Wichmann, at the Hamburg outpost on Sophien Terrace, regarded Johnny as the Abwehr's ace spy in Britain. Owens had reached a position of trust with the German spy master over the years by sending a regular stream of high-grade intelligence to Hamburg.

Owens, a high-living free spirit accustomed to curvaceous mistresses (he was married and had a family in Britain), expensive clothes, and fine wines, had been known to MI-6 since 1936. At that time the young businessman had approached MI-6 and offered to spy against Nazi Germany, where he often traveled on business. MI-6 gave no reply. So

Owens's "loyalties" did a flip-flop: he contacted the Abwehr and went to work for Germany spying against England. His motive was uncomplicated—financial greed to support his high style of living.

Johnny had long suspected (rightly) that MI-5 had been keeping him under surveillance. So early on September 4, one day after England declared war, he telephoned an inspector at Scotland Yard and asked the sleuth to meet him at Waterloo Station. The detective kept the rendezvous, promptly arrested the spy, and ensconced him in Wandsworth prison. This was precisely what Owens, who was playing a subtle game of poker, with his life at stake, had expected.

Now he played another trump card. He figured that if he revealed to MI-5 the location of the rooming house where he stashed his Afu radio transmitter that his captors would be appreciative and release him. MI-5 recovered the Afu, but they displayed no sign of benevolence. To the contrary, Johnny now found himself confronted with the specter of a hangman's noose.

But there was a way out, his MI-5 captors told Johnny. He could become a double-agent and furnish misleading information to the Germans.

Owens's transmitter was brought to his cell, and on September 6, with MI-5 agents hovering over him, Johnny radioed Hamburg the weather information his Abwehr controllers had asked for as a high priority. The false data was accepted as authentic by Hamburg, as MI-5 had based the information on facts it knew were available to the Germans. There was good reason for the Abwehr's urgency. General Hermann Goering and Hitler were toying with the idea of a massive bombing raid on London.

Captain Wichmann in Hamburg was delighted with Johnny's detailed report and did not suspect that his ace spy had been "turned." Mi-5 operatives were delighted too—they had apparently hoodwinked the Germans in this first wartime duel of wits. Owens (code-named Snow by the British) was the most elated of all. In one fell swoop he had saved his own neck and ingratiated himself with both his British and German masters.

Snow was released from Wandsworth the next day and permitted to resume his role as a seemingly hardworking

London businessman. He would prove to be an intelligence bonanza for the British in the months to come, continuing to send fake, misleading information to an unsuspecting Abwehr. It would be through instructions dispatched to Snow by Hamburg that MI-5 would be able to intercept and arrest scores of German spies stumbling into England.

During these frantic early weeks of the war, when the British dragnet was hauling in large numbers of German agents, a similar scenario was unfolding in the Third Reich. A special branch of Abwehr, known as IIIF, was responsible for destroying the extensive British espionage apparatus in Germany, one that had sprouted its roots six years earlier.

Back in 1934 the British Secret Intelligence Service (S.I.S., later to become MI-6) had been headed by Admiral Hugh Sinclair, who delegated day-by-day operations to a pair of colonels, Valentine Vivian and Claude Dansey. The colonels disliked each other intensely, and finally Dansey arranged for an assignment in Switzerland to get away from Vivian. This suited Admiral Sinclair fine, as he had become involved in several disputes with the irascible, sharp-tongued Colonel Dansey.

As if to upstage Colonel Vivian from afar, Dansey, acting on his own, organized a remarkable network of spies in Germany, with satellite groups in Belgium, Austria, and The Netherlands. Bred on cloak-and-dagger connivances, Dansey attached a succinct name to his network: Z.

Z was organized into scores of independent groups, each with its own agents, codes, couriers, and missions. Often a Z ring did not know that another Z ring was operating in its territory. Dansey's growing espionage apparatus meant that the British had competing networks operating on the Continent. The original one, supervised by Colonel Vivian, consisted of S.I.S. stations in capitals surrounding Germany: Brussels, The Hague, Vienna, Copenhagen, and others. Vivian's posts were housed in the various embassies under the facade of Passport Control Offices, and the S.I.S. chief in each capital was outwardly the Passport Control Officer. From these outposts spies were recruited to work against Germany.

As war clouds gathered over Europe in August 1939, Captain Traugott Protze, the IIIF chief, was confident that he could rapidly wipe out the spy network within the Reich once hostilities erupted. He had already penetrated the British espionage outpost in The Hague.

One of Protze's pipelines into The Hague's spy station was Folkert Van Koutrik, a young Dutchman who for two years had been spying against the German espionage network in Holland. Just before war had broken out, Van Koutrik became dissatisfied with the amount of money being paid him by the British, so he approached Captain Protze and agreed to spy for the Germans against the British—for double the money he was getting from the English secret service.

But Van Koutrik hated to give up his British pay, so he spied for both sides. Then his loyalties tilted toward the Germans (with their much higher pay), and the Dutchman began tipping off Protze to each British spy being slipped into the Third Reich from The Hague. Inside Germany the Gestapo and Abwehr kept tabs on these British agents and their contacts, and as soon as Hitler went to war with England, the German agencies swooped down on the spies.

However, Captain Protze's dragnet had not scooped up all the spies in the Reich. But an Englishman, John "Jack" Cooper, fingered the remainder of the agents. Cooper had been a trusted aide to a top officer at the British secret outpost in The Hague and had been fired for stealing its funds. He had had access to secret files and used that knowledge to sell out his country to Nazi Germany—for a modest amount of Abwehr gold.

As a result of the treachery of Van Koutrik and Cooper, Captain Protze and his IIIF branch wiped out the remarkable British espionage network in Germany within thirty days.

Meanwhile, the German blitzkrieg had demolished the 800,000-man, poorly equipped Polish army, whose soldiers fought with great gallantry, in only twenty-seven days. Adolf Hitler, sneered at behind his back by many of his generals as the Bohemian Corporal, had directed the Wehrmacht to a spectacular victory, one that in his mind rivaled the greatest triumphs of his Teutonic idol, Frederick the Great.

Hardly had the smoke of battle cleared from tortured Poland than the fuehrer, on October 9, directed that *Fall Gelb* (Case

Yellow)—an invasion of France, Belgium, and The Netherlands—be launched during the first half of November, barely a month away. Colonel Hans Oster, Canaris's Abwehr deputy, quickly tipped off the Allies through his friend Major Gijsbertus Sas, the Dutch military attaché in Berlin. Sas and Oster often dined together at the German colonel's home in the prestigious suburb of Zehlendorf, so no suspicion would be aroused if prying eyes spotted the pair together.

Hans Oster held a curious position in the Abwehr. He and his boss, Admiral Canaris, did not like each other. Canaris had no interest in human relationships, but found companionship in his pair of dachshunds. Oster, for his part, had no gift for cloak-and-dagger work and little interest in secret connivances, except insofar as he could use them to further his all-consuming passion—ridding Germany of Adolf Hitler.

Canaris had created an Abwehr post for Oster, which placed the entire apparatus of the agency at the colonel's disposal, but the two men were hardly brothers-in-arms in the conspiratorial plot against the fuehrer. They were different in both character and in viewpoint. Canaris was a firm advocate of disposing of Hitler through constitutional and morally acceptable means, while Oster was prepared to go to any length to eliminate the fuehrer and his Nazi cronies.[1]

Canaris was impassioned in his hatred of Hitler and Nazism and never doubted that Germany would eventually lose the war and be destroyed in the process. Each Wehrmacht triumph, Canaris was convinced, would merely prolong the holocaust and multiply the woes of the people.

Y day for the German onslaught in the West was set for November 12, a fact Colonel Oster relayed promptly to Dutch Major Sas. Four days prior to the attack, Adolf Hitler delivered a fire-and-brimstone speech to members of the Nazi Old Guard (those who had backed the fuehrer ever since his early days in politics) at *Buergerbräukeller* (beer cellar) in Munich. The fuehrer gave a much shorter talk than was customary and rapidly left the cellar. Moments later a bomb planted near the speaker's platform exploded, killing seven and wounding sixty-three of the Nazi faithful.

The attempt to murder Adolf Hitler was providential to the warlord on the eve of his sending the Wehrmacht into battle in the West, and Josef Goebbels, Hitler's propaganda genius, set about gaining maximum returns from the episode. The *Voelkischer Beobachter* carried blaring headlines pointing out the culprit: the British secret service. As Goebbels had expected, the inflammatory media blitz throughout the Reich whipped up intense hatred for the British and rallied German public opinion to the fuehrer's side.

Goebbels was not concerned over the fact that anti-Hitler Germans may have been responsible for the bomb. A propaganda bonanza had been tossed into his lap, and he intended to make the most of it. What was needed was "proof" that the British secret service had pulled off the murderous stunt.[2]

Adolf Hitler was seething with rage. Hardly had the smoke cleared from the Buergerbräukeller before he phoned Heinrich Himmler and demanded that the SS chief expose the British as the assassins. Himmler promptly contacted a rising star in his SS, 28-year-old Walter Schellenberg, at Duesseldorf and gave him a bizarre mission. By direct order of the fuehrer, Himmler declared, Schellenberg was to slip into Holland and kidnap a pair of British secret service agents with whom Schellenberg had been in covert contact.

It was a tall order. But Himmler had confidence in Schellenberg, whose character blended an intellectuality with the instincts and morals of a gangster—the precise traits Himmler wanted in his SS leaders.

Since the outbreak of war ten weeks earlier, Schellenberg had been sneaking into Holland in civilian clothes to meet secretly with the pair of British agents who were now his abduction targets, Captain R. Henry Stevens and Captain S. Payne Best. On these incursions into Dutch territory, the SS officer posed as Major Schaemmel, a staff officer in the *Oberkommando der Wehrmacht* (OKW, the high command). Knowing that the British secret service would check out his assumed identity, Schellenberg took the name and rank of an actual officer at OKW. Bright and articulate, Schellenberg had convinced Stevens and Best that he was the emissary of a group of German generals plotting to overthrow the fuehrer.

Best and Stevens provided Schellenberg with a radio receiver and transmitter so he could establish contact with the British secret service in London. What the conspirators wanted, "Major Schaemmel" stressed, were assurances from the British government that it would deal fairly with a new anti-Nazi regime.

Both sides had hoped to gain from the cat-and-mouse game in Holland. Heinrich Himmler and Hitler had been hearing rumors that some German generals were conspiring against the fuehrer, and the SS chief was trying to unmask them. The British had been attempting to learn the names of the conspiring Wehrmacht generals in order to assist them. Now Hitler and Himmler had a new objective: kidnap the pair of British secret service agents and bring them into the Third Reich to stand trial for the Munich bomb-blast "murders."

Alfred Naujocks, the SS thug who had carried out the fake Polish attack on the Gleiwitz radio station, now got into the act. He rounded up twelve heavily armed German secret police who were to assist Schellenberg in the kidnapping.

At 4:00 P.M. on November 9, less than twenty hours after the bomb had exploded in the Buergerbräukeller, Walter Schellenberg was sipping wine on the terrace of a small cafe in Venlo, The Netherlands, a stone's throw from the German border. He was there to keep an appointment with Henry Stevens and Steven P. "Payne" Best. The two British agents drove up, parked their car behind the cafe, then got out to be greeted by a hail of bullets fired by Naujocks and his men. A Dutch intelligence officer named Klop, who was with Stevens and Best, was killed by a bullet through the head. Naujocks's men overpowered the British agents and pitched them, along with the dead Klop, into a car, then headed hell-bent for the nearby German border and on into the Reich. For unknown reasons the "trial" of Best and Stevens would never be held.[3]

His fury over the bomb blast cooled, Adolf Hitler had other matters on his mind: the destruction of his enemies in the West. The weather had been bad, however, and the November 12 Y day had to be postponed. When the weather continued to be especially nasty that fall, winter, and early spring of 1939 and 1940, Hitler was forced to cancel one Y day after the other—fourteen of them in all. Each time Colonel Hans Oster provided the Allies with the latest target date, but as time went by and no attack materialized, London lost confidence in the Schwarze Kapelle activist. Some in MI-6 became convinced that Oster was perpetrating a psychological warfare hoax against the British at the behest of the fuehrer.

For eight months now on the Western Front, the French and British on one side and the Germans on the other had coexisted peacefully. Hardly a shot had been fired. World newspapers labeled it the Sitzkrieg or the Phony War. Belgium, The Netherlands, and Luxembourg remained neutral. Then on April 2, 1940, Hitler invaded Denmark and Norway, and within twenty-four hours the Wehrmacht occupied tiny Denmark. Mountainous Norway proved to be a tougher nut to crack, but in a few weeks the Nazi warlord would be in control there also.

Now Hitler was ready to unleash the full power of the Wehrmacht against the Western Allies.

A Ghost Army Arises

There had been a mountain of evidence that Adolf Hitler was ready to strike on the Western Front. In early May 1940 persistent warnings had come to the Allies from the Schwarze Kapelle and anti-Nazi sources in the Vatican. Turned spies working for the French had pilfered documents that designated the objectives of Case Yellow. A few months earlier the tactical plan for the German offensive in the West had fallen into the hands of the Belgian general staff when a Luftwaffe plane was forced down in Belgium because of bad weather. French and British air reconnaissance reported heavy concentrations of troops and panzers just behind the Reich frontier. Yet in one of history's most stunning failures to evaluate and respond to a mass of intelligence, the French and British high commands dawdled.

On the night of May 9, a few hundred miles from the powder keg along the western borders of the Reich, old friends Colonel Hans Oster and the Dutch military attaché Gijsbertus Sas were dining at Oster's home. It would be their last meal together. Oster was both depressed and furious. He told Major Sas that Hitler earlier that evening had given the final order to launch the offensive in the West. There were 2.5 million German troops, formed into 102 divisions, 9 of them armored and 6 motorized, massed along the French, Belgian, and Dutch borders. Zero hour would be 3:30 A.M. the next day, May 10.

After dinner Colonel Oster drove to OKW headquarters to

see if there had been a change in plans. There had been none: the attack was on. Returning to his home, Oster exclaimed to Sas, "The swine has gone to the Western Front." The "swine" was Adolf Hitler.

Sas telephoned the Belgian military attaché in Berlin, then rushed to his own embassy. He placed a call to Dutch military headquarters in The Hague, and by means of a prearranged code, told his superiors, "Tomorrow at dawn! Hold tight!"[1]

A few hours after Major Sas spread the alarm, a cavalcade of blacked-out vehicles rolled up to a huge concrete bunker located in a heavily forested mountaintop south of the ancient German city of Aachen. It was 3:00 A.M. on Y day for Case Yellow. Code-named *Felsennest* (Aerie on the Cliffs), this structure would be Adolf Hitler's command post for directing the offensive.

Only thirty minutes after the Nazi warlord had arrived, swarms of screeching Stukas began pounding targets in neutral Belgium and The Netherlands. Two hours later German infantry and panzers surged over the frontier. Despite the flood of warnings received by the Allied command, the Wehrmacht gained total surprise all along the line.[2]

Across the English Channel early on that Y day morning, 70-year-old Neville Chamberlain, who for two years had been trying to appease Adolf Hitler, resigned as prime minister. A few hours later King George VI summoned Churchill to Buckingham Palace and asked him to take over the reins of government, an offer the First Lord of the Admiralty accepted eagerly. The two men held a brief discussion of the bleak war picture, kissed hands, and Churchill, in a series of bows, withdrew.

Churchill plunged into his new duties with customary vigor, but there was nothing he could do about the Allied catastrophe unfolding across the Channel. In only three weeks the German juggernaut forced The Netherlands and Belgium to surrender, shattered the once-vaunted French army, and trapped the British Expeditionary Force at the small Channel port of Dunkirk. On May 27, under a pounding by the Luftwaffe, some 850 vessels of all shapes and sizes began evacuating British soldiers to the small southern ports of Margate, Dover, and Ramsgate. The desperate operation was code-named Dynamo.

On June 5, less than one month after the fuehrer had struck in the West, Prime Minister Churchill was in his bombproof command post deep beneath the pavement at Storey's Gate in London. Drawing on a long, black cigar and peering through eyeglasses resting near the tip of his nose, Churchill was scanning reports on Operation Dynamo. On the previous day the last waterlogged soldier had been snatched off the fire-swept Dunkirk beaches. The prime minister was stunned.

Dynamo had brought out 337,131 men of the British Expeditionary Force that had been sent to France to whip Adolf Hitler, but coming out with the Dunkirk refugees were only 25 of 600 tanks, 12 artillery pieces, and a handful of machine guns. Left behind along the French coast were 120,000 vehicles, 2,300 artillery pieces and mortars, 8,000 Bren guns, 90,000 rifles, and 7,000 tons of ammunition. Great Britain had suffered a shocking military disaster, one of the worst in her history.[3]

On June 26, three weeks after the British had fled Dunkirk, Hitler was making a sentimental pilgrimage to the old battle-fields on the border of northern France where he had fought as an infantry corporal more than two decades earlier—Ypres, Fromelles, Messines, and Langemarck. The fuehrer was on a victory honeymoon: France had surrendered, and he reigned as overlord of an empire stretching from the Arctic Circle to the Pyrenees at the Spanish border. With Hitler on the tour was Max Asmann, who had been the fuehrer's sergeant in World War I. As the car passed through Peperinge, Asmann pointed out that Dunkirk was only a few miles away, and Hitler agreed to a detour.

Forty minutes later the conquering warlord was standing at the water's edge. On all sides were twisted, blackened skeletons of hundreds of vehicles, grim evidence of the debacle that had befallen Great Britain. The fuehrer peered intently toward the horizon of the Strait of Dover, as though he were trying to see the famed White Cliffs along England's coast, a bare thirty miles away.

When planning the blitzkrieg in the West, Hitler had given no thought to invading England. But now with a hapless Great

Britain floundering, the fuehrer began toying with the idea of leaping the English Channel and bringing that nation to her knees. The fuehrer had no way of knowing that at that moment, on the sands of Dunkirk, he was as close to the British Isles as he would ever venture.

In late June 1940 England was an island under siege. She stood alone against the awesome threat of the Wehrmacht poised on the far side of the Channel. Contingency plans had been drawn up to evacuate the royal family and the government to Canada, to which some eighteen hundred million pounds sterling worth of gold ingots had already been shipped secretly on the cruiser HMS *Emerald*. Unprepared for total war, Britain reeled in tumult and confusion.

Rumors of the most fantastic nature swept the British Isles. In the invasion of the Low Countries, German paratroopers had landed dressed as nuns—or so rumor had it. Now nuns were suspect, and ecclesiastics in Britain ventured out only for necessities. The BBC stoked the mania fires by reporting that German parachutists dropping into England wearing other than German uniforms were to be shot immediately. To guard against paratroopers, all road signs were taken down, and in towns and villages, street names, railroad station names, and other identifying markings were removed.

In order to thwart Luftwaffe bombers, the government ordered that the roofs of London's red double-decker buses be painted battleship gray to make it more difficult for them to be seen from the air. The edict implied incredible skill on the part of German pilots and bombardiers and conveyed the belief that the Luftwaffe had peculiar notions as to what constituted a worthwhile bombing target.

Having heard tales of fifth columnists and spies paving the way for the Wehrmacht in Belgium, The Netherlands, and France, the people of Great Britain grew **highly** suspicious. Constabularies were flooded with reports of "odd-acting strangers" and of men who "looked German." "Queer" conversations overheard in pubs were promptly reported to police. Civilians grew panicky. They persisted in seeing all sorts of strange happenings: smoke signals, flashing lights, even unidentified men signaling in trees (who turned out to be telephone linemen).

Directives flew from government bureaucracies. Flying kites or balloons was forbidden. Civilians were admonished in the sternest tone never to shoot carrier pigeons, leaving unanswered why they would want to shoot a carrier pigeon or how a carrier pigeon could be distinguished in flight from any other pigeon.

To help repel the looming invasion and to guard against German paratroopers, one million Britishers, mainly boys and old men, rushed to join the Home Guard. They wore armbands in lieu of uniforms. For lack of anything better, they were armed with theatrical sabers, axes, weighted golf clubs, bludgeons, pitchforks, assegais (Berber spears), cutlasses, kukris (Gurkha knives), ancient rifles, and sporting shotguns. Guardsmen without even these weapons were instructed to carry packets of pepper and to hurl the stinging spice in the eyes of German soldiers.

A motley collection of men made up the Home Guard. London newspapers labeled them "Parashots." Retired generals, some quite elderly, resplendent in old dress uniforms dripping with decorations, took their places in the ranks as privates. One Sussex company had six former generals serving as corporals and privates. The Bishop of Truro was roundly cheered in the House of Lords when he disclosed that he had been going out nightly on patrols with his Home Guard unit.

It appeared that the Nazis considered the Home Guard to be a real threat to their ambitions. In Hamburg and Bremen Propaganda Minister Josef Goebbels's radio stations howled against its mobilization as "a wanton violation of international law."

As the Home Guard diligently patrolled and watched over bridges, railroads, and public utilities, millions of Britishers had developed the habit of listening to Lord Haw-Haw over Radio Berlin. Lord Haw-Haw was a notorious traitor who had left England for Germany just prior to the outbreak of war and had begun propaganda broadcasts for Goebbels. His real name was William Joyce. Most Britishers paid no attention to Lord Haw-Haw's Nazi nonsense; they tuned him in for amusement. But many were fascinated with the German propagandist's intimate knowledge of what was taking place in the British Isles. Haw-Haw would even report that a church-steeple clock in a specified village stopped at a certain time when a German bomb exploded near it. Townspeople in the village concerned knew the statement was a lie, but millions of others in the British Isles accepted it as gospel.

One Lord Haw-Haw listener, Anna Wolkoff, was furious over the fact that Englishmen were laughing at the broadcaster's Nazi propaganda. Wolkoff, daughter of a one-time admiral in the Royal Russian Navy, had long been an ardent admirer of Adolf Hitler and his Nazi ideals. Joyce's communications problem, Wolkoff was convinced, was that as an Irishman he did not comprehend the true concerns of the British people. If only Haw-Haw could penetrate the minds of the British people, the invading German army would be received in a much more cooperative manner.

Wolkoff, who had been engaged in a torrid love affair with a member of Parliament, Captain Archibald Ramsay, was determined to take action to remedy Lord Haw-Haw's shortcomings. The attractive (seductive, many said) Anna Wolkoff sat down and penned Lord Haw-Haw a letter of advice, which was to be shuttled to him by a clandestine source: "Stick to plutocracy. Avoid Kind." (Meaning, aim your verbal volleys at the rich and privileged; stop slurring the royal family, which only made English men and women mad.) That was sound advice. Then Wolkoff let her emotions take over and proved that she was as ignorant about attitudes of the British people as was Lord Haw-Haw. "*Kriegshetze* [war fever] only among the Blimps [the rich and powerful]. Workers fed up. Wives more so. Troops not keen. Churchill not popular. . . . ."

Unbeknownst to Anna Wolkoff, agents of MI-5 had long been hawking her every move. They intercepted her letter to Lord Haw-Haw, and after examining it let it proceed to its intended recipient in Germany. MI-5 concluded that Haw-Haw would be more harmed than aided by the would-be Mata Hari's words of advice. Then British secret service agents conducted a sweeping roundup of thirty-three activists in the pro-Nazi British Union of Fascists. Among those caught in the dragnet were Wolkoff and her lover, Captain Archibald Ramsay.

* * *

During the hectic period since Dunkirk, Winston Churchill had made daily inspections of probable Wehrmacht landing beaches in southern and southeastern England. He was shocked by what he saw—or didn't see. Almost sixty miles of coastline were lightly fortified with mines and wire entanglements, but several hundred miles were unprotected. Along one 5-mile strip there were only three guns, each with four shells. Britain was nearly defenseless.

One of England's top soldiers, highly decorated, hawk-nosed General Alan Brooke, was put in charge of the southern coast after his evacuation from France. On June 26, the same day that Hitler had stood on the beach at Dunkirk, Brooke penned gloomily in his diary: "The more I see of conditions at home, the more bewildered I am over what has been going on in this country since war started [ten months earlier]. The shortage of trained men and equipment is appalling. . . . The ghastly part is that we have only a few weeks before the *boches* [invaded England]."[4]

Four days later, on June 30, spirits were high at the Oberkommando der Wehrmacht in Zossen, twenty miles outside Berlin. The generals were convinced that Churchill, hat in hand, would surface soon to seek favorable terms of surrender. General Jodl wrote in his diary: "The final victory over England is now but a question of time."[5]

Surrender to Adolf Hitler had never entered Churchill's mind, for he knew the harsh fate that would befall his countrymen under Nazi rule. But the prime minister had no way of knowing that the fuehrer had plans for subjecting England to savage brutalities. A thick compendium of instructions had been drawn up in Berlin (and approved by Hitler) to guide the German Military Government of England. Males between the ages of seventeen and forty-five were to be shipped to Germany as slave laborers. Aided by the stalwarts of the SS, British women were to be forced to produce a new race of Anglo-Germans. England's intelligentsia and Jews were to be liquidated.[6]

A former faculty dean at the University of Berlin, 31-year-old SS Colonel Franz-Alfred Six, would be the Gestapo chief in conquered Britain. Dr. Six, like Alfred Naujocks and Walter Schellenberg, had the qualities Heinrich Himmler sought in his SS and Gestapo leaders—brains, utter ruthlessness, and no scruples.

By July 1, 1940, Colonel Six had completed *die Sonderfahndungsliste, G.B.* (Special Search List, Great Britain). It contained the names, occupations, and addresses of twenty-three hundred statesmen, clergymen, educators, and "undesirables" who were to be seized at once and turned over to the Gestapo for "processing."[7] On the list were prominent editors, publishers, and reporters, including Norman Ebbutt and Douglas Reed of *The Times* of London, who when they were correspondents in Berlin infuriated Nazi bigwigs with their stories. Names were in alphabetical order. Number 49 on the list was: "Churchill, Winston Spencer, Ministerpresident, Westerham/Kent, Chartwell Manor, Amt VI." This signified that the prime minister was to be turned over to Amt VI (Foreign Intelligence).[8]

Meanwhile, Winston Churchill had reached an inescapable conclusion: if Great Britain were to survive as a nation against the threat of history's mightiest war machine, he would rapidly have to mount a campaign of subterfuge of unprecedented scope and ingenuity. The prospect of baffling and bluffing the fuehrer appealed to the prime minister's imagination and intellect.

Hardly had the dust settled on the Dunkirk debacle than Churchill began mobilizing the intellectual brains of England into a clandestine force that would number nearly one hundred thousand persons. They would be warriors in a great ghost army whose weapons would be intrigue, deceit, fakery, deception, stealth, and periodic bloody mayhem—known collectively to the British by the ominous term "special means."

Men and women of the ghost army were to conceive and implement devious, always intricate, delicately subtle, and sometimes brutal, schemes to mask Britain's glaring deficiencies, to ferret out German intentions, and to cause Adolf Hitler to reconsider plans for invading Britain. In this duel of wits with Nazi Germany, a war within a war, there would be no holds barred.

Churchill would place his ghost army intellectuals in new cloak-and-dagger agencies: Special Operations Executive (SOE), to bedevil the Germans behind their lines; the XX-

Committee (Double-Cross Committee), to mislead the enemy by "turning" captured German spies; Political Warfare Executive (PWE), to demoralize the Reich home front and Wehrmacht. MI-5 and MI-6 would be greatly expanded.

In this hour of dire peril for Great Britain, MI-6 headed by 49-year-old Stewart Menzies, had at its disposal two extraordinary sources of intelligence that were direct pipelines into the Oberkommando der Wehrmacht, the Abwehr, and Hitler's councils of war. One source was the German conspiratorial group Schwarze Kapelle, and the other was Ultra, an ingenious device that intercepted and deciphered secret German wireless messages.

Ultra had evolved over a period of years. Prior to Hitler's invasion of Poland, the Wehrmacht had adopted an encoding machine called Enigma, whose ciphers were considered unbreakable. Even if an enemy were to steal or capture an Enigma, it would be of no use to him without knowledge of the keying procedures, which were changed almost daily. In 1938 Polish intelligence, which had been working with MI-6 against Germany and Russia, stole an Enigma. A British officer, Commander Alistair Denniston, smuggled the device to London from Warsaw.

Leading British scientists, mathematicians, and cryptanalysts concluded that there was but one way to penetrate Enigma: develop another machine that could imitate the changes in keying procedures that the Germans would be making. Intelligence gained from Enigma would be of little value if it had to be painstakingly deciphered by humans, a function that could consume many weeks or months. So the envisioned British machine would also have to be capable of making an almost infinite series of intricate mathematical calculations within the space of minutes.

Could such a machine be built? It existed only in theory. Work on the project began in 1938 in an old Victorian mansion at Bletchley Park, a serene little town forty-two miles north of London. A team of Britain's foremost thinkers labored under the most intense security month after month, never knowing if the project would succeed. The development team was headed by Alan Turing and Alfred Knox, a pair of mathematical geniuses who were considered to be as eccentric as they were brilliant. [9]

The specialists at the old mansion referred to their creation as The Bomb. As time rolled past, they began to despair. Then on the eve of Great Britain's going to war, they hit pay dirt. The Bomb was able to match the electrical circuits of Enigma, permitting the device to imitate each change in keying procedures by the Germans. But it was not until April 1940 (eight months later) that bugs were eliminated from The Bomb and the first significant Wehrmacht intercepts were unbuttoned.

Development of The Bomb would prove to be an intelligence bonanza of unprecedented magnitude. Information deciphered by it was code-named Ultra. From this point onward, the British (and later the Americans) would know the precise strength and location of German units and be advised in advance of enemy plans.

Propaganda and Rumor

Three thousand miles west of the English Channel on the morning of June 12, 1940, Hans Thomsen, chargé d'affaires in the German Embassy in Washington, excitedly dispatched a coded message to Berlin. A well-known Republican Congressman "who is working closely with the [German] Embassy" had offered, for three thousand dollars, to invite fifty isolationist congressmen to the (forthcoming) Republican convention "so they can influence" delegates to adopt an isolationist foreign policy platform, Thomsen reported.

Furthermore, the Nazi chargé d'affaires disclosed that this same Republican Congressman asked for thirty thousand dollars to help defray the cost of full-page newspaper ads to be headlined: "Keep America Out of War."[1]

Thomsen was playing a role in the massive propaganda campaign aimed at the United States by Nazi Germany. With the Soviets neutralized by a Friendship Treaty, Hitler knew that there remained only one nation in the world with the potential power and industrial might to throw a monkey wrench in his plans to conquer England—the United States of America.

During the preceding two decades, America had allowed her armed forces to disintegrate to those of a fourth-rate power, as her citizens were convinced that the nation was protected by wide oceans to the east and west. America in 1940 was a sleeping giant—and Hitler intended to lull her into even deeper slumber. So the fuehrer conceived a propaganda blitz to be aimed against the United States that was to be orchestrated by two masters of fraud and deceit, Minister of Propaganda Josef Goebbels and Foreign Minister Joachim von Ribbentrop. It had been Ribbentrop's devious mind that had concocted and helped implement several of the fuehrer's bloodless takeovers of other nations. And it had been Ribbentrop, who was roundly hated for his arrogance in the Nazi hierarchy even by men such as Heinrich Himmler, who had negotiated and signed the Treaty of Friendship with the Soviet Union, thereby extracting the claws and teeth from the Russian bear until the fuehrer had completed his conquest of the West.

The Nazi campaign to influence American public opinion had no shortage of domestic allies. New York City's *Daily Worker*, parroting the party line from Josef Stalin (now Hitler's bosom buddy) in Moscow, screeched constantly: Don't send American boys to die for the warmonger Churchill and the ill-gotten British Empire. The *Daily Worker* rantings made an impact on thousands of dispirited, jobless Americans caught in the center of the Great Depression.

Hans Thomsen, the German Embassy official, energetically sought out American reporters and authors to enlist them in the Nazi campaign. On June 13 Thomsen again wired Berlin; he was negotiating a deal through a New York City literary agent in which five "well-known American authors" had agreed to write "keep out of war" books. This propaganda bonanza, Thomsen added, would cost only twenty thousand dollars. Ribbentrop promptly approved the expenditure.[2]

Many American newspapers, patriotic but isolationist in viewpoint, were perhaps duped by Dr. Geobbels's media machinations. When the fuehrer gave a speech in Berlin in mid-June, Hans Thomsen arranged to have advance copies of a news release distributed widely to American newspapers and radio stations. He wired Berlin that he had personally slipped an advance (translated) text of the fuehrer's address to a New York City reporter for a chain of large American newspapers.

Only a few hours after the final echo from the fuehrer's Berlin speech had died down, millions of Americans were greeted by blaring newspaper headlines that declared: Hitler Wants Peace. Few editors bothered to probe into the Nazi warlord's price for "peace": the capitulation of Great Britain and the permanent merging of the conquered nations into Hitler's Greater Reich.

Thomsen was ecstatic over the German propaganda bonanza. He wired Berlin that he had arranged for "an isolationist Congressman" to enter the fuehrer's "peach speech" in the congressional record on June 22. The German Embassy official was especially elated over the dramatic play given the Nazi dictator's views in Hearst's New York *Journal-American*. He had one hundred thousand reprints made and distributed to opinion leaders throughout the States, Thomsen informed his boss, von Ribbentrop.[3]

On the same day that the American congressman was entering Goebbels's propaganda into the congressional record, in southern England a new breed of warriors, known as Commandos—tough and resourceful with killer instincts—was preparing for a hazardous mission. The Commandos were the outgrowth of one of Churchill's first orders: create "troops of the hunter class" to launch "butcher and bolt raids" across the English Channel. Their function was to keep German soldiers along the far coast jittery and awake nights and to gather intelligence to help the ghost army to implement its schemes.

The task of organizing the Commandos was given to 41-year-old Lieutenant Colonel Dudley Clarke. There was no time to lose. Churchill was demanding that the cross-Channel raids be launched within three weeks. Clarke hastily recruited the toughest men he could find, and by June 15 a training base was established on England's south coast. There were only forty-one submachine guns in the British Isles, and the fledgling Commandos were loaned twenty of them—but only after Clarke took a blood oath that he would return the weapons following the first raid.

Assault boats were nonexistent. So Royal Navy Captain Garnons-Williams quickly scraped up a motley collection of small boats that had been used for sailing in quiet inland waters. Their seagoing qualities and the reliability of their engines were open to question.

The first raid was laid on for the night of June 23/24—barely three weeks since Dunkirk. A party of 120 Commandos under Major Ronald J. F. Todd, carried in four small boats, would strike at beaches to both sides of Boulogne, opposite Dover.

Lieutenant Colonel Clarke would accompany the raiders, but he had received strict orders not to go ashore. A movie company furnished the Commandos with black makeup, and at dusk the raiders set sail for the far shore.

Just before reaching the dark coast of France, the four boats split, according to plan, each heading for its own beach. There were patches of fog, and the pale rays of the moon were filtering through a haze. Overhead could be seen the dim silhouettes of Luftwaffe airplanes. One boat stumbled into the center of a German seaplane anchorage, was detected, and had to pull out before reaching shore. Commandos in two other crafts stole inland, trekked for hours, and failed to locate a single German soldier. Men in the boat carrying Lieutenant Colonel Clarke and Major Todd were spotted by a German bicycle patrol. A brief shoot-out erupted, and a bullet pierced Clarke's ear, causing a stream of blood to cascade down his neck and saturate his clothing. The Commando leader was angry and roundly cursed the Germans: they had ruined his uniform.

The Commando force reached England in broad daylight, each boat returning independently to a different port. At one harbor, permission was denied for a boat to enter; no one knew the identity of the sinister-looking, black-faced men in a craft with no identifying markings. The boat had to lay off the boom at the entrance; all the time it was covered by shore gun batteries. The Commandos were soaked to the skin, exhausted, and famished. They unfurled their most colorful profanity for the idiots in the port who would not let them dock.

As the morning rolled by, the waiting men got drunk, having consumed jars of rum that someone had stowed on board. Finally, the Commandos were allowed to enter the port, and as they staggered onto the docks, the raiders were arrested as deserters by red-capped British military police.

Eager for any scrap of favorable war news, London newspapers hailed the Commando raid with blaring headlines. Detailed stories, embellishing on the brief communiqué handed out by the War Office, told how Britian's new "butcher and bolt" warriors had stormed ashore in Nazi-occupied France and wreaked havoc before pulling out according to plan. Actually, the raid had been a minor one, but it set the groundwork for much larger and more devastating incursions, and it gave an enormous boost to British morale, which had hit rock bottom.

Three days after the Commando raid, Adolf Hitler concluded his nostalgic tour of World War I battlefields and was relaxing at a mountain retreat in Germany's Black Forest. On July 2 he called in his confidants, Generals Wilhelm Keitel and Alfred Jodl. Keitel, Oberkommando der Wehrmacht chief of staff, was stiff, humorless, and thought by many German generals to be a toady to the fuehrer. As OKW operations chief, Jodl's function was to translate Hitler's decisions into precise military directives. Hitler had selected Keitel and Jodl for these two top posts because they were known to be *fuehrertreu*—blindly loyal to the supreme commander, Hitler.

The OKW, the fuehrer stated, was to begin preparations at once for the invasion of the British Isles, with Y day to be no later than mid-September 1940. A few days later Keitel and Jodl presented Hitler with an outline of an invasion plan. It had been code-named *Löwe* (Lion), but the supreme commander altered it to *See Löwe* (Sea Lion).

Two days later at Abwehr headquarters in Berlin, Admiral Wilhelm Canaris frowned as he read a directive from the *Wehrmachtfuehrungsstab*, Hitler's headquarters staff. For the first time the Schwarze Kapelle leader learned that Hitler had made up his mind to invade England. Canaris was given specific instructions: the Abwehr was to concentrate on obtaining intelligence to support Sea Lion. Canaris passed along the order to key officers in the five-story, graystone building at 72–76 Tirpitz Ufer that housed the Reich's secret service. Then, donning his Schwarze Kapelle mantle, he arranged to have word of the invasion date rushed to MI-6 in London.

On July 16 Canaris was summoned to OKW headquarters by General Jodl, chief planner for Sea Lion. Jodl got right to the point, "Do you have any agents in England?" Canaris fidgeted. He could not afford to disclose that the British secret service had rounded up nearly all of his spies at the outbreak of the war. "Well, yes," the Abwehr chief replied in a tone of uncertainty. He told in glowing terms of the valuable work being done in England by this nonexistent agent and that one.

Jodl cut him off sharply. What was needed, the OKW general told Canaris, were several brand-new spy networks in

Britain to furnish "hot" intelligence on the spot to the Wehrmacht before and during the invasion. "The landings may take place as early as September 5," Jodl stated. "Your target date is August 15 to have your spies at their stations in England. Can you do that?"

"Undoubtedly," Admiral Canaris replied.[4]

Fuming, Canaris left the OKW headquarters. Jodl's order had been an absurd one. Even if the admiral were to make a serious effort to comply, it would take months, perhaps years, to establish spy networks in Britain of the type outlined by Jodl. Canaris had been given thirty days to get the job done.

However, the hot breath of Adolf Hitler was gusting down his neck, so Canaris rushed to the Abwehr station in Hamburg where spies were being trained. There the admiral handed the hot potato to his station chief, Captain Herbert Wichmann. "I want you to locate a platoon of [spy] candidates at once, train them, equip them, and get them to their posts in England—no later than September 7," Canaris ordered.

"But, Herr Admiral," the officer protested, "*that* is impossible."

Canaris was in a foul mood. "This is one time when the impossible must be possible," he snapped.[5]

Before departing Hamburg, Canaris telephoned his office in Berlin to inquire as to the state of health of his two beloved dachshunds. No matter if he was traveling in Germany or abroad, it had long been his habit to telephone daily and, from an aide at Tirpitz Ufer, receive a detailed rundown on the dachshunds' eating habits and bodily functions. When his dogs were ill, Canaris plunged into deep depression. At Abwehr headquarters an ambitious officer's chances for promotion would be squashed if the admiral only heard that he had spoken disparagingly about dogs. Consequently, 72–76 Tirpitz Ufer was crammed with outspoken dog lovers.[6]

During the drive back to Berlin, Canaris was racked with despair over the looming invasion of England. He felt that each German military victory was a defeat for the German people. Then he erased Sea Lion from his mind and concentrated on matters in other parts of the world.

At the Chancellory in Berlin, Adolf Hitler's time was consumed with plans for Sea Lion. He was astonished over the enormous expenditure of effort required by the general staff to solve logistical problems. And he was besieged by those with unorthodox ideas for getting across the English Channel. Gottfried Feder, the Minister of Economics, got into the act. Feder proposed that the English Channel be crossed by concrete submarine barges which would crawl along the seabed. Each would carry about ninety soldiers or two tanks or a few artillery pieces. "Think how terrified the British would be if they suddenly saw hundreds of concrete barges crawling onto their beaches," Feder stated enthusiastically.

Hitler was fascinated by the concept of "concrete crocodiles" and ordered the *Kriegsmarine* (navy) to make a thorough study of their possible use. The German admirals went through the motions of an inquiry, then quietly let the idea die a natural death.

On July 16 the fuehrer signed General Order No. 16:

> Since England, despite her hopeless military situation, still shows no sign of any willingness to come to terms, I have decided to prepare for, and if necessary carry out, an invasion of England.
>
> The aim of the operation will be to eliminate the English homeland as a base for carrying on the war with Germany.
>
> Preparations for the entire operation must be completed by mid-August.
>
> —Supreme Commander of the Wehrmacht

Even as the fuehrer signed orders to unleash the Wehrmacht across the English Channel, Great Britain's psychological warfare was getting into full swing. Sefton Delmer, the 35-year-old son of an Australian who had lectured at the University of Berlin, took regular stints on the German service of BBC to taunt and subvert the Wehrmacht on the far side of the Channel. As head of the Berlin bureau of the London *Daily Express* before the war, Delmer had rubbed shoulders with Hitler, Goering, Goebbels, Himmler, and other Nazi big shots.

Speaking as fluently as any Berliner, Delmer's chats were pleasant and upbeat, designed to impress on the *Feldgrau* (field gray, the average German soldier) that the people of Great Britain had their heads held high. In mid-July Delmer told the would-be invaders that he would teach them a few useful English phrases before they started across the Channel.

"For your first lesson," Delmer said cheerfully, "we will take *Kanalüberfahrt* . . . the Chan-nel cross-ing . . . the Chan-nel cross-ing.

"Now, repeat after me: *Das Boot sinkt* . . . *Das Boot sinkt* . . . the boat is sink-ing . . . the boat is sink-ing.

"*Das Wasser ist sehr kalt* . . . the water is ver-y cold. Now here is a verb that will be most useful. Please repeat after me: *Ich brenne* . . . I burn . . . *Du brennst* . . . you burn . . . *Wir brennen* . . . we burn. And now I suggest that you learn another phrase: *Der SS Sturmfuehrer brennt auch ganz schoen* . . . the SS captain is al-so burn-ing quite nice-ly."[7]

The theme of Germans burning to a crisp in the English Channel had not been used at random. It was tied in with rumors planted with the Abwehr by British deception services, using turned spies. This same rumor was being whispered in neutral embassies in Lisbon, Madrid, Stockholm, Washington, and elsewhere in the world where it was known German sympathizers would quickly pick it up and pass it along to local Nazi contacts who would whisk the report on to Berlin. The Big Lie was that the barbaric British had developed a devious apparatus with which they were going set the Channel afire as soon as German assault boats neared English beaches.

Sparring Across the Channel

While Sefton Delmer was giving English-language lessons to
German soldiers on the far side of the Channel, Adolf Hitler in
Berlin was beginning to have second thoughts on the invasion
of England. He had a bear—or rather a Sea Lion—by the tail.
Even the capricious waters of the English Channel seemed to
haunt him. In an offhand remark the fuehrer told Field Marshal
Keitel (he had been promoted), "On land I am fearless, on sea
I am a coward."

Part of the fuehrer's qualms resulted from the work of the
new but eager British deception agencies that through a myriad
of machinations had subtly planted in Hitler's mind that
Britain's defenses were far stronger than was actually the case.
In fact, as August 1 neared, Great Britain was nearly as
militarily bankrupt as she had been following the debacle at
Dunkirk two months earlier.

Abwehr chief Wilhelm Canaris added to the fuehrer's
growing concerns by telling him darkly, "In my opinion, even
the Dunkirk [evacuees] are not inclined to peace." And, of
course, Canaris felt it his duty as head of Hitler's secret service
to remind the fuehrer of the ominous reports of the British plan
to set the English Channel ablaze when assault boats approached.

The Nazi dictator ranted to confidants that "Churchill and
his clique," and King George to a lesser degree, were obstacles
to his granting Great Britain magnanimous peace terms. Hitler

held the notion that there was a large "peace movement" in Britain. So if Churchill and the king could be disposed of, peace would return to Europe—with Adolf Hitler reigning as lord and master.

In mid-July the fuehrer's nimble brain concocted an idea for disposing of the pair of "obstacles to peace"—Churchill and King George. Hitler called in his foreign minister, von Ribbentrop, and told him of his wild-eyed scheme that revolved around the Duke and Duchess of Windsor.

The duke, who as King Edward VIII, had abdicated the British throne in 1937 in order to "be with the woman I love," a commoner, and the duchess had been in Paris when France surrendered. The couple had then moved to Madrid, where they were now living.

According to Hitler's plan, the duke and duchess would be kidnapped, and in some undetermined manner the Nazis would return the duke to the British throne, presumably whether he wanted to wear the crown or not. With King Edward VIII ruling once again, the comic-opera script went, he would bounce Churchill from office (or have him arrested), boot out his brother, King George, and, presto, Sea Lion could be canceled, and peace would be restored to Europe.[1]

The 47-year-old Ribbentrop was enthused over the abduction plot and called in Walter Schellenberg, who had kidnapped the pair of British secret service agents in Holland, to mastermind the covert operation. During the last week of July, Schellenberg flew to Madrid to begin work. But by that time the duke and duchess had gone on to Lisbon, Portugal. Schellenberg followed them there.

In the meantime the Nazi plotters learned that the duke had been appointed by Churchill to be the governor of the Bahamas and would be sailing to the islands in the near future. Word of this development caused Ribbentrop to fire off a coded telegram marked "Very Urgent, Top Secret" to the German ambassador in Madrid, who was involved in the machinations. Ribbentrop stressed that the duke should be prevented from going to the Bahamas by being coerced back to Spain. Then the duke and duchess "must be persuaded to remain on Spanish soil," Ribbentrop declared, and if necessary "Spain could intern the Duke as an English Officer" and "treat him as a military fugitive."

Effectively restrained—that is, kidnapped—in Madrid, the duke could be convinced that England's well-being could best be served by the duke's returning to the throne. The Nazi foreign minister knew that he could count on the "cooperation" of the Spanish dictator, Francisco Franco. Spain had remained officially neutral in the war, but Franco and his cohorts had long been conniving with Hitler and the Nazis.[2]

At this point, Ribbentrop concluded, what was needed was a scheme to get the Duke of Windsor back to Spain so that Walter Schellenberg and his SS associates could kidnap the former king. So it was arranged for Franco to send to Lisbon an old friend of the duke, Miguel Primo de Rivera, to invite the kidnap target to Spain for "a little hunting" and to discuss Anglo-Spanish relations. While in Lisbon, Rivera was to pass along a tidbit that the Abwehr had invented: the British secret service had hatched a plot to assassinate the duke once he had arrived in the Bahamas. This disclosure of his imminent demise would, Ribbentrop hoped, both frighten the duke and duchess into canceling their trip to the Bahamas and place him in the proper anti-Churchill frame of mind to "cooperate" with Schellenberg.

Next Ribbentrop contacted Schellenberg in Lisbon and instructed him to launch "scare tactics" against the duke and duchess to encourage the British couple to return quickly to Spain. Schellenberg eagerly went to work. One night a few SS thugs (in civilian clothes) slipped up to the Windsors' villa and pitched stones against the windows. Rumors were then planted with the servants as to who was responsible for the nocturnal terrorism: the British secret service.

Schellenberg canceled plans for having pistol shots fired into the Windsors' home, apparently on the theory that such a racket might result in the SS perpetrators being unmasked. But the following day a beautiful floral arrangement was received by the duchess, with a card saying: "Beware of the machinations of the British secret service. From a Portuguese friend who has your interests at heart."

On July 30 Eberhard von Stohrer, the Nazi ambassador in Madrid, fired off an urgent message to Ribbentrop in Berlin: a

German spy had just learned that the duke and duchess were going to sail for the Bahamas on August 1. "Why not," Stohrer suggested, "emerge from our reserve and arrange a face-to-face meeting between the duke and fuehrer?" As it was highly unlikely that the Duke of Windsor would voluntarily travel into Germany, a nation at war with his country, Ambassador Stohrer presumably was proposing that the duke be physically abducted in Lisbon and flown to Berlin. The world would not know that the former British king had been kidnapped by SS men (and no doubt drugged in the process), and it would appear that the duke had gone to Berlin in a dramatic effort to seek peace and to announce his opposition to "the warmonger" Churchill and to his brother, King George. It could be a propaganda bonanza for the Nazis.

Before the conspirators could carry out such a plot, however, the duke threw a monkey wrench into the proceedings. Much to the consternation of Ribbentrop and Schellenberg— and presumably to Hitler as well—the duke and duchess sailed for the Bahamas on the night of August 1 on the American line's *Excalibur*. Right up to the moment of the *Excalibur*'s departure, the tenacious Walter Schellenberg had labored to prevent the Windsors from leaving. The SS leader frantically arranged for the Spanish ambassador in Lisbon, a brother of dictator Franco, to make a final, last-minute appeal to the Windsors not to sail. German agents infiltrated the dock and spread reports that a bomb had been planted on the *Excalibur*. The ship's captain delayed sailing until the vessel had been searched from bow to stern. The vehicle carrying the Windsors' baggage to the dock was sabotaged by Schellenberg's men, but the luggage was transferred to another truck and hurried to the ship.

The bizarre kidnap plot had failed. Schellenberg had failed. The ambitious SS officer had to come up with a sound reason for his shortcoming: he blamed it on "the Duke's mentality."[3]

Kroll Opera House in Berlin was decorated in dazzling colors on the night of July 16. The cavernous hall was filled with bemedaled generals and admirals, the Nazi hierarchy, the Party faithful, and exquisitely groomed and gowned wives. It was a gala affair: Adolf Hitler, conqueror of Europe, would appear to speak and to bask in the type of worship and adulation once showered upon Frederick the Great, Caesar, Napoleon, and Alexander the Great.

Thunderous applause rocked the opera house as the fuehrer strode to the rostrum. He took the occasion to make "one final peace appeal" to Great Britain. Speaking in a calm, almost pious tone, Hitler said, "It almost causes me pain to think that I should have been selected by providence to deal the final blow to the edifice which these men [Churchill and King George] have already set tottering. . . . In this hour I feel it my duty before my conscience to appeal once more to reason and common sense in Britain. I see no reason why this war must go on!"[4]

Six hundred miles away in London, staff members of BBC's German service had been monitoring the fuehrer's final appeal for peace (on Hitler's terms). One hour later, without the knowledge of the British government, a German-speaking BBC announcer took to the airwaves to beam an unauthorized reply to the Third Reich.

At that same moment William Shirer, the bearded American correspondent, was at the *Rundfunk* (broadcast station) in Berlin. He had arrived just as the BBC broadcast replying to the fuehrer came on the air. Listening intently were junior officers of the Oberkommando der Wehrmacht and officials from assorted ministries. As the voice began speaking in impeccable German, Shirer glanced at the listeners and saw astonishment written in their faces. The voice, using crude and undiplomatic language, said in effect, Go to hell! One Wehrmacht officer, his face flushed red with fury, shouted at Shirer: "Can you understand those British fools? To turn down peace now? They're crazy *Schweinhunde!*"[5]

That was the only reply the fuehrer received. For his part, Winston Churchill ignored Hitler's "final offer of peace."

The Nazi hierarchy was enraged by the impudent British reaction. Hitler told the chief of the German navy, Admiral Erich Raeder, "We are confronted by an utterly determined enemy" who would stop at nothing to prevent an invasion.[6]

Meanwhile, the pragmatic Churchill prepared for the worst. Shrouded in secrecy almost as intense as that surrounding

Ultra, a large force of British guerrillas was being formed, an underground army whose function would be to surface when the invasion struck and contest the Germans for every foot of English soil. The organizer and head of the underground army was 44-year-old Major General Colin McV. Gubbins, a Scotsman regarded as Britain's foremost expert on guerrilla warfare.

Most of Gubbins's military career had been spent in special means—sabotage, deception, intrigue, guerrilla warfare. After World War I he had fought in Russia against the Bolsheviks and later with the Irish rebels. He had been sent to deal with insurrections in India. Gubbins had authored several handbooks on guerrilla tactics, and his theories were invariably blunt: the way to handle an informer is to kill him immediately.

Moving with customary vigor, General Gubbins set up a training center for guerrilla leaders at Coleshill House, a country estate belonging to the family of the Earl of Radnor, located about seventy-five miles west of London. The rolling fields, thick forests, and streams that belonged to the estate made ideal grounds for training guerrillas.

Even before the first recruit arrived at Coleshill House, Gubbins had decided on the tactics to be used. Since the German invaders would be the most vulnerable during the first few days of landing, the guerrillas would be concentrated in a strip of terrain some thirty miles deep running along England's southern and southeastern coasts.

Guerrilla recruiting had to be top secret, so Gubbins decided to draw on the Home Guard. A guerrilla was selected in a manner that kept others in his guard unit from knowing the purpose of his leaving them. The prospective guerrilla was told only that he would be involved in "special defense duties."

Guerrilla recruits reached Coleshill House on Cole River through a series of mysterious steps. Each man was told to report to his post office, where he handed papers of unknown (to him) contents to the postmaster. The postmaster made a telephone call, and after a long wait, a staff car drove up to collect the new—and by now mystified—guerrilla.

The recruit was driven to Coleshill House, joined a large number of other equally curious Home Guardsmen, and awaited developments. Soon the entire group was called together and told by a grim-faced army officer that in the event of a German invasion they were to be guerrilla leaders. It was impressed on the recruits that their function was top secret and that they were not to as much as mention that a British underground army was being formed.

Training was arduous. The men were armed with Tommy guns (a large shipment having arrived covertly from the "neutral" United States) and with British bazookas. They learned how to handle plastic explosives, "tie pencils" (innocent-looking writing instruments packed with an explosive that was set off by acid that ate through a thin wire), and special mines that were built to look like horse dung or lumps of coal.

Guerrillas were taught how to construct devious explosive devices from materials that could be found in the home. They learned how to fill milk cans with explosives and attach a fuse, so that when a German soldier pulled off the lid, his head would be blown off. Thousands of Molotov cocktails were made at Coleshill, shipped throughout the British Isles in trucks marked as carrying food or medical supplies, and hidden for the day they would be needed.

When each new batch of guerrilla recruits completed its training in sabotage techniques, mayhem, and killing, each man returned home, where he recruited his own team of fifteen men who in turn were taught what the leader had learned at Coleshill. Molotov cocktails and explosives were hidden in the homes of guerrillas. Their job now was to prepare themselves to either defend the areas in which they lived or to rush to the invaded coast if summoned.

Meanwhile, many guerrillas were planting mines in country homes in the coastal areas. These houses, it was presumed, would be used by the invading Germans as headquarters for their push inland. Explosives were laid in bridges which when blown would delay the Wehrmacht's advance.

Throughout the British Isles, hundreds of patrols, as the 16-man guerrilla units were called, set up their own headquarters, which were usually camouflaged dugouts in the woods. In Wales, abandoned coal mines were used; in Cornwall, old tin mines. By the end of the year, there would be hundreds of these guerrilla hideouts, most of which could house 10 to 15 men for extended periods. Lamps, beds, stoves, and other necessities were installed, and stocks of food and water would make it possible for an entire patrol to remain underground for a month or longer. General Gubbins had no illusions that his irregular force could do more than bedevil the invaders. So when the Wehrmacht overran the British Isles, his guerrillas, who would wear neither uniforms nor insignia, would gather at their bunkers and from there harass the Germans indefinitely.[7]

While Britain's underground army awaited the pealing of church bells across the land signifying the arrival of the Wehrmacht, Operation Sea Lion was beginning to falter. At a council of war in Berlin late in July, General Franz Halder and Admiral Erich Raeder of the Kriegsmarine got into a bitter dispute. Overestimating British strength by eight divisions (because of Admiral Canaris's machinations), Halder wanted to land thirty-nine divisions over a 140-mile stretch of coast. "Impossible," Raeder snapped. He suggested a landing front of only 70 miles and urged a postponement for nine months. "All things considered," the admiral declared, "the best time for the invasion would be May 1941."

General Halder bristled at the narrow front proposal. "I might just as well put the troops through a sausage machine!" he exclaimed.

The *Heere* (army) and Kriegsmarine chiefs did agree on one point: England could not be invaded until the Royal Air Force had been wiped out. They were almost visibly relieved when Adolf Hitler, on August 1, signed General Order No. 17 placing the brunt of Sea Lion on the broad shoulders of Hermann Goering, who had recently been promoted to the specially created post of *Reichsmarschall*. The bombastic Goering was delighted. His Luftwaffe alone would bring England to her knees.

Goering set August 2 for *Alder Tag* (Eagle Day). Across the English Channel and on up into Norway were 3,358 Luftwaffe planes. While this air force, unprecedented in numbers and striking power, poised to smash England, the fuehrer insisted on making one more "final" peace offer.

On the night of August 1, Eagle Day minus 1, a flight of Luftwaffe bombers winged over London and southeastern England, but not a bomb was dropped. Instead, the aircraft scattered hundreds of thousands of leaflets printed in English and headed: A Last Appeal to Reason. The last-ditch effort to subvert Britain through psychological warfare proved to be a failure. A Dover dockworker read the leaflet and summed up the reaction of most Britishers: "Ol' Hitler has come to our rescue. With all the rationing here, he's showered us with toilet paper!"

Rain squalls and murky weather postponed day by day the launching of the Luftwaffe blitz. Reichsmarschall Goering paced about like a tiger in a cage, but finally his meteorologists gave him good news: the weather was clearing. Goering, rubbing his hands in glee, set Eagle Day for August 13.

6

Radar Duel of Wits

Reich Marshal Goering (Fat Hermann to subordinates behind his back), the most pompous of the Nazi bigwigs, anticipated with a great deal of confidence the impending Luftwaffe blow designed to wipe England off the map. Not only did his warplanes far outnumber those of the Royal Air Force, but German technicians, who had closely studied Hurricane and Spitfire fighters captured in France, pronounced them to be far inferior to their counterparts in the Luftwaffe, the Messerschmitt 109s and twin-engined 110s.

In addition, files of Goering's own intelligence service, *Abteilung* (Department) 5, bulged with a mountain of photographs and detailed data on bombing targets in the British Isles. This information had been gathered clandestinely during the previous three years. All through 1937 and 1938, unarmed German aircraft had crisscrossed Britain, purportedly gathering weather data for the Reich's civilian airline, Lufthansa. Actually, the planes had been on photographic missions for the Target Data Unit Information Department of the Air Ministry in Berlin (later to become Abteilung 5).

The "weather flights" had paid special attention to RAF fighter and bomber fields in southern England, to Royal Navy facilities, and to the bustling commercial ports of London, Glasgow, Bristol, Southampton, and Liverpool.

German intelligence officers studying hundreds of photographs were puzzled by the twenty strange-looking steel lattice

45

towers, each 350 feet tall, that were strung out at wide intervals along the southern and southeastern coasts of England. The Abwehr, on the basis of reports from agents all over the world, concluded that the new towering plumes of steel were merely radio stations, erected to deploy RAF planes in the event England were attacked.

But the Abwehr had been bamboozled by the British secret service that for two years had been conducting a subtle worldwide campaign of *sibs* (false rumors whispered in scores of embassies to deceive the Abwehr). For the towers, one of Britain's most intensely guarded secrets, were not radio stations, but rather a revolutionary electronic device called radar, a tracking system to determine the number, altitude, and direction of enemy aircraft.

In 1936 a noted British physicist, Robert Watson-Watt, had perfected the electronic process whereby a plane could be located by wireless methods. This discovery would become known as radar, a technique for detecting airplanes in flight by echoes from reflected radio waves.[1] As a result, the British government launched a crash program to erect a chain of twenty towers, whose function was the source of the most intensive curiosity, not only in Hitler's intelligence agencies, but among British civilians as well.

One month before the onset of war, Major General Wolfgang Martini, chief of Luftwaffe Signals, began to have serious doubts over the true nature of this chain of towers. He was fearful that the British had developed radar, which the Germans thought they possessed exclusively. Martini decided to have a look at the steel structures, and on August 2, 1939, the big dirigible *Graf Zeppelin*, with General Martini in the gondola, cast off from Friedrichshafen, crossed the North Sea, and made landfall along the eastern coast of England. Crammed into the gondola was a vast array of high-frequency receivers to monitor the towers.

All day the *Graf Zeppelin* floated up and down the British coast, causing great anxiety among lighthouse keepers and coast watchers. Martini returned to Germany greatly relieved. His instruments had not picked up any radar pulses, and there seemed to be no indication of a British reflector technique, which would have been revealed had this mysterious chain of towers been radar.

Wolfgang Martini and German intelligence had been outwitted. When the *Graf Zeppelin* had headed across the North Sea, it had made a huge blip on British radar screens, and to foil the spy in the sky, the radar had been switched off.

Unbeknownst to each other, both Germany and Britain had been working feverishly through the 1930s to develop radar, and both thought they had monopolies on it. Then in mid-1937 the British secret service picked up an alarming report: the Germans had erected a number of tall steel towers near the village of Neukirchen. What was their purpose? A hurried conference was called by British intelligence, whose first thought was: *radar!*

That conference resulted in a decision to send the physicist Watson-Watt, traveling incognito and under a false name and with a phony passport, to the Neukirchen region of Germany to clandestinely inspect the reported towers. Watson-Watt, brilliant, tireless, often irascible, utilized every means but a fake beard to mask his true identity as he furtively combed the suspected area for several days. Fears that he would detect German radar facilities were unfounded. Watson-Watt returned home satisfied that Great Britain still held a monopoly in this vital field of electronic surveillance.

What Robert Watson-Watt had no way of knowing was that there was indeed a German radar station such as the one he had painstakingly searched for; only it was in another region: near Pelzerhaken, in the Bay of Lübeck.

German radar experiments had begun in late 1934, and it was known as *Dezimeter Telegraphie*. To mask its development from foreign eyes, the system was placed under cover of the German post office. A few years later, while the British were busily building their radar towers, a large German commercial firm, Telefunken, got into the Dezimeter Telegraphie field and began producing a device called a Würzburg. It had a range of twenty miles and could track a swiftly moving airplane with great precision.

Würzburg was far ahead of its time and would prove to be a boon to the German war effort, but at the time of its unveiling in 1937, Luftwaffe chief Goering greeted it with a jaundiced eye. He commented to General Martini, his top Signals officer: "Radio aids contain boxes with coils, and I do not like boxes with coils."[2]

After Europe was plunged into war, bizarre developments began unfolding in Oslo, Norway. Late in October 1939 the Royal Navy attaché at the British Embassy received an anonymous letter in which the writer said that if the British wanted important information on German technical and weapons developments it could be arranged. The embassy was to give an affirmative reply by altering the beginning of the regular BBC German Service broadcast to insert the words: *"Hullo, hier ist London . . ."*

After an intense discussion—it could be some sort of psychological warfare gambit by the Abwehr—British authorities approved changing the BBC preamble. On November 4, 1939, a guard at the British Embassy in Oslo detected a small parcel half-buried in the snow just outside the gate. The bundle was addressed to the naval attaché, but the guard opened it—very gingerly, for it might contain a bomb. The package contained eight pages of typewritten text detailing German technical innovations being developed and a number of sketches of what appeared to be revolutionary new weapons. The parcel was rushed to London in the sacrosanct diplomatic pouch and eventually reached the desk of another physicist, Professor Reginald V. Jones.

Jones, twenty-eight years of age, had been educated at Oxford and was on the scientific staff of MI-6. With an eagerness typical of his breed, Jones began examining the parcel's contents. It was clear immediately that the mystery writer who assembled the report had an extensive technical and scientific background. Jones was startled by the extent of the disclosures: the Germans were developing long-range rockets, radio-controlled glider bombs, at a remote place called Peenemünde, proximity fuses that would cause a shell to explode as it neared its target, a torpedo that homed in on its target acoustically, a system of radio ranger measurement that would permit German bombers to hit targets blind, and two radar systems (which later appeared with the code names Würzburg and Freya).

Professor Jones's report on his findings in the Oslo mystery parcel sent shock waves reverberating throughout British officialdom. If true—a big if—the German scientists had begun to develop an entire new dimension of warfare. The bizarre episode set off an intense behind-the-scenes debate among scientists. Some thought it to be another of Admiral Wilhelm Canaris's schemes. If the Abwehr chief's devious hand was not involved, then who in Nazi Germany would be so high placed as to have the entire secret German weapons development program at his disposal? Always the finger pointed at one man: Wilhelm Canaris.[3]

Official British interest in the Oslo report waned, and eventually the documents were pigeonholed, but Reginald Jones continued to piece together a mosaic that indicated Great Britain was faced with a crisis: the Germans had developed a radio beam by which Luftwaffe bombers could be guided to targets in bad weather or in the blackness of night. The disclosure sent ripples of alarm through the Air Ministry. RAF bombers were relying on conventional (that is, primitive) methods of astronavigation, and it had been presumed that the Luftwaffe was using the same techniques.

Jones's sleuthing had begun in March 1940 when he studied a translated transcript of a conversation between two Luftwaffe prisoners of war. (The discussion was apparently obtained by an electronic "bug" concealed in a POW barracks.) The POWs talked about something called X-Gerät (X-Apparatus). Jones had never heard of X-Gerät, but it seemed to be a device for guiding airplanes by a series of radio pulses.

A short time later a small piece of paper, recovered from a crashed Heinkel, reached Jones's desk. The translation contained the words: Radio Beacon Knickebein (Crooked Leg). That added evidence convinced the scientist-sleuth that the Germans had developed a guidance technique that could tilt the course of the war farther toward the enemy unless countermeasures were developed by the British. The Luftwaffe, with the new technology, would be able to pound English cities with devastating accuracy, while the RAF bombers, Jones knew, often got lost over Germany while trying to locate their targets at night.

On May 23 Reginald Jones submitted to the Air Ministry an official analysis of his investigation: "It is possible that the

Germans have developed a system of intersecting radio beams so that they can locate a target such as London accurately . . . something like one-half mile from the frontiers of Germany."[4]

Jones had discerned the nature of Knickebein (the beams' intersection marked the target), but crucial questions remained. Intersecting beams meant that there had to be two German transmitters, but where were they located? What frequency did they operate on? What was the technology of the system?

Partly because of Reggie Jones's relative youth, but mainly because of hidebound viewpoints, brass in the Air Ministry were skeptical of his findings. Prior to the war, the Air Staff had flatly turned down proposals for a radio guidance system for RAF night bombers. In effect, the brass had held that what had been good enough for Christopher Columbus was good enough today. So why would the Germans squander enormous amounts of money and time on these complicated contraptions for their bombers when using the stars would get the job done?

Undaunted, Jones continued to probe into radio beams. On June 12 he was summoned by Britain's most highly placed scientist, Professor Frederick A. Lindemann (soon to be elevated to the peerage as Lord Cherwell), who was scientific advisor to Prime Minister Churchill. Lindemann asked if Jones truly believed that the Germans had a radio beam to guide bombers. Jones said he held such a view. Lindemann disagreed. He stressed that radio waves on the 30 megacycles frequency (or near there) traveled in a straight line through space rather than curving to follow the earth's surface. (That frequency had been in a log found in a crashed German bomber.) Therefore, Lindemann argued, it would be impossible for Knickebein beams to penetrate throughout the British Isles.

Persevering, Jones returned the next day and showed Professor Lindemann a graph and analysis that had been produced by a respected scientist in the Air Ministry, Thomas Eckersley, a report that had been gathering dust for weeks in a bureaucratic pigeonhole: "There seems to be reason to suppose that the Germans have some type of radio device with which they hope to find their targets . . . It is vital to investigate and to discover what the wavelength is. If we knew this, we could devise a means to mislead them."[5]

On the morning of June 20, a Heinkel III was shot up by a Spitfire over southeastern England, and the radio operator landed by parachute. Rapidly shucking his chute, the German airman's first action was to rip us his working notes in tiny pieces. He was burying them when a squad of the Home Guard, waving axes, swords, and a few old shotguns, dashed up and captured the parachutist. Hundreds of tiny scraps of paper were uncovered, laboriously pieced together, and the finished pasteup was rushed to London.

The precious package reached its destination at three o'clock in the morning, and shortly after dawn Reginald Jones was examining the German radio operator's notes. The scientist was elated. Here was a wealth of crucial information. It confirmed data taken from another downed Heinkel that one beam transmitter for Knickebein was set up at the ancient town of Cleves, just inside the German border, and it fixed a second beam transmitter in Schleswig-Holstein, up near the North Sea.

Within the space of forty-eight hours, two more shot-down Heinkels provided Jones with the pieces he needed to complete the intricate jigsaw puzzle that he had been assembling tediously for six months. Notes found in the wreckages revealed that the Cleves Knickebein transmitter operated on a frequency of 31.5 megacycles per second and the Schleswig-Holstein beam was 30.0 megacycles.

On June 21 an urgent meeting was called at 10 Downing Street to discuss the alarming beam situation. Jones found himself seated among the high and the mighty of the British Empire: Churchill, puffing on a long, black cigar; the prime minister's scientific advisor, Professor Lindemann; Lord Beaverbrook, the war production minister; a clutch of the nation's most distinguished scientists; and several air marshals. The conference was so secret that secretaries were not allowed to be present to take notes.

Jones felt ill at ease, as all eyes seemed to be on him. The whole affair had a sense of confrontation. Almost at once the Knickebein investigator grew alarmed, as a few of those present made remarks that indicated they had only a hazy grasp of the situation. Finally, Churchill began to direct questions at

Jones, who asked, "Would it help, sir, if I told you the story right from the start?"[6]

The implication of the question—that neither Churchill nor others in the room knew what they were talking about—caught the prime minister off guard. After a short hesitation, he cleared his throat and replied, "Well, yes it would."

Although everyone in the room was Jones's senior by far in age and in every other way as well, the German radio-beam threat was too serious for anyone to take exception to the Knickebein sleuth's seeming impudence. For his part, Jones drew strength from the fact that, judging by the earlier remarks of others, he knew more about the enemy's beam technology than did any of those present.

Twenty minutes later, when Jones had finished his presentation, there was an air of incredulity. A hush had fallen over the room. Finally, Churchill asked Jones, "What can be done about it?" The prime minister was told that the first course of action would be to confirm the existence of the Knickebein beam, which was still only theory, by discovering the beam then flying along it. Once that was done, countermeasures could be developed.

The conference broke up after Professor Jones had been given the green light to try to locate the Knickebein beams—a task similar to finding the proverbial needle in a haystack.

Knowing that enormous stakes were involved, Jones lost no time in launching his search. On the night following the Churchill meeting, Flight-Lieutenant H. E. Bufton, an officer experienced in radio-guidance systems, and a special team lifted off in an Anson from Wyton airfield in Huntingdonshire in east-central England. Professor Jones had calculated that the Knickebein beam—if there was one—could be found in that locale. Bufton had been directed to search for the beam on the 30.0 and 31.5 megacycle bands (the bands mentioned in the notes recovered from the crashed Heinkel bomber).

As Bufton searched the sky, a sudden shout of exultation rang out in the Anson. Its radio band had picked up clear signals that told those aboard that they were winging through a narrow radio beam (some 400 to 500 yards wide). The Knickebein beam had been located. Later in the same flight a second beam was detected, and the bearings on both beams were the precise locations of the transmitters thought to be at Cleves and Brestdt in Schleswig-Holstein on the North Sea.[7]

Under Dr. Robert Cockburn, a team of scientists plunged into the task of developing radio countermeasures (RCM). In a desperate emergency action, Cockburn commandeered diathermy sets from scores of hospitals and used them to distort Knickebein beams with sound. Then the team developed equipment that transmitted its own beam (code-named Aspirins) that jammed the Knickebein transmission.

Aspirins proved highly successful, as the garbled Knickebein signals confused German bomber crews, causing some aircraft to fly in circles through the black skies of England while seeking their target. One Heinkel, out of gas after a night of circling, crashed-landed on a Channel beach in southern England in the belief that it was coming down in France.

Word that the British had succeeded in jamming the Knickebein caused Luftwaffe morale to plunge. But the device would remain in use for two months. No one could summon up the spunk to inform the highly volatile Hermann Goering that on the brink of his mighty offensive to crush England by airpower alone that Knickebein was useless.

Decoys to Confound the Luftwaffe

As Great Britain, a lion at bay, braced for the invasion, German psychological warfare agencies launched a war of nerves. On the night of August 12, a Luftwaffe plane flew over southern England and dropped several containers by parachute into an open field. As anticipated, the containers were discovered after daybreak. Local police rushed to the site and found wireless sets, rubber dinghies, explosives, maps, lists of addresses of prominent Englishmen, and instructions to German spies on actions to be taken when the invasion was launched.

The parachute drop was a deception ploy. To an extent it achieved its purpose, as word of the German containers spread like wildfire, causing many persons to believe that England was infested with German spies. Most of the Abwehr agents had been rounded up eleven months earlier, but now the butcher, the baker, and the candlestick maker had become suspect.

Josef Goebbels's radio broadcasters, who spoke fluent, unaccented English, flooded British airwaves with advice to civilians, advice that left many of them jittery and badly frightened. Confused listeners were told to keep straightjackets handy, as many persons would go stark, raving mad once Goering's Luftwaffe began all-out bombings. A Radio Hamburg voice, identified as that of a prominent German doctor, gave helpful instructions on how to give first aid to those who would be hideously burned or mutilated by the impending rain of German bombs. The "doctor" was a member of the propaganda station's staff.

The British population was also made privy to Wehrmacht military secrets. Goebbels's broadcasters revealed that *Fallschirmjaeger* (paratroopers) were equipped with "fog tablets," allowing each man to turn into a small cloud after he leaped from his airplane. Hitler's scientists, so said the German announcers, had developed dirigible parachutes that were to be unveiled during the invasion. The huge parachutes would allow dirigibles to remain hovering in the air for as long as twelve hours, and were indistinguishable from clouds.

Josef Goebbels, known in Germany as the Propaganda Dwarf, was aware that British intelligence remained mystified over how "impregnable" Fort Eben-Emael, near Liège, Belgium, had been captured at the outbreak of war. (In history's first assault of its type, the Germans had landed troops by glider in the center of Eben-Emael's defenses.) Now Goebbels's broadcasters disclosed to the British how the Belgian fort had been seized: it had been destroyed by the use of electronic rays, a revolutionary weapon that was currently being readied for the impending invasion of Great Britain.

On August 12—Eagle Day minus 1—General Wolfgang Martini, the Luftwaffe Signals chief, was a worried man, possibly the only member of the German armed forces not radiating confidence. Martini had gone to the French coast a month earlier and had set up several Würzburg and Freya radar stations. All during July the Luftwaffe had been bombing English Channel shipping and pounding British targets inland. Martini's radar in France had regularly been picking up signals beamed from the 350-foot-high "radio" towers strung out along the British coastline.

As Luftwaffe squadrons knifed over the White Cliffs of Dover, General Martini and his technicians monitored the constant radio chatter from the other side of the Channel, causing the Signals chief to grow bewildered. It appeared that the RAF was "seeing" German warplanes as they lifted off from airfields deep behind the French coast, and then Hurricanes and Spitfires were "talked" to the locales where they could intercept Luftwaffe squadrons as they approached the English coast.

Martini, realizing that the British had developed an innovative technique of air defense, promptly conveyed his concerns to the Luftwaffe high command. Tut, tut, said the German brass. On the threshold of Eagle Day, General Martini had simply come down with a bad case of the jitters. Major Beppo Schmid, chief of Abteilung 5 (Luftwaffe intelligence) hurried to pitch cold water on Martini's gloomy revelation. Schmid fired off to the Wehrmacht brass an appreciation of the British air-defense system, as he viewed it from six hundred miles away in Berlin.

RAF fighters, Major Schmid trumpeted, were controlled from the ground by radiotelephones, a process that restricted the planes' operations to the sky above their respective radio stations. (This was precisely opposite the true situation. British radar was capable of gathering Hurricanes and Spitfires from throughout the British Isles to a narrow, threatened front.) Schmid concluded his analysis with: "The forming of a strong [RAF] fighter force at crucial points at crucial times is unlikely. There will be confusion in the defense during massed [German] air attacks."[1]

The two-year campaign by British deception agencies to "hide" the chain of tall steel radar towers (now numbering thirty) had hit the jackpot. Major Beppo Schmid, as well as the Abwehr, had been totally hoodwinked into believing that these towers were radio stations. When the Luftwaffe struck on the morrow (through Ultra, the RAF high command knew when they were coming), the intruders would be confronted by a radar system that could range, fix, and read the altitude of aircraft many miles distant.

It was a system that existed nowhere else on earth. Invisible walls twelve miles high had been built around the British Isles, walls shored up by far-outnumbered but grimly determined Royal Air Force pilots. Even though the construction of the chain of towers had to be funneled through public firms, contractors, power and telephone companies, and the bureaucracies, the Germans knew nothing. The concealment of the true purpose of these big towers had been one of history's most masterful deceptions.

Shortly after dawn on August 13, thousands of German airmen began climbing into Junkers, Dorniers, Heinkels, Stukas, and Messerschmitt 109s and 110s at scores of airfields in France, Belgium, The Netherlands, Norway, and Denmark. Armed with photographs, sketches, and maps of their targets (obtained before the war in the Lufthansa "weather flights" over England), the German airmen were brimming with confidence. As their planes sped down runways and set a course for England, those aboard were unaware that radar on the far side of the Channel was "watching" them.

All across southern England, RAF pilots leaped into their Spits and Hurricanes and soared skyward to meet the challenge. These fighter pilots were a breed apart—brash, scrappy, courageous—the elite. A few years earlier many had been avowed pacifists. Some had signed the controversial Oxford Pledge, in which they swore that they would never fight "for King and Country." But now, with the survival of the empire at stake, they fought.

Air Marshal Hugh Dowding, chief of Fighter Command, had been forewarned by Ultra that Goering was unleashing an all-out onslaught. Armed with that knowledge, the miracle of radar, and an excellent radio-control system, the 58-year-old Dowding would direct what Churchill had called the Battle of Britain from an underground room (known as The Hole) at Fighter Command headquarters at Bentley Priory in Middlesex.

Ultra had provided Dowding in advance the Luftwaffe's targets and tactics, permitting RAF tactical officers to gather their fighter squadrons at the right places, at the right times, at the right altitudes, concentrating RAF power against the main assaults, rather than frittering away the slender British air reserves chasing madly across the skies after secondary or decoy attacks. All that day, fierce, murderous clashes raged over the Channel ports and southern England.

As the days and nights wore on, German air attacks grew heavier, scores of RAF planes were destroyed, and British pilots, fighting bitter air duels constantly, were near exhaustion. In the crucial period between August 23 and September 6, the RAF lost 466 fighter planes, 103 pilots were killed, and 128 were seriously wounded. In that fortnight the Luftwaffe lost 214 fighters and 138 bombers but could more easily absorb those losses, being much larger than the RAF. The scales had turned against Fighter Command. There was deep anxiety in official British circles. A few more weeks of this carnage in the sky and Goering would succeed in his boast of bringing Britain to her knees with his Luftwaffe alone.

In this hour of peril, Britain fell back on a ploy as old as warfare: decoy targets. The task of rapidly creating dummy facilities to draw off at least a portion of the explosives being rained on England was handed over to Colonel John F. Turner, who was regarded as an officer of exceptional enterprise. Turner's mission was born of desperation.

Colonel Turner first concentrated on RAF airfields that were being pounded by German bombers at night. He had two rows of parallel flares set in open country about two miles from the airfields. The flares were to simulate emergency airstrips. German airmen, it was hoped, would conclude that British planes were using these strips because their nearby airfields had been knocked out.

Few in the RAF held out much hope that the hoax would work. But German night bombers were attracted to the flames of the flares as a moth to a candle, and as ground ack-ack fire burst around them, the Heinkels and Dorniers plastered the fake strips with bombs. There was one phony flare-lighted strip in southeastern England that the eager Luftwaffe came back the following night to bomb again.

In the days and nights ahead, as deadly clashes raged in the skies, Colonel Turner and his men raced about southern England expanding their Trojan Horse operations. The flares on dummy emergency landing strips were replaced by dim electric bulbs called Q Lights. These bogus airfields were growing more elaborate. Near major airfields, the decoy fields were provided with taxi aprons and phony recognition beacons. At night, when the Luftwaffe was overhead, salvaged automobile headlights mounted on wheels were dragged up and down the false airfields, conveying the impression that RAF planes were landing.

Within a few weeks there were scores of these dummy

airfields scattered throughout southern England. Luftwaffe navigators and bombardiers, coming across the Channel from France, Belgium, and The Netherlands, were often confused by the Q Lights and dropped hundreds of bombs on open fields, explosives that otherwise might have wreaked havoc on genuine RAF airfields.[2]

All the while, Josef Goebbels's English-speaking radio announcers continued to bombard Britain with another type of weapon: propaganda. On August 22 the Hamburg station warned off an impending assault on London in which one of Hitler's "secret weapons"—air torpedoes—would destroy the British capital. These torpedoes, the announcer declared, would be guided to targets with pinpoint accuracy by a wireless device operated from aircraft flying four or five miles away from the target.[3]

At OKW headquarters at Zossen, outside Berlin, on August 27, final orders for Sea Lion had been drawn up. The Germans would strike at four main points on Britain's south coast between Folkestone and Selsey Bill, just east of Portsmouth. Seaborne landings would be preceded by jumps of five thousand paratroopers just behind the bridgeheads. At 0 hour the Luftwaffe would heavily pound London in order to cause tens of thousands of panicky civilians to flee, clogging the roads and thereby hampering the movement of British reserves to the German landing beaches.

To mask the true points of assault, the Germans would launch an elaborate hoax code-named *Herbstreise* (Autumn Journey). It would be a feint against Britain's east coast, where Winston Churchill had initially expected the blow to fall. Four ocean liners—including Germany's largest, *Bremen* and *Europa*—ten troop transports, and four cruisers were to sail from the Heligoland Bight and southern Norwegian ports on Y day minus 1. German intelligence knew that these areas were kept under constant surveillance by RAF scout planes, so the convoy would certainly be spotted.

Without any troops aboard, the flotilla would set a course for a point between Newcastle and Aberdeen. As darkness fell, the "invasion convoy" would reverse direction and hurry back to its ports. The British high command, it was hoped, would swallow the bait, rush forces to the threatened eastern beaches, and leave the true invasion sites to the south denuded of defenders.[4]

German deception agencies that had concocted this Sea Lion hoax were unaware of a crucial point that would doom their efforts to failure: at Bletchley Park, The Bomb had unbuttoned Enigma messages that revealed to the British precisely where the invaders planned to come ashore.

When the Germans came, there would be a massacre on both sides, with no mercy asked or given. The Wehrmacht could be expected to be brutal, and Winston Churchill and his advisors were ready to retaliate in kind. On August 27 the prime minister, after intensive Cabinet discussion, reached a painful decision: if conventional methods failed to halt the invasion, the German beachheads would be drenched with mustard gas sprayed from low-flying aircraft.[5]

Shortly after midnight on September 3, four men in two rubber dinghies were paddling silently toward the black coast of Kent, thirty-five miles across the English Channel from Boulogne. They had left a German trawler seven miles off the southeastern coast of Britain only an hour earlier. These men were Abwehr spies, the vanguard of a team code-named Operation Lena, which Captain Herbert Wichmann had hastily scraped up when ordered by Admiral Canaris to infiltrate agents to support Sea Lion.

Leader of the spy band was Jose Rudolf Waldberg, who was fluent in French and German, but spoke not a word of English. Waldberg had performed outstanding service as a spy in France before the Wehrmacht overran that country. The others were Charles van den Kieboom, a 26-year-old, mild-mannered Dutchman who had been a bookkeeper at the YMCA in Amsterdam; 24-year-old Carl Meier, a German who had been involved with the Nazi underground in The Netherlands; and 28-year-old Sjord Pons, a former ambulance driver in the Dutch army.

Their training as spies had been minimal—a couple of weeks. At the Abwehr station at Hamburg the four men had been given a crash course in basic cryptography (their codes were childlike in simplicity) and on "recognition"—how to identify British guns, aircraft, equipment, and unit insignia.

Each Nazi agent had been given a specific mission. Waldberg, by far the brightest of the lot, was to ferret out which British divisions were in position along the southern coast, the type of fortifications there, and the number, caliber, and range of coastal and antiaircraft artillery. Meier was to collect information on the status of the RAF, while Pons and Kieboom were told to snoop in a general way.

All four spies had one common denominator: difficulty with the language of the nation they were now trying to infiltrate. Waldberg neither spoke nor understood English, and the others knew only a few words of English and could understand it only if it was spoken extremely slowly.

Now, in the blackness, Waldberg and Meier in one dinghy slipped ashore outside Dungeness, near Lydd. Pons and Kieboom landed at Romney Marsh, fourteen miles north of Lydd. Shortly before dawn all four spies were ashore. Each pair carried an Afu radio set and an incredible amount of luggage, as though on an extended vacation.

Waldberg, the most eager of the group, quickly set up his Afu and signaled his controllers in Hamburg that he and Meier had landed safely "even though a British patrol was just down the beach." As a pleasant autumn sun ascended into the bright blue sky, Waldberg became extremely thirsty. Since he did not speak English, he asked Meier to go into nearby Lydd and bring him back some cider.

Carl Meier unwittingly walked into a trap of his own making. He was unaware that British pubs had regulated open hours, and when he strolled confidently into a bar and ordered two bottles of cider and some cigarettes, the landlady was immediately suspicious. She explained what every Englishman knew: that nothing could be bought until mid-morning.

"Why don't you wait around, sir?" the proprietress suggested pleasantly. "You might want to have a look at the old church just down the street." When Meier returned to the pub an hour later, two constables, summoned by the proprietress, took him into custody. His career as a spy in England had lasted five hours.

Meier admitted that he had landed in a dinghy, but said he

had slipped out of Nazi-occupied Holland to come to England to join the new Dutch army. He said nothing about Waldberg, who presumably was still on the outskirts of Lydd awaiting a refreshing drink of cider. But early the next morning Waldberg was spotted by a police search party and arrested.

Fourteen miles to the north, Pons and Kieboom were jolted by an even more abrupt finale to their spy mission. Within one hour of sneaking ashore, the two men walked right into a unit of the Somerset Light Infantry. Pons was caught, literally, with his pants down. He was apprehended in the act of taking off his wet trousers to change into dry ones.

Carl Meier, Jose Waldberg, and Charles van den Kieboom, all brave men, but not too bright, were hanged a short time later at Pentonville prison. Sjord Pons, curiously perhaps, convinced a jury that he was really a Dutch patriot who had joined the spy band for the cross-Channel trek merely to escape from Nazi oppression in The Netherlands. Pons was exonerated.

Meanwhile, the bitter aerial clashes over England continued to rage. After two months of slugging it out with the Luftwaffe, the Royal Air Force was on the ropes. In Berlin on September 14, Adolf Hitler was damning with faint praise the pilots that Air Marshal Dowding affectionately called "my chicks." The fuehrer complained, "The enemy [RAF] recovers again and again. . . . Enemy fighters have not yet been completely eliminated." Then he added, "Our own reports of successes do not give a completely reliable picture."[6] (Translation: Luftwaffe intelligence officers have been lying about RAF losses.)

An embarrassed Reich Marshal Goering, his customary bombast subdued, exclaimed, "All I need is four or five days of good weather to wipe out the remnants of the British air force."[7]

Later that same day six hundred miles west of Berlin, Ultra unbuttoned an alarming Luftwaffe signal: Goering had proclaimed September 15 as Eagle Day, the day on which all the awesome power of the German air force would be unleashed in one unprecedented trip-hammer blow to wipe out what was left of the RAF. (This was Goering's second Eagle Day, the first having been on the opening day of his campaign, August 13.)

On this day all the chips would be on the table—and both the Germans and the British knew it. If Eagle Day succeeded in destroying the battered RAF, Hitler's legions would invade; if the Luftwaffe failed, Sea Lion would be postponed at least until the spring of 1941 because of the equinoctial gales lashing the Channel.

Shortly after dawn on September 15, Air Marshal Dowding (called Stuffy by his colleagues) was in the underground operations room at Bentley Priory, making final-minute preparations to meet the Luftwaffe onslaught. Dowding was a worried man. Through Ultra intercepts, the air marshal knew Goering's plan: London was the main target, and it would be struck by one thousand bombers escorted by seven hundred fighters.

Stuffy Dowding, as did other British officials from Churchill on down, knew that the weather, the moon, and the tides were right for a massive crossing of the Channel by German armies in France, Belgium, and The Netherlands. All that barred the way were a few hundred of Dowding's chicks, the RAF pilots.

Through the magic of radar, Marshal Dowding looked on grimly as swarms of German warplanes assembled over the coast on the far side of the Channel. And he watched as twenty-five squadrons of Spits and Hurricanes, gathered from all over England, raced to the southern approaches to London.

By noon the bright blue skies over southeastern England were aflame with countless duels between equally determined German and British pilots. There was the constant chatter of machine-gun fire, the throb of powerful bomber engines, the roar of diving and maneuvering fighters. Bits and pieces of aircraft spun crazily earthward. The sky was laced with the crisscross patterns of contrails. Planes caught fire, plummeted, and crashed in huge, fiery balls. Here and there a British or German parachute opened and drifted lazily to the ground. The fierce, murderous clashes raged all afternoon. By sundown the Luftwaffe's back had been broken. Spunky RAF pilots still controlled the skies over Great Britain.[8]

Two days later, on September 17, Winston Churchill, at his bombproof headquarters at Storey's Gate, was handed an Ultra intercept. It was a message from the Oberkommando der Wehrmacht, a signal of enormous portent. German paratrooper units posted on the alert at Dutch airfields were given orders to begin dismantling their equipment. Sea Lion had been called off by the fuehrer.

For the first time in months, the British Bulldog allowed himself the luxury of a broad smile. But Great Britain's ordeal was far from over.

Camouflage and Hoax

Adolf Hitler, after three years of dazzling successes, had at last met failure. But to save the fuehrer's face, the Oberkommando der Wehrmacht would keep up the pretense that England would still be invaded that autumn.

At his headquarters outside Berlin, corpulent Reich Marshal Hermann Goering was stunned by the Luftwaffe's Eagle Day disaster. Fifty-six of his planes, including thirty-four bombers, had been shot down. On the next day the Nazi air baron ordered a drastic change in tactics. His black-coated bombers would still be sent over Britain in daylight, but the heaviest attacks would be carried out under the protective veil of night. For fifty-seven consecutive nights, London would take an awesome pounding from a daily average of two hundred bombers, and many other cities would be ground into rubble.

Despite this torrential rain of bombs, neither British morale nor armament production was destroyed, as Hitler had predicted. Aircraft plants, prime targets of German bombers, would outproduce the Reich in 1940 by 9,924 to 8,070 airplanes.

A key ingredient in the ability of British armament factories to thrive under the relentless threat from the sky was the work of thousands of unheralded warriors who were camouflaging the face of England. Weapons used were such mundane items as chicken wire, paint, smoke, fishnets, canvas, plaster, lights, and papier-mâché.

Where a factory might be an inviting target for Luftwaffe bombers, an inexpensive structure was erected a short distance away. The genuine factory was blacked out and sometimes covered by natural foliage or other concealment. But the fake plant gave the subtle impression that its blackout was haphazard, for here and there a dim light could be seen from the air. As a result, many German bomber crews returned to base after a night raid and reported destruction of a British factory, whereas the bombs had blown to smithereens the bogus plant.

Tricks of camouflage were astonishingly imaginative. Often professional set designers from Britain's movie colony contributed their expertise. Entire British factory complexes were painted to resemble apartment houses, and military facilities were disguised as innocuous filling stations. To confound German bombardiers, fake highways cut across empty fields. Dummy airfields sprang up all over southern England. One genuine airfield, bordering a housing development, concealed the hangars by painting them to look like more housing, with doors, windows, and flower boxes precisely like those in the development.

A camouflage, or *ruse de guerre*, was expected to be unmasked eventually, but the important thing was that it cause delay, confusion, and, it was hoped, an extravagant waste of Luftwaffe bombs. Camouflage psychology-in-reverse was even successful for a few nights on some occasions. Dim lights were placed on dummy airfields and the nearby real field was lighted up to where it glowed for miles. The Germans took the bait—and plastered the dummy field with bombs.

Camouflage was often successful if it merely blurred the target from the view of the approaching bombardier. He had to spot the target from about ten miles away and, at nineteen thousand feet, drop his lethal cargo at three miles. Then as he flew over the target, the bombardier would recognize that it was a dummy, but could only watch as his bombs obliterated a fiberboard building.

A novel creation of British camoufleurs and Royal Engineers was fake bomb damage on airfields. The day after a night attack, the Germans would dispatch reconnaissance planes to photograph the destruction. When the photos were developed, they revealed that large numbers of bombs had scored bull's-eyes on runways and hangars. Actually, in many cases little damage had been inflicted, sometimes none at all. As soon as the night raiders had departed, camouflage crews began rapidly distributing around the field large piles of debris that they had previously collected for the purpose.

On occasion old rubber tires placed at points about the targeted airfield would be set on fire the next morning, and the Luftwaffe recon pilot could report—and be backed up by his photos—that the airfield was still burning from the night's bombing. Adding to the "carnage" that greeted the eyes of Luftwaffe photo interpreters across the Channel were the blackened skeletons of Spitfires and Hurricanes, testimony to the accuracy of German bombardiers. These were indeed British planes, ones that had crashed earlier in southern England and had been collected in stockpiles by camoufleur warriors. Then after an airfield's bombing, the hulks were rushed to the site and placed about the premises.

If a British airfield truly had suffered the heavy damage camoufleurs tried to convey to the Germans, it would have had bomb craters, so artists were put to work painting crater likenesses on hundreds of large pieces of canvas. After the Luftwaffe had paid a night visit to an airfield, a number of these painted craters would be fastened to runways. From the air they looked so realistic that on occasion a passing RAF pilot would report that a certain airfield's runways had been heavily bombed and were useless. Actually, the pieces of canvas had been fastened so securely that pilots in the know could continue to take off from and land on the "bomb-pocked" runways.

In a few days German recon photos would show that the craters had been repaired—meaning that camoufleurs had removed the pieces of canvas.

All over England, particularly in the southern half, Royal Engineers and Colonel John Turner's wizards of deception had created a vast web of bogus targets that protected real facilities. The camoufleurs built dummy shipyards, erected phony docks, and set up fake oil storage complexes and gasoline tanks. The face of England had been altered to the point that one beaming camouflage officer chortled to colleagues, "Even her own mother wouldn't recognize her!"

While hundreds of British camoufleurs were laboring like eager beavers to confuse, baffle, and mislead the Luftwaffe, in Hamburg a harried Captain Herbert Wichmann was still trying to sneak more spies into England. His first four agents in Operation Lena, who had landed from rubber dinghies in southeastern Britain on September 3, had vanished. A realist, Wichmann presumed (rightly) that they had been caught. Undaunted, Wichmann, three weeks later, was preparing to dispatch to Great Britain three more agents.

The spy team was led by 34-year-old Theo Druecke, a sophisticated intellectual and son of a noted German lawyer. Druecke, the playboy type, had traveled extensively throughout the world before the war. On one of those junkets, Druecke had fallen in with an international ring counterfeiting American one-hundred-dollar bills. He told an Abwehr officer friend of the excellent forgeries, and the German secret service acquired a large supply to bankroll skullduggery in the war looming over the horizon.

Going along on the mission would be a shadowy character named Waelti and a mystery-shrouded, well-proportioned female known variously to her Abwehr friends as Vera, Viola, and The Countess. Even Wichmann did not know her family name, but he did know that she had been involved periodically in the world's oldest profession. Actually, The Countess was Vera de Witte, the daughter of a White Russian naval officer who had been killed while fighting the Bolsheviks.[1] Bright, vivacious, and beautiful, The Countess was considered by Wichmann to possess the qualities to become one of his ace operatives.

On September 21 the Lena team, headed by the playboy Druecke (who was also The Countess's current lover), were flown to Stavnger, Norway, and at dawn on September 30 the trio climbed aboard a seaplane and flew to a point off Banff in Scotland. They transferred to a rubber dinghy to paddle ashore, but halfway there the water was so shallow that they had to get out and wade the rest of the way.

Reaching land, they had not the slightest idea where they were. As they were to carry out their missions separately, they split up and set out to find some sign of habitation. Waelti located a tiny station and caught a train to Edinburgh, from which point he would take another train to London, his destination. Druecke and The Countess independently came to another small station and found themselves together in the waiting room.

When the ticket window opened at 7:30 A.M., The Countess, who spoke English fluently, asked the clerk, "What town is this?" The startled Englishman replied, "Why, it's Port Gordon." Druecke meanwhile had located a timetable, and he sauntered to the ticket window and told his female companion in thickly accented English, "Buy two tickets for Forres."

The clerk grew more suspicious. Here was a pair of strangers who did not know where they were or where they were going. The man spoke with a heavy accent, and the Englishman noted that although it had not been raining, the man's pants were wet, as were the woman's stockings.

While the two strangers waited for the train, the clerk telephoned the constabulary. Moments later the police arrived and took The Countess and Druecke into custody. A search of Druecke's suitcase revealed a German Mauser pistol, a cardboard-disk coding device, a list of RAF air bases in southeastern England (his destination), and an Afu radio set.

Meanwhile, in Edinburgh Waelti went to a movie theater while waiting for the train that would carry him to London. Earlier a clerk at the station where Waelti had stored his suitcase had become suspicious and summoned police. The spy's luggage was opened and found to be crammed with espionage apparatus. When Waelti returned, two policemen arrested him.

Altogether in Operation Lena fifteen Abwehr spies slipped ashore or parachuted into the British Isles at remote, widely separated locales. One reached London and after his first meal at a Soho restaurant handed the waitress food coupons for his dinner. Minutes later the spy was arrested. He had been unaware that food coupons were not required in restaurants.

Another spy was caught when he asked a clerk in a train station the price of a ticket to Bristol, his assigned base of operations. When told the cost was "ten and six," the man did not know how much money that was. Police were called, and the Abwehr agent was hauled away.

One Lena operative posing as a Dutch refugee came to a

mysterious end. He was found shot to death in a bomb shelter in Cambridge. Police inspecting his Abwehr-created papers saw that his name—a phony one—was Jan Villen Ter Braak. At the dead man's side was a suitcase. When police opened it, they found that the case contained an Afu set.

Yet another German spy parachuted into the Manchester Ship Canal in Lancashire and drowned. His espionage career in Britain had lasted less than five minutes.

Two more parachuting Lena agents crashed hard into a small woods near ancient Salisbury in Wiltshire. One, named Schmidt, broke his ankle. His companion, who went by the name Caroli, managed to get the injured man to a British doctor who, displaying no curiosity over the pair of unkempt strangers who spoke in thickly accented English, placed Schmidt's ankle in a cast. Leaving the physician's office, the brash Schmidt quipped: "This was lucky for me. The British don't hang spies with broken ankles."[2]

Returning to the site where they had landed a short time before, Schmidt and Caroli recovered the radio that had come down with another parachute and contacted Major Ritter, their control officer, at the Hamburg Abwehr outpost. Advised of the predicament of his two Salisbury spies, Ritter promptly radioed his ace agent, code-named Johnny, in London. The Abwehr officer pleaded with Johnny to go to the aid of the stranded Schmidt and Caroli.

Major Ritter, in his anxiety over the well-being of his Salisbury spies, threw caution to the winds; he was not talking on the radio to Johnny (the double-agent code-named Snow by the British), but rather to an MI-5 man. Details were worked out for Johnny's rescue of Schmidt and Caroli.

Later that afternoon, accompanied by a doctor and an ambulance, Johnny (that is, Snow) reached the designated point of rendezvous outside Salisbury. Spotting the approaching ambulance, Schmidt and Caroli issued sighs of relief: good old Johnny had come through again, just as Major Ritter had assured them he would. Moments later smiles vanished from their faces. Several British secret service men concealed in the rear of the ambulance leaped out and handcuffed Schmidt and Caroli.

Young Schmidt (who also went by Hansen and Hansen-

Schmidt) told MI-5 that he was Danish. Bright, personable, and energetic (he had studied to be an industrial engineer), Schmidt was an ardent Nazi. But when given a choice by MI-5—the gallows or working for the British as a double-agent—the Dane began to develop a different philosophical point of view. Perhaps the British were right after all. MI-5 quickly gave Schmidt a code name: Tate, after a popular comedian. Tate would become Britain's ace double-agent of the war.

Caroli, much rougher hewn and far less intelligent than Schmidt, was also a fanatical Nazi. He held out much longer than his companion before he, too, agreed to become a double-agent. His code name would be Summer.

All fifteen Operation Lena spies were caught—including the corpse of the luckless one who had parachuted into the Manchester Ship Canal. Most were hanged at Wandsworth prison—unmourned by either side. Vera de Witte (The Countess) remained a woman of mystery. Even though in British custody, she would eventually vanish.[3]

Early in October 1940 the Foreign Office in London received a request from Franco's Spanish government: could a Falangist who was associated with youth movements in Spain come to study the British Boy Scouts and their wartime activities? "Yes, indeed, come right ahead," replied the Foreign Office. They knew this man well and were positive that everything he heard and saw would reach Berlin within twenty-four hours after his return to "neutral" Spain.

The red carpet was rolled out for the Spaniard. A few British secret service men, posing as Boy Scout officials, met him at the airport, then escorted him to the posh Athenaeum Court Hotel and all but tucked him into bed in an ornate suite, one that was an intricate maze of concealed microphones and tapped wires. His gracious hosts provided him with expensive whiskey and whatever else he might want. Jolly good fellows, these Englishmen.

Most of Britain's limited number of antiaircraft guns were protecting the coasts or the approaches to the capital. There were only about four heavy ack-ack batteries in all of London. One of these batteries was quickly moved into the park across from the hotel. Orders had been given to the puzzled ack-ack gun crews: fire continuously through every air raid, even if there are no targets for miles.

German bombers pounded London almost every night, and the antiaircraft guns in the park barked constantly. The racket was terrific, and the sleepless Spaniard across the street must have thought London was honeycombed with ack-ack guns. His hosts permitted the Spaniard to inspect the gun battery, where one of its officers (actually a secret service agent) was careless enough to let slip the altitude these weapons could reach (he gave a figure thousands of feet higher than these antiquated ack-acks could attain).

Next the British escorts took the Spaniard to Windsor to inspect the activities of a large group of Boy Scouts there. By coincidence (it wasn't) one of the few fully equipped regiments in the British Isles and possibly half the tanks the army possessed were drawn up in parade formation outside Windsor Castle. The Spaniard's hosts mentioned casually that these tough-looking men constituted but a small force that could be spared from defense of the islands to act as a ceremonial bodyguard for the king and queen. The incredulous look on the Falangist's face told his escorts that he had swallowed the hoax.

Next day the Spaniard was taken to a Channel port to see more Boy Scouts. By now he must have been sick of Boy Scouts. His hosts were. As the little group drove onto the docks, they viewed a harbor jam-packed with British navy vessels of all types. With knowing grins the escorts hinted to the Spaniard that the Home Fleet was much larger than Britain's enemies realized and that what they were seeing in the harbor was typical of the naval force that protected each major port. The visitor's eyes bugged out.

Within an hour after the Spaniard's departure, the harbor was almost devoid of ships. During the hours of darkness, the navy units had congregated in this one port. Now they rushed back to their regular assignments all along the southern coast of England.

Later in Madrid, double-agents working for MI-5 managed to copy the eyewitness report the "Boy Scout official" had sent to the Abwehr in Berlin. It was a stunning document. Great

Britain obviously was an armed camp, and the British, crafty fellows, had been portraying the islands as a being weakly defended in order to entice Hitler into the invasion that would meet with bloody disaster.[4]

SOE and Double-X

At the unpretentious Buckinghamshire village of Tempsford, forty miles up the Old North Road from London, the whistling gales of November 1940 foretold the arrival of a bitter winter. About a mile away through the fields and low-lying hills snuggled a secret airfield and a complex of Nissen huts, collectively called Gibraltar Farm. This was the base of the new RAF Moon Squadrons, so named because most of their flying would be done over occupied Europe in periods of moonlight, when conditions were favorable to clandestine operations.

On this gray day George Noble and two comrades were steeling themselves for the ordeal that confronted them: that night they would be parachuting "blind" into Nazi-held France. They were spies, the first of hundreds (it was hoped) to follow during the long war years ahead.

George Noble had been in the original group of ten potential spies recruited by the cloak-and-dagger Special Operations Executive (SOE) that Churchill had created five months earlier with the stirring directive: "You are to set Europe ablaze." Noble had been one of six candidates to survive the rigorous physical and mental tests conducted by SOE (known to its members as The Firm). As pioneer parachute spies, Noble and his two comrades had staked their lives on one unknown factor: their ability after landing in France to locate a friend of Noble's who, he felt, would provide the British agents with shelter and concealment.

George Noble had long been out of contact with his French friend. Was he still alive? Was he in a Nazi concentration camp? In the volatile climate in Europe, had he switched loyalties and gone over to the Germans? These crucial questions could not be answered.

Noble, a quiet, unassuming man, and his two comrades had been living in a house some distance from Gibraltar Farm, awaiting the arrival of the proper moon period. At noon that mid-November day they received the word that their mission was on for that night. A short time before leaving for the secret RAF field, Noble left the house to run an errand. As he departed the eerie moan of air-raid sirens wafted over the locale, followed by the throbs of Luftwaffe engines, then the kerplunk, kerplunk of exploding bombs.

Returning to his house, Noble found it demolished. A bomb had made a direct hit. Sprawled under the rubble were his two dead friends. Noble, badly shaken, was determined to go to France alone. He was driven to the airfield, where SOE men gave him a painstaking final search. A forgotten English bus- or theater-ticket stub, a grocery receipt, a handwritten note, any one could doom him to a Gestapo gallows.

Noble had already been given his cover story and been forced to repeat it endlessly while shouting members of The Firm, acting as Gestapo agents, browbeat and threatened him. Now he was handed his forged papers and a radio set and a parachute. Then The Firm's first spy scrambled aboard his airplane.

The RAF crew hardly acknowledged Noble's presence. For security reasons no Moon Squadron airmen would ever know the real or code names of the spies they were carrying across the Channel. The RAF men merely called them "the Joes." George Noble was the first of the Joes.

Minutes later, with a raucous revving of engines, the aircraft sped down the runway and lifted off into the glowing rays of an ascending moon. Noble, grief-stricken over the death of his two friends, did not say a word during the entire flight. When the plane reached the designated spot, a signal was flashed to the spy, and he bailed out. Some ten hours later there was elation at SOE headquarters. A message had been received from George Noble. He had landed safely and found his friend.

Special Operations Executive, under its "D" (code cipher for the chief), Sir Charles Hambro, had taken its first wobbly steps in mid-1940. It settled into sparsely furnished offices at 64 Baker Street in London, not far from the fictional home of the legendary Sherlock Holmes. From the beginning, SOE was clothed in secrecy. The true name of the fledgling spy agency, its correct address—even its existence—were known to but a handful of high-level officials. SOE gave out different names and addresses to chiefs of the armed forces. The Air Ministry knew SOE by a different set of initials, the Admiralty knew it by another set. Both thought SOE was located at addresses other than the correct one. Only the few in the know could even find SOE headquarters, for there were no markings or signs anywhere in the building at 64 Baker Street to indicate that the agency was housed there.

Even as George Noble, without benefit of ground signals or friendly reception committee, was parachuting into France, the D was diligently drawing up plans for the enormous expansion of SOE. Each country that had been overrun and occupied by the Wehrmacht would have its own section in SOE—the French Section, the Belgian, the Dutch, and the Polish. Each section would direct espionage and sabotage operations within its own country and recruit, train, and infiltrate its own agents. The SOE-dispatched spies, in turn, would recruit their own agents and organize them into clandestine networks.

Chief Hambro's ultimate goal was to organize in occupied Europe such a widespread and sophisticated organization of zealous, heavily armed, well-trained spies and saboteurs that when Allied forces eventually invaded the Continent, a clandestine army of men and women would rise up to attack, disrupt, and bedevil the Germans from the rear and in their midst. In the intervening months (or years) the SOE's secret force in Europe would provide detailed intelligence and sabotage the Wehrmacht to keep the Germans in a constant state of jitters.[1]

Early in November Prime Minister Churchill called an urgent midnight conference at Number 10 Downing Street. The Luftwaffe, having failed in its all-out effort to destroy the RAF, was continuing to blitz London and other key cities, each night sending over from 160 to 220 Heinkels and Dorniers. Means for striking down the hostile bombers were high on Churchill's priority list.

Present at the session was a group of freewheeling naval scientists who operated in an agency known as the Directorate of Miscellaneous Weapons Development (DMWD). Its chief and guiding spirit was Lieutenant Commander Charles F. Goodeve. A Canadian in his mid-thirties, Goodeve had been brought up in Winnipeg and was the son of a Church of England parson. He had come to Britain on a scholarship twelve years earlier, excelled in science, and joined the Naval Reserve while prospering as a civilian scientific consultant.

As a temporary, wartime agency manned mainly by reserve officers, DMWD was far from touchy about stepping on the toes of hidebound brass, if the brass was holding up their work. None was worried about postwar promotions. They called themselves the Wheezers and Dodgers, and the "Miscellaneous" in the organization's title gave these enterprising men the wide latitude they needed to develop innovative, unorthodox, sometimes bizarre weapons to help thwart the ambitions of Nazi Germany.

Now, at his midnight meeting, Winston Churchill, a cigar clamped firmly between his teeth, was discussing one of his pet weapons projects: a gigantic wire trap in the sky to snare German bombers. The prime minister listened impatiently as the Royal Navy scientists and others argued back and forth over the technical difficulties involved. But Churchill was not concerned with the problems.

"I want a square of wire in the sky as big as the Horse Guards Parade, with parachutes holding it in place," Churchill snapped. "Just think of the difficulties of an aircraft trying at the last minute to avoid a thing that large."[2]

Continuing discussion produced a vague concept of the "mousetrap in the sky." Wire cables would have to be shot into the air by rockets, it seemed, and held there by parachutes. High-explosive mines would be attached to the cables. At 3:00 A.M. Goodeve and his Wheezers and Dodgers were dismissed to meditate on the technical problems, and with orders to report back at a later date.

Shortly afterward Commander Goodeve learned that the

RAF had been experimenting with a similar apparatus. It consisted of a network of wire and bombs and was to be dropped by RAF bombers in the path of attacking Luftwaffe fighters. Goodeve studied the device carefully, as it might give him a head start on his own mousetrap-in-the-sky project. However, intensive experiments with the RAF apparatus revealed a major flaw: it wouldn't work.

Experimentation continued, and a device called the Free Balloon Barrage was developed. The apparatus had a few hundred components, and each had a large balloon filled with hydrogen. Suspended below each balloon was a metal container, a wooden spool with two thousand feet of piano wire, and a parachute.

The operating procedure for the device was simple—in theory. The balloons would be sent aloft in an area of perhaps two miles square, and when they reached a specified height a mechanism would release the two thousand feet of thin, sturdy piano wire under each balloon. A parachute at the bottom of each wire would hold it taut. Moments later the metal containers, which held bombs and were dangling beneath the balloons, became activated.

At the split second that a German bomber struck a wire, things would begin to happen in rapid-fire order, theoretically. Air blasts pouring into the parachute would cause the wire to tighten and the dangling bomb to slide down the wire and detonate on impact with the hostile aircraft. But in trials the Free Balloon Barrage proved to be highly temperamental. A leak could cause the balloon to drift to earth—perhaps in a populated area—with an active bomb ready to explode on contact with any object.

However, the DMWD scientists worked feverishly to iron out the kinks in the apparatus, and while so doing, on December 29, 1940, orders came down for the Free Balloon Barrage to be given its first full-scale tryout. Ultra had unbuttoned Luftwaffe signals indicating that London was to be saturated with firebombs that night. In an enormous expenditure of effort, hundreds of British RAF and Royal Navy men transported the balloons, hydrogen, bombs, an other components to the windward side of the capital. More than eight hundred trucks and trailers were used in the operation.

Charles Goodeve and his naval scientists feared a disaster, as they felt much more testing was needed on the Free Balloon Barrage. Their fears would prove to be justified. But British authorities from Churchill on down were desperate. London was steadily being reduced to rubble. Any device that might bag a few Luftwaffe Heinkels had to be tried.

While German bombers were setting huge swaths of London on fire that night, some two thousand of the bomb-loaded balloons were launched in less than three hours. Reports flowing into the DMWD control center confirmed the disaster fears. Balloons broke loose or leaked, coming down with their lethal bomb loads all over southern England. One landed on the grounds of Buckingham Palace. Other balloons came down in France.

Those balloons straying as far as France caused a flap in that country. One balloon-carried bomb exploded near a German army barracks, and the device—or rather, its remains—was rushed to Berlin for inspection by experts. Had the British developed a new type of weapon with which to bombard the Channel coast of France and the Low Countries? French newspapers reported "mysterious objects in the sky," and a high-ranking policeman, sent to retrieve a balloon that had lodged in a tree, was wounded when he tugged on the dangling piano wire and the bomb exploded.

The results of the first major Free Balloon Barrage test poured a thick layer of depression over the Wheezers and Dodgers. They had worked hard to perfect the ingenious mousetrap in the sky, but the exigencies of war had caused it to be used before it had been perfected. Experimentation continued, however, and future trials, notably one at Liverpool, resulted in an 80 percent efficiency, although it could not be determined if any Luftwaffe bombers had been ensnared. But by then the mass air raids on the British Isles had ceased, and the mousetrap was no longer needed.[3]

In the meantime the hangman at Wandsworth prison had not been lacking for work. By late 1940 seven German spies had gone to the gallows and several more were awaiting execution. What a waste of potential benefit to the British Empire, thought Major Thomas A. Robertson, a young officer in MI-5 who had served with the Seaforth Highlands before mysteriously "vanishing." Robertson had joined MI-5 and gone under such deep cover that his name was stricken from British army rolls. Still in his late twenties, articulate, handsome, and considered to be a devastating charmer, Robertson conceived an idea for a deception system whereby captured German spies, instead of being hanged, buried, and forgotten, would be put to work double-crossing their former Nazi masters. Already the British had used this technique a couple of times, but only on an unorganized basis.

Major Robertson lobbied for his pet scheme with the Air Staff and with Naval Intelligence. Then the young officer finagled an appointment with Colonel John H. Bevan, who was in charge of a super-hush-hush deception bureau in the Cabinet Office under Winston Churchill's principal military aide, General Hastings "Pug" Ismay. Using his ample powers of persuasion, Tommy Robertson convinced Bevan that a live double-crosser would bolster the war effort far more than would a dead German spy.

Colonel Bevan, a quiet, very private man and the son of a prominent London stockbroker, bought the concept. He promptly set the wheels in motion to create the finely tuned instrument with which MI-5 double-crossers would mislead and confuse Adolf Hitler and his high command. It would set the stage for a relentless wireless duel of wits across the English Channel, as the Germans were also using turned Allied spies in what they called the *Funkspiel* (radio game). The British were much more direct in naming their new deception apparatus: the XX-Committee, or Double-Cross Committee.

The XX-Committee was set up in Colonel Dick White's B-Division in MI-5. It was a perfect home for the Double-X, as White was one of the more innovative and energetic of the younger officers in MI-5. John C. Masterman, a tall Oxford intellectual fifty years of age, would mastermind the fledgling operation.

On December 20, 1940, shortly after Major Robertson had sold his double-cross concept to the powers that be, a 30-year-old Yugoslavian businessman, Dusko Popov, was aboard a Royal Dutch Airlines plane winging toward England from Lisbon. As the aircraft approached the English coast, panels were placed over the portholes to thwart spies who might be aboard. Popov was precisely that—an Abwehr agent.

Popov, a member of a wealthy Yugoslavian family, was contacted by the Abwehr in Belgrade at the outbreak of war. It was suggested that Popov's family's extensive commercial interests in Europe would be "protected" if the young man became a spy for the Third Reich. Popov, grasping the implied threat, agreed to serve Adolf Hitler.

Now the Dutch civilian airliner touched down at Felton Airport near Bristol. As soon as Popov cleared customs, he was approached by a stranger who said he was to take the Abwehr spy to London. After a breakneck drive through the blacked-out countryside, the two men reached the capital, and Popov was dropped off at the Savoy Hotel. Although an air raid was in progress, the lobby and bar were filled with people. No one was paying attention to the falling bombs.

While Popov was registering, he was approached by his London contact, a handsome young man whom the Abwehr spy judged to be about thirty years of age. The newcomer introduced himself, and the pair went into the crowded bar for a beer, a sandwich, and a get-acquainted chat. When the man excused himself, he told Popov, "We'll get down to business in the morning."[4]

Popov did not feel nervous strain, as did most spies when suddenly finding themselves in the midst of the enemy. For Dusko Popov, while ostensibly ferreting out British secrets for the Abwehr, was actually a double-agent. The young man who had met him in the lobby was Major Thomas Robertson, conceiver of the XX-Committee and known to friends as Tar.

Popov had been playing the double-game for more than a year. After agreeing to spy against Britain for the Germans, the Yugoslav had sought out an MI-6 agent in Belgrade, revealed his Abwehr connection, and volunteered to work for the British as a double-agent.

Popov went to bed feeling that he had been accepted as a full-fledged and trusted associate of MI-5. He had been put up at the posh Savoy and had even been welcomed warmly by Major Tar Robertson. Popov would have a rude awakening. Not long after dawn there was a knock at his door, and he climbed sleepily out of bed to be confronted by a collection of grim-faced men, some in uniform, others in civies. They were from MI-5, MI-6, Air Intelligence, and Naval Intelligence.

The Yugoslav soon learned that they were there to conduct an inquisition. He was neither accepted nor even trusted. Popov could be a clever, genuine German spy who had managed to slip through Britain's first line of defense. No one could trust anyone in the espionage business.

In the comfort of the Savoy suite, the twelve intelligence officers took turns in grilling Popov, stopping just short of the third degree. This continued for four consecutive days. During that period he was free to come and go at night as he wished, but Popov was aware that the shadowy figures trailing him were British agents.

One of those boring in on Popov was the XX-Committee chief, J. C. Masterson, a former member of the British Olympic hockey team and a Wimbledon tennis player. Masterson's questioning—cool, calculated, incisive—apparently "cleared" the Yugoslav. But it was not until two nights later that Popov knew for certain that he had been accepted as genuine. A British officer took him to the lobby of White's, telling him that there was someone who wanted to meet him. Popov was escorted into the dining room, where a thin, blond man of perhaps fifty, wearing a civilian suit, was seated alone at a table. The officer introduced the pair with "this is Stewart Menzies." Popov knew at once who he was: Major General Stewart Menzies, "C," the chief of MI-6.

Popov, code-named Tricycle, would be the XX-Committee's first double-agent—and he would prove to be one of the best. Under the pretense of being a businessman buying goods for Yugoslavia, Popov was instructed by the Double-X to go through the motions of snooping out British secrets in the event another Abwehr agent had been assigned to shadow him.

At this point the XX-Committee's stress was upon misleading Hitler as to British strength (which was still woefully weak). The Germans instructed Popov (code-name Ivan by the Abwehr) to probe and photograph a certain RAF fighter airfield. He motored to the vicinity of the airfield, sat in a pub drinking ale for two hours, then drove back to London. That night Ivan mailed to an Abwehr drop in Lisbon five photos of the targeted field. The snapshots had been taken a day earlier by British agents and showed portions of the airfield crammed with RAF fighters. Actually, this was one of Colonel John Turner's dummy strips, and the Spits and Hurricanes had been on the field only long enough for hasty photos to be taken.

A week after Ivan had mailed his photos, Luftwaffe night bombers plastered the empty dummy strip, churning up huge clouds of dust and badly frightening nearby cattle.[5]

Much of Popov's information was sent to Lisbon in secret writing. It consisted of a witch's brew of data cleverly created by men of the Double-X. The deception strategy was to reveal truths when it was judged that they would cause no harm and would strengthen Popov's credibility with the Germans, half truths based on data the Abwehr was known to possess, and outright lies in matters that the Germans could not check.

In the months ahead Popov utilized "contacts high up in British officialdom" to send misleading reports on British defenses. The Abwehr apparently never doubted such lofty contacts, for Popov had often visited England in prewar years and as a wealthy man had rubbed elbows with Britain's high and mighty. On one occasion the XX-Committee provided Popov with documents he was supposed to have obtained from "a source in the Ministry of Transportation." These documents revealed that thirty thousand antitank rifles had just been distributed to British troops. The documents were authentic (for they would undergo intense scrutiny by Abwehr experts in Berlin), and the figures were accurate. The Double-X decided that it would be beneficial to let the Germans know that the British army was getting stronger. What the documents did not reveal was that the thirty thousand rifles were useless: there was hardly any ammunition for them.

Because of the wealth of high-grade intelligence (or so it seemed to the Abwehr) that Ivan was pumping into Berlin, it did not take long for him to establish himself as the ace German spy in the British Isles. That reputation was enhanced when the XX-Committee, without Popov's prior knowledge, arranged to have him arrested on suspicion by police not in the know either. After Popov had been grilled and released, he sent his Abwehr controller in Lisbon a detailed report on the episode, including the authentic names of policemen who had taken him into custody—just in case the Abwehr would send another spy to check on the truth of Ivan's account.

That night Dusko Popov was reminded forcefully that along with cloak-and-dagger activities there was also a violent side to the war. A German bomb blew off the corner of his Savoy Hotel.

Measure and Countermeasure

That fall and early winter of 1940 Goering's Luftwaffe continued savagely to bomb British cities, factories, ports, and RAF airfields (as well as a large number of dummy plants, fake airstrips, and bogus docks). Royal Air Force heavies, in turn, were raiding German cities, raids that were little more than pinpricks. Nearly all bombings took place at night, for both the RAF and the Luftwaffe had found that daylight assaults were too costly.

Under the relentless stress of creating innovative measures and countermeasures in what Churchill called The Wizard War, German and British scientists began conjuring up wild theories as to what devious device or technique the other side might have developed.

In late November German scientists theorized that members of the British Royal Observer Corps were switching on red lights when they heard Luftwaffe night bombers approaching. This procedure, it was speculated, permitted RAF night fighters to rush to the locales being threatened and intercept the hostile flights. At an airfield outside **Vannes**, France, the commander of Luftwaffe *Kampfgruppe* 100 (**Battle Group** 100) was ordered to investigate the red-light theory.

For three weeks German bomber crews studied the red-light

warning system and reported that based on their eyewitness observation the British indeed were using this technique. When Ultra picked up the German report, British air scientists were amused. There was no red-light warning system. So many red lights were winking and blinking in violation of the blackout that German air-crews had concluded that this was a coordinated operation.[1]

During this same period of time, Ultra unbuttoned a chilling German message that stated a certain locale in France would be ideal for storing "Flak Gas." Earlier Ultra intercepts had indicated that the Germans were filling antiaircraft shells with gas. Now it was the British scientists' turn to break out with the jitters. They theorized that the shells were intended to explode in front of British bombers, and the released clouds of gas would paralyze engines as the planes flew through them.

After a flurry of investigations, it was found that a single missing letter in the German message had caused the commotion. The letter *t* should have been at the end of *Gas*, as it was meant to read *Gast* (for *Geräte Ausbau Stelle*), merely an antiaircraft depot.[2]

The red-light warning system fantasy of the Germans and the great gas flap of the British were but interludes in the relentless twilight war of deceit and deception, of move and countermove. Neither adversary could relax or let down its guard for one minute. The immutable laws of challenge and response were constantly in operation. That is why Dr. Robert Cockburn and his team of scientists had no time for rejoicing when they succeeded in jamming the Knickebein beam. For hard on Knickebein's heels came an even more accurate German technique for guiding bombers to targets at night or in cloudy weather—the *X-Gerät* (X-Apparatus).

Shortly before midnight on November 5, 1940, bombers of Kampfgruppe 100 lifted off from Vannes in Brittany, winged northward over the dark waves of the English Channel, and headed for the large industrial city of Birmingham. Aboard the black-coated heavies was the X-Gerät, equipment so complicated that only the elite KGr100 was trained in its use. Birmingham was bombed heavily, and on the way home a Heinkel crashed on England's southern beaches. From the wreckage the X-Gerät was salvaged. It was rushed to the Royal

Aircraft Establishment (RAE) at Farnborough in Hampshire, where it was studied minutely by Dr. Cockburn, Reginald Jones, and their associates.

Jones and the others had been aware from German POWs' conversations the previous March that the Luftwaffe was developing X-Gerät. Now they determined that it consisted of a primary radio beam aimed at a target and three crossbeams. The main beam (code-named *Weser* by the Germans) was transmitting from Cherbourg on the Channel coast of France, and the three crossbeams (*Oder, Elbe,* and *Rhein*) were being sent from Calais, opposite Dover.

As a result of the scientists' findings, an alarmed Dr. Frederick Lindemann sent Prime Minister Churchill a memorandum on X-Gerät's capabilities: "Bombing accuracies on the order of 20 yards are expected."[3]

While Churchill was pondering suggested countermeasures to the X-Gerät threat, including a Commando raid on Kampfgruppe 100's base at Vannes, Ultra intercepted signals that revealed the Luftwaffe would launch a massive assault (Operation Moonlight Sonata) to wipe off the map three British cities code-named *Einheitspreis, Regenschirm,* and *Korn.* Weather permitting, Moonlight Sonata would be launched on November 14/15 and continue on successive nights. But which were these code-named cities?

An ant heap of activity erupted as British scientists tried to find the answer. Speed was essential; the blow would strike in only five days. Reginald Jones's hunch was that they were the Midlands cities of Wolverhampton, Birmingham, and Coventry. A few thought London was the target. All sorts of wild guesses came out of the Air Ministry. No one knew for sure.[4]

Whatever the targets were, they lay naked to night bombings. There would be insufficient time for Farnborough to produce enough X-Gerät jammers. RAF night fighters, without built-in radar to locate the hostile bombers, would be helpless. What antiaircraft guns were available to protect the three unidentified cities had no sophisticated aiming devices and could bring down a bomber at night only through sheer luck.

As late as early evening of November 14, all that anyone in Great Britain knew was that the Luftwaffe was up to something big. Among those speculating about Moonlight Sonata targets was Winston Churchill. Shortly after dusk the prime minister, with his confidential secretary, John Martin, drove off from Number 10 Downing Street to spend the night at a retreat outside London. During full-moon periods, Churchill's residence Chequers, not far from the capital, would be a clear and tempting target to German bombardiers.

At about 5:00 P.M. Kampfgruppe 100 lifted off at Vannes and, following the main X-Gerät beam (Weser), made a beeline for ancient Coventry. Shortly after 7:00 P.M. KGr100 bombers began showering thousands of incendiaries on the doomed city, transforming it into a roaring inferno.

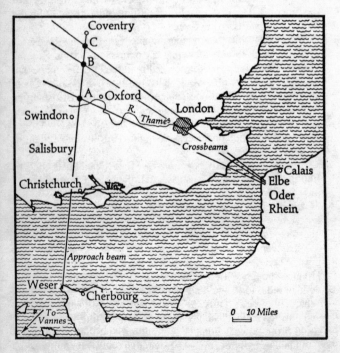

X-Gerät Beams Target Coventry

(Courtesy Prof. R. V. Jones)

Meanwhile, a few hundred Luftwaffe bombers had taken off from airfields at Chartres, Evreux, and Orly, in France, from Antwerp, Cambrai, and Brussels, in Belgium, and from Amsterdam and Eindhoven, in The Netherlands. Masses of flame leaping hundreds of feet into the black sky over Coventry served as a homing beacon that could be seen forty miles away by approaching German bomber crews. Within a few hours one hundred fifty thousand incendiaries and fourteen hundred high-explosive bombs were dropped. Historic Coventry had been pulverized. Sprawled in death beneath the rubble were 554 men, women, and children. Nearly 5,000 civilians were injured or burned.

Soon after daylight RAF officers descended upon the smoking ruins and learned that the Luftwaffe had employed a new technique for mass-bombing raids: a pathfinder group equipped with X-Gerät to mark the target with incendiaries for the main force of bombers.[5]

Moonlight Sonata continued, and Birmingham was struck the next night, but the damage was not as severe as at Coventry. Wolverhampton was not bombed, as British Intelligence had conjectured it would be.

Scientists at the Telecommunication Research Establishment near Swanage worked feverishly to develop countermeasures to X-Gerät (code-named *Wotan 1* by the Germans, Wye by the British). The horrible specter of Coventry's incineration spurred on Cockburn, Jones, and the others. Bad weather protected the British Isles from heavy German raids during the next few weeks, and by the end of 1940 British scientists had created a technique for jamming X-Gerät. But there was no time for celebration. Through Ultra, the British learned that German scientists had come up with an even more precise night-bomber radio beam, code-named *Wotan 2*.

Wotan 2 was a remarkable invention. The beam not only guided the bomber to its target, but told the bombardier when to release his cargo. However, scientists at TRE were soon eagerly inspecting this new electronic guidance equipment that had been salvaged from three Heinkels that had been shot down over England. Wotan 2 proved to be remarkably easy to jam, and BBC television transmitter at Alexandra Palace in London was ideal for the task—it worked on the right frequency band.

What the transmitter did was to reradiate the German bombers' own signals. This countermeasure was code-named Domino.

Now the customary cat-and-mouse game began. British scientists tried by subtle means to cause hostile bombers to stray slightly from their courses and drop their explosives off-target. The trick was to bamboozle the Luftwaffe without its discovering that it was being bamboozled. During the first few nights of the BBC transmitter's use, a minimum of power was injected into the Wotan 2 system, just enough of a signal to give approaching bomber fleets a slightly false course without arousing the suspicions of crews. Gradually the BBC power was turned higher to deflect German bombers even farther from their targets, and eventually the Luftwaffe realized that Wotan 2 had been compromised and was useless.

The rapid jamming of Wotan 2 had been one of Britain's most notable achievements. But this did not stop the bombing of London, a target so huge German bombers could find it without radio beams. Nor did it halt raids on ports in southern England, which the Luftwaffe could reach before the British had time to jam their guiding devices.

By January 1941 Great Britain had been bombed heavily for five months. There was little the British could do to retaliate against the Luftwaffe for the destruction of many cities and the loss of thousands of civilian lives. There was one man, however, Major Grant Taylor of the British army, who was determined to gain at least a measure of revenge. But what could one man accomplish?

Major Taylor was a freewheeling Englishman who had fought in France in World War I, been decorated, and left for the United States at the close of hostilities. Rumors reached old friends back in England during the next two decades that Taylor variously was a hit man for the mob, an undercover agent for the FBI (he was said to know its director, J. Edgar Hoover), and a bodyguard for the infamous Chicago gangster Al Capone. Reports flowed back home that Taylor, during 1937–1938, had set up small-arms schools in Chiang Kai-shek's Chinese army that was fighting the Japanese.

Whatever may have been the true activities of this swashbuckling adventurer, there were those in high places (legal and otherwise) who regarded Grant Taylor as a master in teaching the fine art of killing a foe or foes—quickly and efficiently.

At the outbreak of war in Europe, Taylor hurried back to England, was commissioned, and began organizing "killer schools" for elite units and for British spies who were to be parachuted into German-occupied nations. He taught how an armed man in a sudden confrontation with six armed men in a small area (a guardroom, for example) could kill all six foes in six seconds or less—one shot for each, in the right sequence, taking the most alert or dangerous man first, using the elements of surprise and speed. (It was said that Taylor had done this—in three seconds.)

Now, in January 1941, Major Grant Taylor was going to put his techniques into action. Through underground sources across the Channel, he learned that a group of Luftwaffe pilots who had been engaged in bombing London met each Friday night at a certain restaurant in a small town along the French Channel coast to dine, drink, and make merry. Taylor decided that he would crash their party.

Armed with a .45 Colt automatic, another pistol, and a trench knife, Major Taylor crossed the Channel in a launch (provided by Charles Hambro's SOE) during the early hours of darkness. Reaching the targeted town, the craft slipped into the black harbor and tied up at a deserted dock. Disguised as a French fisherman, Taylor, noiseless as a jungle cat, leaped onto the dock hards and began stealing through the streets toward the restaurant where the German pilots gathered.

Arriving at his destination, the major paused briefly and checked his weapons. Blackout curtains covered the windows, but he could hear raucous singing and boisterous talk from within. No doubt the German bomber pilots' party was in full swing. "Enjoy yourself, you bastards," Taylor reflected, "for you won't be able to sing much longer!"

Clutching tightly to his pistols, one in each hand, Major Taylor threw open the front door, spotted his adversaries across the room, and squeezed off several bursts. He was right on target. A couple of the startled Germans reached for their pistols, but it was too late. All six pilots crumpled to the floor and died. Taylor raced back to the dock, leaped into the waiting launch, and by sunrise was back in England. [6]

Although it had wiped out six skilled German pathfinder pilots and infected Feldgrau in that locale with a case of the jitters, Grant Taylor's one-man rampage was mainly a gesture of defiance. British cities continued to be bombed heavily, and it was touch and go as to whether Great Britain could survive. No matter how farfetched any deception idea may have seemed, the British had to try every conceivable means to thwart enemy bombers. Railroad tracks, bridges, and roads were used as orientation points, so many of these were camouflaged to confuse Luftwaffe navigators. But German airmen could count on one unfailing aid to pinpoint English targets—the iridescence of the moon reflecting off rivers, lakes, reservoirs, and canals.

Consequently, Charles Goodeve, leader of the Wheezers and Dodgers of the Directorate of Miscellaneous Weapons Development, was handed a difficult task: hide the moon. Goodeve promptly formed a team under Lieutenant Commander Duncan Bruce to solve the urgent problem of masking England's waterways. Early attention was given to the use of large nets held up by floating corks. This proved to be adequate only on ponds and small lakes.

After extensive experimentation, Bruce's team developed a mixture of coal dust and fuel oil that could be sprayed over bodies of water. It would cling to the surface, resulting in a dark, nonreflecting coating, thereby "hiding the moon." Now came the trials. The majestic Thames River in London was selected. Winston Churchill himself suddenly appeared on Westminster Bridge to view the demonstration.

A cigar clamped between his teeth, the prime minister watched as four launches carrying spraying apparatus began plying slowly along the Thames and depositing the oily concoction onto the surface. The trial seemed to be successful. Churchill looked on in fascination. But it was not just the broad Thames that was being coated with the sooty substance, so were the Wheezers and Dodgers on the launches, to the point that they had difficulty in recognizing one another.

Then Mother Nature got into the act. The winds began to gust, the current grew brisk, and the oily concoction on the

Thames began to break up and scatter. Matters went from bad to worse. A disappointed Churchill, flicking specks of oil from his clothing, strolled rapidly off the bridge. A naval craft had to be rushed into service to pick up dead dogs and cats floating in the river. Housewives downstream protested bitterly that the oily substance blowing from the water had ruined washings hanging on outdoor lines.

Regretfully, for the Wheezers and Dodgers hated to admit defeat, the Thames River project had to be dropped. But Commander Bruce's team persevered. Outside Coventry, where they did not have to contend with the tides, they camouflaged the Coventry Canal (which the Luftwaffe was using as an orientation point) so effectively that an elderly man and his dog, out for an early evening walk, fell into the body of water, having mistaken the canal for a newly built road.

But this had been an isolated case. The expenditure in money, time, and manpower to "hide the moon" would be enormous. Even the most ardent advocate of water camouflage among the Wheezers and Dodgers had lost faith in the practicability of the ambitious project.[7]

Not far from where the eager beavers of the DMWD were conducting ill-fated trials on the Thames, Sefton Delmer, the former Berlin correspondent for a London newspaper who had been with the German service of the BBC for several months, was growing increasingly frustrated. Each day he sat hunched over an empty desk in a small office in a top-secret building just off Berkeley Square. In his impeccable German, he delivered two or three brief talks each week over BBC transmitters beamed to the Wehrmacht across the Channel and to the Reich home front, but that was all.

Delmer's frustration was laced with anger, for he was convinced that the German service of the BBC, as it was being conducted, was a waste of time and effort. Wheel spinning. The German service news bulletins, while well written, sounded to Delmer like one Nazi refugee talking to a few other Nazi refugees. What was needed was to reach the minds of the great mass of Germans who supported the fuehrer and his war, not the tiny sliver who wanted Hitler to lose the conflict.

For many weeks Delmer had been hounding his bosses at BBC, trying to persuade them that it was necessary to stimulate

Germans into thoughts and actions hostile to Hitler. The *herrenvolk* (civilians) and the Wehrmacht would have to be tricked. Trickery and deception. Those were the keys. But BBC executives recoiled at the suggestion. What, use staid, circumspect BBC for purposes of trickery? Preposterous.

Suddenly, in mid-1941, Delmer was jolted from his dejection. Leonard Ingrams, an innovative official in the cloak-and-dagger Ministry of Economic Warfare, sent for Delmer. Speaking in conspiratorial tones, Ingrams revealed that the British had been operating a radio station called *Sender der Europäischen Revolution* (Radio of the European Revolution), which supposedly was based in some Nazi-occupied country, but was actually beamed from transmitters near London. It was run by a group of German Communists and appealed to Reich workers to throw off the Nazi yoke and join in one Europe (under Communism, of course).

Frowning, Ingrams said that the German Communists were allowed to run the station and its doctrine however they saw fit. "Not really a terribly good idea," he exclaimed.[8] The "European revolutionaries" (as they called themselves) resented any hint of British editorial suggestion. All they wanted from the British were radio facilities and money with which to operate.

Now, Ingrams said, the ministry felt that it was vital to start a right-wing station aimed at the Third Reich and that Sefton Delmer had been selected as the man to run it—with total editorial control. Delmer was elated and accepted immediately. But why the decision to launch a German right-wing station? The Nazis, Ingrams replied, had recently begun operating a British left-wing radio station they called The Workers Challenge, in which Germans speaking flawless English tried to undermine the British and turn them against Winston Churchill and his "war party."

Smiling, Ingrams added: "Little old ladies in Eastbourne and Torquay are listening to it avidly, because it is using the foulest language ever. They enjoy counting the *F*'s and *B*'s."[9] He said that Dr. Hugh Fulton, Minister of Economic Warfare, thought that the British should reply in kind, using gutter language and crude expressions.

"Go to it, Tom," the ministry official enthused. "It's a great chance for you to show your ingenuity. There are no limits. No holds barred!"

That's the kind of talk Tom wanted to hear. No holds barred! Delmer had become the Chief High Priest of "black radio."

In April 1941 a group of some of Britain's most illustrious figures—and devious intellects—began convening daily in a small conference room in Prime Minister Churchill's headquarters beneath the pavements at Storey's Gate in bomb-battered London. The existence of this group would be one of the most closely guarded secrets of the war, comparable to the intense security masking Ultra. This body was known by the innocuous title London Controlling Section (LCS), and it was the brainchild of Churchill.[10] Charged with developing deception stratagems and coordinating activities of the myriad cloak-and-dagger agencies that had mushroomed under the prime minister's inspiration, LCS was the first bureaucracy created in Great Britain's history whose sole function was deceit.

In implementing stratagems to deceive the Germans, LCS would meld techniques used for centuries with the special means of modern technology and psychological and economic warfare, using any or all arms of the government and the military. LCS methods would not only be secret and intricate, but ruthless. Under its chairman, Colonel Oliver Stanley, a prominent Tory minister, the LCS would see that each British war-planning staff had a deception section linked directly to LCS. As the result of this network, the sum of all intelligence data could be utilized by LCS to create stratagems that would have enormous impact on current and future military operations.

"Peace Proposal" Mission

*England has already lost the war. It is only a
matter of having the intelligence to admit it.*
                                        —Adolf Hitler
                                        March 27, 1941

On the night of May 10, 1941, an enormous red glow
shimmered in the sky over burning London. The city was
suffering the heaviest bombing it had known and was fighting
for its existence. Searchlights sent up long, slender fingers of
white, and ack-ack guns barked constantly—and futilely. RAF
night fighters rose to challenge the Luftwaffe heavies, but
could not locate them. Amidst the harsh cacophony of exploding shells and the thunder of guns came the urgent clanging of
bells on fire trucks and ambulances trying to pick their way
through piles of rubble that had cascaded into the streets.

Far removed from the fiery London holocaust, some 350
miles to the north in Lanarkshire, Scotland, 40-year-old David
McLean, a bachelor farmer who lived with his sister and
mother in a white-washed cottage, was undressing for bed. In
the hush of the night, his ears discerned the throb of an airplane
engine. He stuck his head through the open window, scanned
the sky, and saw the craft's shadowy silhouette. Moments later
his heartbeat quickened as, in the pale rays of a half moon, he
saw a billowing white parachute and, dangling beneath it, the
dark blob of a figure. McLean awakened his mother and sister,

crying out that a man had bailed out of an airplane almost directly overhead and that "it might be a German."

Unarmed, the farmer dashed outside and raced to a pasture. Reaching its gate, McLean could see that the man had already landed and was gathering up his parachute. The Scotsman ran to the intruder, who was sitting on the ground and breathing hard, and exclaimed, "Are ye a Nazi, or are ye one o' ours?"[1]

The man replied in a friendly voice, "Not a Nazi enemy, but a British friend." McLean sensed that the German pilot was in pain, and he was, for he had baldly jammed his ankle on landing.

The Scotsman put a supporting arm around the German, and the pair set off toward the cottage. How strange, McLean reflected. He had long conjured up the mayhem he would inflict upon any German airman unfortunate enough to parachute onto his farm. As the two men reached the cottage, 68-year-old William Craig, puffing hard from exertion, rushed up. From his adjoining farm, he had seen the parachuting figure. "Go fetch the soldiers!" McLean called out.

With his wide-eyed mother and sister staring at the tall, beetle-browed German by the light of a flickering lantern, the farmer for the first time realized that there was something unusual about his "captive." Although over hostile territory, the pilot had been unarmed and seemed to be too old for a fighter pilot, perhaps in his late forties. What's more, McLean observed, the German's uniform was of expensive material, unlike that worn by other captured pilots.

In the spic-and-span kitchen, the German identified himself as *Hauptmann* (Captain) Alfred Horn, and he asked how far away Dungavel House was, home of the Duke of Hamilton. Told that it was ten or twelve miles distant, Captain Horn asked pleadingly if McLean would take him there. "It's urgent," the German declared. "I have to speak to the Duke of Hamilton."

There was a knock at the door. Mrs. McLean opened it to a pair of British signal soldiers who said that they had been searching for a parachutist. McLean was startled; neither soldier was armed. Another knock. Two more men crowded into the small kitchen. One wore civilian clothes and a steel helmet with the word *Police* scrawled across it. The other man, who wore civilian trousers and an army battle jacket and who was armed with a World War I Webley revolver, seemed quite nervous over the sudden confrontation with The Enemy. He whipped out his sidearm and in a loud voice shouted menacingly: "Hands up!" The fierce command was aimed at the docile German, who had been sitting peacefully for thirty minutes, but it was so shrill that others in the kitchen, including the two McLean women, threw up their hands.

Captain Alfred Horn, who gave his age as forty-seven, was escorted in a truck to Maryhill Barracks in Glasgow—but not before the entire Home Guard around Lanarkshire had been turned out to "guard" the prisoner. There the German changed his story. "My name is Rudolf Hess," he declared. "And I have come to save humanity!"

His identity would shock the world. Rudolf Hess was Number 3 man on the Nazi Germany totem pole, ranking behind only Adolf Hitler and Reich Marshal Hermann Goering.

The Duke of Hamilton, a wing commander in the RAF, was summoned from his duty station; he had been battling the Luftwaffe for four consecutive nights. The two men met, and Hess claimed that he had met the Duke at the 1936 Olympics in Berlin. The Duke had no memory of having met the Reich minister.

On the following day Ivone Kirkpatrick, who had been a British spy during World War I, flew to Scotland to interview Hess. The Nazi bigwig excitedly poured out details of his self-appointed mission to "save humanity." Hitler was convinced that England had been whipped and no doubt knew it, Hess declared, so the fuehrer was prepared to grant a compassionate reprieve to a doomed nation of Aryans.

Once England had ceased the war in the West, the Reich minister exclaimed, the Wehrmacht would withdraw from all of France except for Alsace and Lorraine. Hitler would evacuate Belgium, The Netherlands, Denmark, and Norway, but would retain Luxembourg. England, in return for these concessions, would assume a benevolent neutrality toward the Third Reich in Hitler's looming "eastern mission."

The British, through Ultra, had already been aware that the fuehrer was rushing huge masses of troops, panzers, and warplanes eastward to invade the Soviet Union in June.

Once Hitler had launched his invasion of Russia "to save humanity from the Soviet barbarians," England and France would become arsenals of free capitalism, and the fuehrer would take over the full production of their war industries, Hess explained. As a humanitarian gesture, the German pointed out, Hitler was eager to halt the "senseless war" with a brother nation (England)—and, of course, thereby protect his rear while fighting the Russians.

Kirkpatrick rushed to London with ten notebooks filled with transcriptions of Hess's remarks. The "peace proposal" was communicated to Washington, which had suddenly grown alarmed over the threat posed by Adolf Hitler's powerful war machine. "Neutral" Washington rejected the offer. So did London.[2]

On May 13, three days after Rudolf Hess had parachuted into a Scottish pasture, a furious fuehrer called a special meeting of his military chiefs at the Berghof in Bavaria. Hitler had known nothing in advance of his disciple's flight to Scotland. If Hess returned to Germany, the fuehrer declared, he was to be shot immediately.[3]

Field Marshal Wilhelm Keitel, Colonel General Alfred Jodl, General Franz Halder, and other army brass sat in stone-faced silence as Hitler paced about, tapping his forehead as though to say Rudolf Hess is crazy. The fuehrer declared that his longtime crony was suffering from hallucinations. "Hess was deeply disturbed because he was not on active [war] duty," Hitler explained.

Meanwhile, Admiral Wilhelm Canaris in Berlin was ordered to launch a probe of the Hess affair to uncover a conspiracy against the fuehrer. The Abwehr chief and Schwarze Kapelle leader found himself in yet another curious position: as a conspirator against Hitler, Canaris had been given the job of investigating a possible conspiracy.

No, Canaris finally reported (accurately), there was no conspiracy. Hess had taken off alone in a Messerschmitt 110 from Augsburg for the flight to Scotland. Although the Number 3 Nazi had been with his wife at the family home in Munich the day he departed, he had not told her of his plan. Hess had informed only his longtime aide, Captain Karlheinz

Pintsch, who had furnished him with maps and weather reports.[4]

Adolf Hitler and his confidants were greatly concerned about the propaganda harvest the British would reap from what could be made to appear as the "defection" of the deputy fuehrer. But Winston Churchill was viewing the affair from a different point of view. A political hot potato had been dropped into the prime minister's lap.

For eighteen months the British people had endured bombs and shortages of food, fuel, and clothing. Perhaps a million people spent nights in cold, damp air-raid shelters, and hundreds of thousands more fled cities each night to sleep fitfully in frigid open fields. They had seen hundreds of RAF planes shot out of the skies and knew that German U-boats in the Atlantic were wreaking havoc with merchant shipping. Thousands of their fighting men had been killed and wounded, as had tens of thousands of civilians. And the Dunkirk debacle had indelibly impressed British minds with the fact that England was an island under siege with no hope of outside assistance.

Now Churchill feared that if the true purpose of Rudolf Hess's bizarre mission became known, the British people would become angered because the government had not considered the Nazi's "peace proposal." So the prime minister erected a wall of silence around the entire affair. BBC was gagged and told it would announce only that Hess had landed by parachute in Scotland and had been taken prisoner. It was "suggested" to the editors of *Luftpost*, a propaganda organ dropped on the Germans by the RAF, that they refrain from any comment on the episode.

Churchill, the shrewd political card player, kept an ace up his sleeve. Hitler had sought to discredit Hess by calling him insane; Churchill went along with that point of view. So if British political opponents raised an outcry and tried to unseat Churchill for not acting on the "peace proposal," the prime minister would declare that the deputy fuehrer had been certified as insane. Hess was placed in the care of psychiatrists, and a whispering campaign was launched to spread the word that the Number 3 Nazi was indeed mentally deranged.[5]

At the same time that Hess had parachuted into Scotland, Sefton Delmer was nearly ready to go on the air with his "black radio" station. Articulate and with a keen grasp of human nature, Delmer had sold his bosses on an innovative concept. Instead of spiels coming from London and beamed to the German people (spiels that would be shrugged off as enemy propaganda), Delmer would give the impression that his was a clandestine station being operated by patriotic Germans who were using a portable transmitter somewhere in Nazi-occupied Europe. These loyal Germans, it would soon become evident, were regularly on the run from the Gestapo.

A master psychologist, Delmer knew that his station would gain far more German listeners if *herrenvolk* believed that they were eavesdropping on radio talk of a secret nature not meant for their ears. And "German" operators would add to the station's credibility in the Third Reich.

The central figure in Delmer's plan to subtly subvert German minds was a crusty, foul-mouthed old Prussian who the station would identify merely as *Der Chef* (The Chief). Actually, Der Chef was neither old nor Prussian. He was 34-year-old Paul Sanders, a Berliner who in 1938 had fled Nazi Germany, come to England, and at the outbreak of war joined the British army.

The clandestine station—with a few million Germans, it was hoped, eventually listening avidly—would relay a series of instructions to the "secret cells" of a nonexistent underground army in Germany. Then Der Chef was to come on the air and, in language laced liberally with four-letter words, give his viewpoints on what was taking place in Nazi Germany and in England. It would soon become clear to Reich listeners that Der Chef was loyally devoted to Adolf Hitler, but felt that the rabble around the fuehrer had seized control of the Reich in Hitler's name. Der Chef would be as scathingly contemptuous of Winston Churchill as he was of those "sycophants" clustered around the fuehrer.

Delmer's "black radio" began operations on the night of May 23, 1941. He called the station *Gustav Siegfried Eins* (George Sugar One, a signaler's phonetic wording for GS-1), a random identity intended to add mystique and to generate widespread conjecture in the Reich as to what the letters stood for, thereby drawing a larger audience. Subject of the initial broadcast: Rudolf Hess's "peace mission."

Delmer, Leonard Ingrams, and others in British psychological warfare had been shocked by Churchill's placing a muzzle on British media concerning speculation over the Hess affair. But Gustav Siegfried Eins had not been included in the restriction, for it was not bound by truthfulness or accuracy; its function was trickery and deceit. Missing facts were no problem to the station: facts could always be invented. Der Chef would exploit the Hess episode.

After a series of phony coded messages to nonexistent cells, Der Chef, with his booming voice, came on the air. He took out after Rudolf Hess. "First, let's get this straight," Der Chef roared. "This fellow [Hess] is by no means the worst of the lot. He was a good comrade of ours in the old days. But like the rest of this bleeping clique of cranks, megalomaniacs, string pullers, and parlor Bolsheviks who call themselves our [German] leaders, he simply has no guts for a crisis."

Der Chef continued to read from the script that had been carefully prepared by Sefton Delmer: "As soon as Hess learns a little of the darker side of the developments that lie ahead, he loses his head completely, gets a white flag, and flies off to throw himself and us all on the mercy of that bleeping flat-footed bastard of a drunken old Jew Churchill."[6]

Der Chef paused for dramatic effect. Then he castigated the bleeps around Hitler who had been passing the word that the fuehrer had sent Hess on the mission. "They're the bleeping obscenities who have taken over Germany in Adolf Hitler's name," Der Chef thundered.

In closing, the "old Prussian" told the "underground army" the times that Gustav Siegfried Eins would be on the air each day. And he cautioned the secret cells that the station would periodically be silent in order to hastily move the transmitter to a new locale. The obscenities in the bleeping Gestapo, he declared, were constantly on the station's trail.

On June 22 Air Vice Marshal Trafford Leigh-Mallory and a group of Royal Air Force intelligence officers were holding a tense conference in a bombproof shelter at Uxbridge. Leigh-Mallory disclosed that British intelligence had received an alarming report (probably through Ultra): the Germans would mount a raid to kidnap (or kill) Rudolf Hess. At 1:00 A.M. the following day, the air marshal said, German planes would bomb Luton Hoo in Bedfordshire as a distraction for a paratrooper force that would land nearby. This was in the locale of Cockfosters, where captured German pilots were held. Apparently enemy intelligence thought (mistakenly) that the former deputy fuehrer was a prisoner there.

A successful German raid to recover Hess from the heart of England could result in a monumental propaganda bonanza for Adolf Hitler. So Leigh-Mallory was determined to repulse the operation. He ordered all available searchlights and antiaircraft guns to get on the road for Luton Hoo within ten minutes. Police and Home Guardsmen in that locale were alerted. Armed with shotguns, axes, sabers, pitchforks, and pistols, the elderly men and fuzzy cheeked boys of the Home Guard were rapidly deployed to meet the German paratroopers.

Minutes after the searchlights and the antiaircraft guns arrived at Luton Hoo, the eerie moan of air-raid sirens floated across the lush green landscape. Then the throb of airplane engines. Searchlights probed the sky and guns opened fire.

The raid proved to be a fiasco. There was only a handful of aircraft, and they dropped their bombs and flew away. For forty-eight hours the eager Home Guard scoured the region for enemy paratroopers, but found only two parachutes.

Far off in East Prussia, Adolf Hitler had no time for recriminations over the botched mission to kidnap Rudolf Hess. The fuehrer was deeply involved in plans for launching the most fateful operation of his life.

12

Underground Escape Lines

In the spring of 1941, Ultra at Bletchley Park began unbuttoning German messages that revealed a startling fact: Adolf Hitler, conqueror of Europe, was postponing plans to crush England and instead would launch a massive invasion of the Reich's ally, the Soviet Union. Already large numbers of German divisions and air squadrons were being moved out of France and the Low Countries and back into Poland and the Balkans. Hitler assured nervous generals that his blitzkrieg would require but two months, three at the most, to bring the Russian army to its knees. *Then* he would unleash the full fury of the German armed forces across the English Channel and wipe out obstinate Great Britain once and for all.

As the Wehrmacht flow to the East gained momentum, Winston Churchill and British high-level commanders were kept abreast of Hitler's moves by Ultra. Even though the Germans had left behind forces strong enough only to guard the Channel coasts in France, Belgium, and The Netherlands, Britain's armed forces were far too weak to attempt to recross the embattled moat.

For several weeks Prime Minister Churchill, although unable to reveal his Ultra source, had repeatedly warned Russian dictator Joseph Stalin, by dramatic messages sent through diplomatic channels, of the German plans. Stalin, who later would be described by Churchill as having "all the charm of a python," ignored the warnings, apparently considering them a devious effort by a doomed England to drive a wedge between him and his close ally, Adolf Hitler.

In the blackness at three o'clock on the morning of June 22, 1941, the fuehrer launched Operation Barbarossa. Along a 2,000-mile front some three million German troops poured across the Russian frontier in the mightiest military maneuver the world had known. Despite Churchill's urgent warnings, the Russians were taken by total surprise.[1]

Besieged Great Britain no longer stood alone against the awesome power of Hitler's legions. But would Churchill, the archfoe of Communism, seek a partnership with the Soviet Union? He would—aggressively. Whatever the cost, Russia must be kept in the fight against the fuehrer and Nazism. "If Hitler invaded Hell," the prime minister exclaimed to John Martin, his private secretary, "I would make at least a favorable reference to the Devil in the House of Commons."[2]

Churchill set about joining up with the devil. On December 12, 1941—the day German spearheads reached the outskirts of frozen Moscow—two British emissaries, Foreign Secretary Anthony Eden and Undersecretary of the Foreign Office Alexander Cadogan, sat down with a stony-faced Stalin in the Kremlin. Almost at once the Soviet leader raised the question: When was England going to launch an attack across the English Channel to relieve the pressure on Russia? He demanded that Britain strike sometime in 1942.

Three days later Eden and Cadogan met with the chief of the Russian secret service, a scowling Lavrenti Beria. "What are your plans for arming underground forces in German-occupied Europe?" Beria demanded. It was as though two suspected "enemies of the Soviet state" were undergoing a third-degree grilling from the head of Russia's dreaded secret police. Cadogan, who had helped organize Special Operations Executive, described the work of that cloak-and-dagger agency.

Finally, on December 20, Winston Churchill's pact with the devil was sealed. In one of history's most curious—and secret—amalgamations of undercover forces, Britain's MI-6 and Special Operations Executive joined with Communist Russia's NKVD (Secret Service) in an agreement to exchange both nations' intelligence on Germany. So secret was the pact that the negotiators on both sides did their own typing. Only

Stalin, Beria, and Foreign Minister Vycheslav Molotov among the Russians, and Churchill, Eden, Cadogan, and a handful of top leaders in Britain would be aware of the agreement.

It was a shotgun marriage laced with mutual suspicion and mistrust. Stalin and his two top subordinates were convinced that MI-6's goal was to destroy Communism. Churchill, who had labeled Communism as "foul baboonery,"[3] and his confidants felt that Russia's purpose in the intelligence alliance was not only to defeat Hitler, but to spread Communism in a postwar Europe weakened by the war.

Even as Eden and Cadogan had been sailing toward the Soviet Union to negotiate the secret pact, Great Britain gained another ally. The Sleeping Giant—the United States—had been bombed into the war at Pearl Harbor on December 7, 1941. It was the answer to Winston Churchill's fervent prayers. The road to victory would be long and bloody, but Great Britain would live.

America, in fact, had been openly involved in the European conflict since March 1941, when President Franklin Roosevelt had proclaimed the United States to be the Arsenal of Democracy. He had rammed through Congress the Lend-Lease program in which guns, tanks, trucks, ships, and munitions began flowing across the Atlantic to beleaguered Britain in return for token payments.

So essential were these supplies to Britain's survival that nearly all German U-boat wolf packs descended upon the North Atlantic trade routes as Hitler sought to strangle the British Isles into surrender. The Nazi submarines inflicted such a terrible toll in shipping that England was faced with as grave a threat to her existence as Sea Lion had been the previous year. Seeking to focus free-world attention on the crisis, Churchill proclaimed it the Battle of the Atlantic.

All through 1941 MI-5 continued to haul in German spies that the Abwehr tried to slip into Britain. Alfred Owens, the double-agent known to the Germans as Johnny and to the XX-Committee as Snow, had fingered many of them. Abwehr Captain Herbert Wichmann in Hamburg trusted Johnny and had advised him of the imminent arrival of new agents.

But Snow's service to the British crown came to an abrupt

halt. In an unusual move the Double-X had allowed him to travel to Belgium to meet with an Abwehr agent. On his return to England, Snow's controllers began to doubt his true loyalties (if any), and he was put in prison, where he would spend the remainder of the war. Despite the high-living, carefree Canadian's sudden incarceration, the Double-X had no shortage of turned German spies. On January 1, 1942, there were nineteen double-agents in its stable.[4]

These nineteen were the elite. All captured Nazi spies were interrogated at Latchmere House, a rambling old mansion near Richmond in Surrey that had once served as a convalescent home for wounded British officers. Most of the scores of Abwehr agents processed there were found to be too unintelligent to become effective double-agents. A handful of Nazi fanatics were turned over to law-enforcement agencies, and most of those concluded their service to the fuehrer on the gallows at Wandsworth prison.

For several months now, a Spanish diplomat who was a member of the exclusive Boodle's in London's St. James Street, had been sitting in the club's venerable bay window pretending to read a newspaper. In fact, he was watching the comings and goings at the large building across the street. That structure housed MI-5. The diplomat sent regular reports to the Abwehr (through its Madrid outpost) on those entering and leaving the building and on unusual activities. But the Spaniard, whatever may have been his diplomatic skills, was a clumsy spy for the fuehrer. Almost from his first day in the bay window, MI-5 had been keeping an eye on him and had arranged to intercept his reports to the Abwehr. The ones containing harmless information were allowed to reach Madrid. Those that held observations that were better left confidential were confiscated by MI-5 and, as far as the Spaniard knew, had merely become lost in the chaotic wartime postal services.

During 1941 Charles Hambro's Special Operations Executive—The Firm—had steadily been infiltrating agents into German-occupied Europe. Some had slipped ashore in rubber dinghies; others had parachuted in from Whitleys of the Moon Squadron. But it was not until late in the year that the Moon

Squadron, based at secret Gibraltar Farm north of London, inaugurated an espionage shuttle service to the Continent.

These would be "set down" and "pick up" flights carried out by Lysanders—small, maneuverable airplanes capable of landing and lifting off in short spaces. In order to provide room for one passenger—a Joe—the Lizzies, as they were called, had been stripped of guns, armor, and other equipment. Only a radiotelephone remained.

Chosen for the first shuttle mission was Flight-Lieutenant "Whippy" Nesbitt-Dufort, a lean, congenial officer with an engaging sense of humor and a reputation as an exceptional pilot. He would be confronted by an operation fraught with peril and difficulty. Without benefit of a navigator, Nesbitt-Dufort would have to locate a flyspeck field in the vast blackness of France, using only a map and whatever landmarks—villages, roads, rivers—he might detect in the moonlight. He would have to avoid Luftwaffe night fighters, ack-ack guns, and searchlights on the French coast; and when he landed, a Gestapo committee could be on hand to welcome him to France. It was not a job for faint hearts and weak knees.

Lieutenant Nesbitt-Dufort was to drop off the Joe at a designated French pasture, then pick up another Joe who was waiting there. The latter agent had been parachuted into France several months earlier and had radioed The Firm to arrange for a Lysander pickup, as the Gestapo was hot on his trail.

Nesbitt-Dufort's little Lizzie trundled down the Gibraltar Farm runway after dark, lifted off, and set a course for Normandy in France. Wedged in next to him was the Joe. Neither knew the name of the other or hardly spoke during the flight across the Channel. Reaching the French coast, Nesbitt-Dufort lost altitude and began skimming over the sleeping moonlit farms and tiny villages. Every few seconds he glanced down at the map on his lap. He seemed to be on course—or was he?

Unknown to the RAF officer, the Joe who was to be waiting at the rendezvous and who was to signal an all clear by flashlight was not at the pasture. He had been arrested that morning by an officious French policeman in a town ten miles away and charged with having improper papers. The Joe had been held at the police station all day, then released only at dusk. He had hopped on a bicycle and and begun pedaling frantically toward the Lysander rendezvous ten miles distant. Could he make it on time? The Joe feared he could not.

Winging toward the flyspeck, Nesbitt-Dufort glanced at his watch. Right on time. Five minutes to go. That was crucial, for the Gestapo-hounded agent could not tarry indefinitely at the rendezvous. Speaking for one of the few times on the flight, the pilot told his passenger that when they landed there would be no time for emotional farewells. Leap from the Lizzie and get the hell going, Nesbitt-Dufort reminded the Joe.

Now the Lizzie was over the field. The pilot began circling, and he squinted through the moonlight for a glimpse of the split-second flashlight glow that would tell him that it was safe to land and that this was indeed the place to touch down. Already, Nesbitt-Dufort reflected, the noise of the Lizzie's engine had roused the Germans in the locality.

At the same moment the bicycling SOE agent was still a mile away. He discerned the dim silhouette of the circling Lysander and knew that he could not reach the field before the pilot, sensing that things had gone awry, aborted the mission and flew back to England. The agent was desperate. If he failed to get aboard the Lysander, he could soon fall into the clutches of the Gestapo.

The spy threw caution to the winds. Perspiring heavily from the exertion, he leaped off the bicycle, scrambled over a hedgerow, and ran out into a small pasture, flashing his light skyward. Much to his relief, a split-second light of recognition flashed from the Lysander.

As Joe concealed himself in the shadows, he was deeply worried. He had previously inspected the designated field and found it suitable for a Lysander landing and takeoff. But this was a strange pasture and might be dotted with tree stumps, boulders, and ditches. The Lizzie touched down, skidded and bumped along grass wet with dew, and ground to a halt. Even before the craft had come to a complete stop, its door flew open, the Joe leaped out, raced away, and was swallowed up by the night. Moments later the Joe on the ground scrambled into the vacated space.

Lieutenant Nesbitt-Dufort, always irrepressible, called out

cheerfully, "Good evening to you—or should I say good morning?"[5]

By January 1942 Hitler's legions were bogged down in a bloody slugging match on the frozen steppes deep inside Russia. In black-bordered columns headlined "Fell for the Fuehrer," Reich newspapers were printing long lists of German soldiers killed in the East. So Tom Delmer, the mastermind of Gustav Siegfried Eins, Britain's black radio, began zeroing in on the culprits in the Wehrmacht disaster.

Der Chef, the crusty, foul-mouthed old Prussian, had built up a large following of Germans who eavesdropped on his rantings to the calls of the nonexistent underground network. Der Chef remained staunchly loyal to the fuehrer (as were his Reich listeners). The catastrophe in Russia was not Hitler's fault, Der Chef thundered, but rather that of the unprincipled bleeps around him.

In writing scripts for Der Chef, Tom Delmer carefully avoided mentioning Goering, Himmler, Goebbels, and other bigwigs, for that would have smacked of enemy propaganda and would have damaged the credibility of Gustav Siegfried Eins as a clandestine radio station operated by German patriots who were always one jump ahead of the Gestapo. For the same reason, Der Chef never referred to the Nazi Party—only to the party.

So the targets were lesser-known Party leaders, the "spineless bastards" conniving behind the fuehrer's back. Where possible, authenticity was injected into Delmer's fabrications by using the true names of minor Nazi officials culled from censored POW mail, Reich newspapers, and British intelligence.

Der Chef ranted against those bleeping Party officials who in order to make big profits delayed shipments of heavy clothing to "our brave boys freezing in the Russian winter." And the old Prussian nearly choked with apoplexy as he raged about the "traitorous whores" married to Party leaders in Schleswig-Holstein. These "filthy tramps," Der Chef bellowed, rushed to stores and bought up all the woolen textiles to which they were entitled by their clothing coupons after learning from their bleeping husbands that the Reich was about to run out of wool.

As a loyal German, Der Chef rolled out his choicest epithets to castigate the bleeping obscenities who permitted transfusions to be given to "our brave wounded boys in Russia" of blood drawn from Russian prisoners without testing the donors for venereal disease. As a result, Der Chef thundered, many of "our wounded boys" had contacted VD, and when they return home "will pass it along to their wives."

While other British cloak-and-dagger agencies, hastily thrown together in 1940, were beginning to bloom by early 1942, a secret organization known as MI-9 was still wrestling with an unprecedented and unforeseen problem that had suddenly burst forth after the Dunkirk debacle. No one in British intelligence had studied how to rescue from under the noses of the Germans the hundreds, perhaps thousands, of troops cut off from their units after the Allied defeat on the Continent.

MI-9, under Brigadier Norman R. Crockett, was the War Office Intelligence Department concerned with Allied prisoners of war. IS9(d) was the section responsible for organizing and conducting covert operations in France, Belgium, and The Netherlands to aid Allied troops to escape and return to England. IS9(d) was located in two rooms in London, and its official mailing address was Room 900, War Office. So the tiny agency (it had one officer for many months; later it would have but three) became known as Room 900.

Within a month of Dunkirk, Room 900 had started organizing underground escape lines. Most of the cutoff British soldiers were in hiding near the English Channel coast, but since the Germans guarded the beaches and ports, it would be impossible to smuggle the escapees directly across to Britain. So the escape lines would have to extend all the way from The Netherlands to the Pyrenees at the French-Spanish border, from where the escapees would be sneaked into neutral Spain and finally taken back to England.

At that time a husky MI-9 agent posted at Gibraltar, Donald Darling, was rushed to Barcelona, Spain, and Lisbon, Portugal, to establish the first clandestine links to France. Darling (code-named Sunday), bright and energetic, knew the Spanish-French frontier area well. His mission was complicated because of the June 1940 armistice that had divided France with a demarcation line. All of France north and west of that line was occupied by the Germans, and the so-called Unoccupied Zone in the south was administered by a pro-German Vichy Government headed by the elderly World War I hero, Marshal Henri Pétain.

So while Darling was forging escape-chain links in Spain, Room 900 arranged for an agent, wealthy young Nubar Gulbenkian, an official of the neutral Iranian Legation in London, to organize a system to smuggle escapees over the Pyrenees and into Spain. Gulbenkian received his instructions at Room 900's secret flat at 5 St. James Street: he was to make contact with a garage owner known as Parker at Perpignan on the French side of the border with Spain. Parker's real name was Michel Pareyre, and he was a contact of Donald Darling.

Room 900 officials told Gulbenkian that he was to arrange with Parker for the payment of guides to escort British escapees over the treacherous Pyrenees. His Majesty's treasury would pay forty pounds for each British officer and twenty pounds for other ranks. The plan was for Parker to hide British escapees in his garage, then turn them over to guides the Frenchman had recruited. The guides would smuggle the escapees into Spain where, it was hoped, they would be freed from Spanish internment by diplomatic means and continue on to England.[6]

As planned, Nubar Gulbenkian met Parker several days later in a cafe at Perpignan. Neither had seen the other before. As recognition signals, Parker was reading a French newspaper upside down, and the Iranian asked him, "Have you a Parker pen?" The discussion was brief, for although this was Unoccupied France, the Gestapo in disguise had heavily infiltrated the region. The Room 900 agent told Parker that he would be paid only on results and that money due him would be held in London until the end of the war. The Frenchman agreed to that arrangement.[7]

Now Don Darling in Spain and Nubar Gulbenkian along the Pyrenees had tied together links at the far end of the escape chain. Meanwhile, Captain Ian Garrow, tall, energetic, and resourceful, had been organizing escape lines in France. Garrow had escaped from the English Channel coast after his Scottish 51st (Highland) Division had surrendered in May 1940. He could himself have tried to flee back to England, but chose instead to remain and help other British fighting men to escape.

During the first ten months of 1941, Captain Garrow established escape lines from Paris (where escapees were collected from northern France, Belgium, and The Netherlands), southward across the demarcation line, and on to the Pyrenees. Obstacles to his work were enormous, including lack of funds, no radio communication with London, and the fact that he did not speak a word of French. But by October 1941, when he was arrested by Vichy French police and sent to prison, Captain Garrow had set the pattern for other escape lines to follow.[8]

By early 1942 the system for shuttling British evaders for hundreds of miles to sanctuary in the consulate in Barcelona was operating effectively. Disguised in civilian clothing, the fugitives traveled singly or in tiny groups by foot, bicycle, horse and cart, bus, car, and train. Along the way they were taken in tow by Dutch, Belgian, and French patriots who risked their lives to escort the escapees, passing them from one "safe house" to another.

Not all British evaders made it home. Vichy France prison camps held hundreds of them who had been captured while trying to reach the Spanish border.

Escape of German Warships

Late in January 1942 Lieutenant de Vaisseau Jean Philippon of the French navy was going about his duties at the Kriegsmarine arsenal at the port of Brest, 316 miles west of Paris at the tip of the Brittany peninsula. Philippon was one of fifteen hundred French sailors and ten officers the Germans had kept on active duty at the arsenal after the 1940 armistice. Kriegsmarine officers were impressed by Philippon, who clearly held an enlightened view that accepted the Nazi occupation of France. Friendly and personable, the French officer had no qualms about fraternizing with German officers at the port, and often he engaged them in long conversations. There were times when the Germans, their tongues loosened by Calvados, would reveal confidential information to the smiling young Frenchman.

German officers at Brest were not the only ones impressed with Lieutenant Philippon. So was Major André Dewavrin (code-named Colonel Passy after a famous Paris subway station), commander of the *Bureau Central de Renseignement et d'Action* (BCRA), Charles de Gaulle's secret service based in London. For Philippon (code-named Hilarion) was one of BCRA's ace spies.

De Gaulle, a relatively unknown French general, had led a division in the futile fight against Hitler's blitzkrieg in 1940, escaped to England, and proclaimed himself head of the Free French. One of the black-haired, six-foot-seven-inch general's first actions was to direct the 28-year-old Colonel Passy to organize an espionage network in France to help pave the way for the Allies' (and de Gaulle's) eventual return to the Continent.

Hilarion belonged to a network called Confrérie Notre-Dame (CND) that was headed by a gifted, energetic Frenchman named Gilbert Renault (code-named Rémy). Rémy, an unlikely spy master, was forty-seven years old and slight of build. He had four children. In mid-January 1942 his wife, Edith, had informed him that a fifth child was on the way. Mr. and Mrs. Renault and their family were living in Vannes, near the airfield from where the Luftwaffe's crack Kampfgruppe 100 had taken off to bomb Coventry in November 1940.

Renault, a deeply religious man, held no illusions as to the fate that awaited him or his family should his espionage activities be discovered by the Gestapo. But his immediate family and closest relatives were among the first to join with the Confrérie Notre-Dame.[1]

Hilarion, the CND's chief in Brest, was operating in one of France's most closely watched cities. The Gestapo, the Abwehr, and the Milice (French traitors and thugs who worked as policemen under the Germans) were everywhere. Gestapo radio-detection vehicles were active. Hilarion and the radio operator assigned to him to dispatch messages to Colonel Passy in London bicycled about the port with dismantled radios in their pockets, for no transmissions were made from the same house.

On January 28 Colonel Passy in London received an electrifying message from Hilarion: three of Hitler's most powerful warships, the *Prinz Eugen, Gneisenau,* and *Scharnhorst,* were preparing to bolt out of Brest and make a daring dash up the English Channel to Germany. The vessels had been bottled up in Brest, under round-the-clock surveillance by British aircraft, for nearly a year while undergoing repair for bomb damage.

The British Admiralty had considered that the three German ships might try to bolt for home ever since they had reached Brest in March 1941. But the Royal Navy was heavily committed elsewhere, so the job of keeping a watchful eye on the enemy vessels had been turned over to the RAF. Bomber

Command had long relished the "unique opportunity" for concentrated air attacks should the Kriegsmarine be so foolish as to try to sneak the big warships up the relatively narrow confines of the English Channel. To meet such a possibility, the RAF had drawn up an attack plan code-named Operation Fuller.[2]

Preparations were indeed underway in Brest for this mad dash up the Channel. The decision to risk destruction of the three ships had been made by Adolf Hitler himself at a tension-filled conference on January 12. Subtle machinations by British secret service agencies had convinced the fuehrer that British forces were preparing to invade Nazi-held Norway. So, to meet that spurious threat, Hitler ordered all heavy German warships and a large flotilla of U-boats to be concentrated off the coast of Norway.

At the strategy session held at the *Fuehrerhauptquartier* (Hitler's headquarters) near Rastenburg, East Prussia, the commander in chief of the Kriegsmarine, Admiral Erich Raeder, declared that an effort by the warships to break out of Brest and dash up the Channel under the noses of the British would be "sheer folly." But the Luftwaffe chief of staff, General Hans Jeschonnek, and 33-year-old General Adolf Galland, chief of fighter planes, gave assurances that their aircraft could cover the ships' breakout.

Hitler overruled his naval chief. "To come through the Channel is risky," the fuehrer exclaimed. "But to stay in Brest is even more so. In any case, the element of risk is reduced if we take the enemy by surprise, which we can do if we send these ships through in broad daylight."

Hitler code-named the breakout Operation Gerberus. "You will see," the fuehrer exclaimed. "This will be the greatest naval exploit of the whole war!"[3]

Secrecy and surprise. Surprise and secrecy. Those were the ingredients on which Hitler was counting for the *Prinz Eugen, Scharnhorst,* and *Gneisenau* to escape from their trap at Brest.

On February 8, however, Hitler's needed element of surprise seemed to burst like a punctured balloon. German electronic monitors intercepted a report from the British Coastal Command that stated the three German warships were planning on bolting out of Brest and that they would make the effort in the period February 10 to 15.

In Brest on February 8, even though the Gestapo was trying frantically to locate his transmitter, Lieutenant Philippon (Hilarion) radioed Colonel Passy in London: "Sailing imminent. Keep close watch at period of the new moon."[4]

Although Hilarion's espionage reports had been remarkably accurate in the past, the British Admiralty ignored the ace spy's prediction that the enemy ships would depart Brest at night. The admiralty was convinced that the departure would be in daylight so that the ships could reach the 20-mile-wide bottleneck at the Strait of Dover, 300 miles to the northeast, some twelve hours later under the protective cover of night.[5]

In the naval cat-and-mouse game between Adolf Hitler and the British Admiralty, the fuehrer had chosen a night departure from Brest because, he reasoned, that was precisely opposite to how the British would expect the breakout to be timed. Hitler hoped that his three battle cruisers could reach the Strait of Dover before the enemy woke up to the fact that they had broken out of Brest.

As the crucial period of February 10 to 15 drew closer, British intelligence detected signs that the escape effort was near. German minesweeping was being conducted in Brest harbor under cover of night. Ultra intercepts and spies in France revealed that Luftwaffe fighter squadrons were moving into airfields along the Channel, presumably to cover a warship sortie from Brest.

In England on February 11, Colonel Robert Wallace of British Signals called on radar expert Professor Reginald Jones. Wallace was frustrated and angry. He told Jones that for more than a week British radar along the Channel coast had been jammed and that the jamming was growing more intense each day. "I am sure that the Germans are up to something," Wallace declared. "But," the colonel complained, "no one will listen to me."

Jones arranged to send a scientist to investigate. Events would prove that the colonel had been the only one to detect the subtle "blinding" of British radar along the Channel coast. In preparation for the bolt up the English Channel, German technicians had slightly increased the intensity of their jamming over a period of two weeks. The increase had been so gradual that British radar technicians did not realize by February 11 that the jamming had rendered their radar virtually useless.

At 10:15 on the night of February 11—under a new moon, as Hilarion had predicted—the *Prinz Eugen, Scharnhorst,* and *Gneisenau,* escorted by a small flotilla of E-boats, slipped out of Brest. Destination: Germany. Almost at once the British encountered a series of incredible difficulties that indicated the gods of war were smiling on Operation Gerberus.

Just before the German flotilla emerged from the harbor, *Sealion,* the submarine assigned to keep watch on the exit, had withdrawn to recharge her batteries. Two Coastal Command planes patrolling outside the harbor had radar breakdowns (possibly due to German jamming). A third British patrol plane was summoned home shortly before the fleeing flotilla neared its search area. None of these gaps in the patrolling system was reported to Coastal Command headquarters. After daybreak, RAF fighter sweeps of the Channel failed to sight any unusual activity.

By this time Vice Admiral Hans Ciliax, the *Flottenchef* (Flotilla Chief) was gaining confidence that the "impossible" feat might indeed be pulled off. His optimism soared when, at 7:32 A.M., the first squadrons of General Galland's fighter planes roared in overhead. It was not until almost three hours later, near the mouth of France's Somme River, that a Spitfire sweep spotted the fleeing ships. But the RAF squadron declined to break radio silence to report its findings.

It was not until 11:23 A.M., more than twelve hours after the flotilla had sneaked out of Brest harbor, that Admiral Bertram Ramsey at Dover was notified that the three German ships were nearing the Dover bottleneck. Taken by total surprise, the British reaction was piecemeal. Singly or a few at a time, RAF planes, motor torpedo boats, and destroyers attacked the escaping flotilla. None hit the *Prinz Eugen, Gneisenau,* or *Scharnhorst* with a bomb or a torpedo. Of the 398 RAF planes taking part in the effort to sink or badly damage the German ships, 71 were lost from the fire of the Luftwaffe air umbrella, guns of the fleeing vessels and their surface escorts, and the heavy ack-ack fire of batteries along the French coast at the Strait of Dover.

At 12:56 P.M. the German flotilla was through the Dover bottleneck and sailed into the North Sea. The *Scharnhorst* was jolted twice, and the *Gneisenau* damaged by exploding mines, but at dawn all three warships had reached friendly ports in Germany and Denmark.

At Rastenburg Adolf Hitler rejoiced. He had overruled his top admiral, who had declared that such a mission would be folly, and outfoxed the British Admiralty.

In Great Britain the public was stunned and furious over the escape of the big German warships, and the War Cabinet was roundly blasted by the press. *The Times* of London bellowed: "Nothing more mortifying to the pride of sea-power had happened in home waters since the 17th Century."

While the great Escape of the German Warships melodrama was being played in the English Channel theater during the first half of February 1942, British scientists were reaching an agonizing conclusion. Based on a flow of evidence, it seemed certain that Germany also had radar, a fact Britain had refused to recognize earlier. And possibly the German radar system was more sophisticated and effective than was England's.

After the RAF had won the Battle of Britain, much of England's war production had turned to offensive bombers. Winston Churchill could order this switch from largely defensive fighter planes because he had learned, through Ultra intercepts, that Adolf Hitler had temporarily abandoned plans to invade England until the Wehrmacht had conquered Russia.

Since late 1940, the RAF had been sending bomber formations over the Reich and German-occupied countries almost nightly in steadily growing numbers. In Germany Reich Marshal Hermann Goering had grown concerned over heavier RAF bombings and had obtained Hitler's approval to increase dramatically the production of night fighter planes. Early in the war, in typical Goering bombast, the Luftwaffe chief had assured the German people, "If a single British bomb ever falls on the Third Reich, you can call me Meier [presumably a Jewish name]!" Now he was having to eat those words.

Despite Goering's personal discomfiture, the RAF was

paying dearly: four out of every one hundred night bombers were being lost. Some British bombers were being shot down by German ack-ack, but two-thirds of the destroyed aircraft were the victims of night fighters.

For many months now Professor Reginald Jones and his colleagues, with the help of Royal Air Force PRU (Photographic Reconnaissance Unit), had been searching diligently for tangible evidence of German radar. How had Luftwaffe night fighters been so deadly unless they were being guided by radar? But if the Germans possessed radar, where were the huge towers such as those strung out along England's southern coast? Could it be that German scientists had developed a radar system that did not require these 350-foot towers—or towers at all?

No stone was left unturned in efforts to unlock German radar secrets. PRU pilots took thousands of photos of suspected radar sites in the Reich and in Nazi-occupied territory. Through Special Operations Executive, the French, Belgian, and Dutch undergrounds were urged to provide information on curious-looking (to the underground) equipment that the Germans might have installed.

RAF bombers were asked to drop carrier pigeons during missions over northern France, Belgium, and The Netherlands. Tiny printed slips were attached to the pigeons' legs requesting finders to report any round, flat, rotating objects in their vicinity. If any were seen, they were to give a brief description of the device and send the pigeon back to England with the report.[6]

Interrogation of Luftwaffe pilots and bomber crews shot down over England, bugging of German POW camps, radio monitoring, and Ultra intercepts all contributed bits and pieces to growing evidence that the Germans not only possessed radar, but that they had established a sophisticated electronic defense line across British bomber approaches to Germany.

These suspicions by British scientists would prove to be well taken, for the Germans indeed had established a radar line running from the northern tip of Denmark and on into Germany, The Netherlands, Belgium, and southward to the Swiss-Italian border. Architect of the electronic defense line was 43-year-old Major General Josef Kammhuber. He had been urgently summoned by a worried Reich Marshal Goering late in 1940, told to build an effective air defense system against RAF bombers, and given the highest priority in Dezimeter Telegraphie (radar), night fighter planes, searchlights, and antiaircraft guns. The resulting development became known as the Kammhuber Line.

By early 1942 the key to the Kammhuber Line's success was the *Würzburger Reise* (Giant Würzburg), one of the Reich's most closely guarded secrets. Beside each Giant Würzburg was placed a cache of explosives, which was to be used to blow up the device in the event of a British raid to capture it. The new equipment replaced the standard Würzburg that had been developed in the late 1930s under cover of the German Post Office to mask its existence. The Giant Würzburg could track a swiftly moving airplane with great precision, and its 24-mile range was double that of the earlier model.

The Kammhuber Line consisted of a series of "radio boxes," with each box about eighteen miles long. Code-named *Himmelbett* (four-poster bed), each box had two Giant Würzburgs and one Freya, a radar that could reach farther than the Würzburg, but which could not determine aircraft altitude. The three radar devices were arranged in a triangle, and in its center was a small building housing the Himmelbett's ground controller.

When early-warning systems along the coast reported the approach of British bombers, one ME-110 or ME-109 night fighter in each box took off and began circling its Himmelbett. The fighter was tracked by one of the Würzburgs, and its pilot was in contact by radiotelephone with his Himmelbett ground controller.

When hostile bombers neared the Himmelbett, the second Giant Würzburg took a fix on them, and they appeared on the controller's screen as a red blob. All the while the first Würzburg continued to track the circling Messerschmitt fighter, which showed as a blue blob on the controller's screen. Then the controller, by radiotelephone, "talked" the fighter plane (the blue blob) into contact with the British bombers (the red blob).

Late in 1941 RAF Squadron Leader Tony Hill, a dashing pilot noted for his flying skill and courage, swooped in low over 400-foot-high cliffs near the French coastal village of Bruneval and, despite sporadic efforts to shoot down his Spitfire, took several clear photos of a suspected radar site. British scientists were at once alarmed and electrified. Tony Hill's photos revealed a large piece of equipment that looked like a saucer standing on its rim. It was a Giant Würzburg, the backbone of Germany's air defenses.[7]

The discovery that the Third Reich had sophisticated radar sent shock waves through the top echelons of British government and the military. Close study of the Bruneval photos indicated that it would be an ideal locale for a Commando raid. Why not dismantle and steal the Würzburg during the raid and bring it back to England for study and the development of countermeasures, British scientists suggested.

It was an audacious proposal. But Lord Louis Mountbatten, the 42-year-old naval commodore who had recently been appointed chief of Combined Operations, eagerly accepted the "butcher and bolt" mission. Not only would the theft of Germany's top-secret Würzburg be a scientific coup, but the raid would be in keeping with Winston Churchill's standing desire to harass the Germans across the Channel.

Conditions for the Bruneval raid would have to be right. The moon had to be full to provide visibility, and the tide had to be high enough for naval craft to reach the beach. And there was a critical need for someone on the ground to reconnoiter the closely guarded Bruneval area. The latter function was entrusted to de Gaulle's secret service chief, Major André Dewavrin (Colonel Passy).

Raid to Steal a Würzburg

It was a blustery, gray morning in early February 1942 when an aging Simca 5 huffed and wheezed into Bruneval, a drab village nestled in a ravine ten miles north of the port of Le Havre. Bundled up against the frigid blasts blowing off the English Channel were Charles Chauveau, who operated a garage in Le Havre and who knew the Bruneval locale intimately, and Roger Dumont, a former officer in the French air force. They were spies, members of Rémy's Confrérie Notre-Dame network. Chauveau, code-named Charlemagne, and Dumont, alias Pol, had been ordered by Colonel Passy in London to reconnoiter and report on German defenses below and on top of the 400-foot cliff that looked down onto a narrow shelf of beach.

It was a mission fraught with peril, for the Bruneval region was closely guarded by the Germans. Neither man had been told why this area was so important to London, and both were putting their lives on the line on faith alone.

Reaching the Hôtel Beauminet, Charlemagne parked the Simca in deep snow, and the spies went inside. The hotel's owner, Paul Vennier, and his wife were staunch patriots, Charlemagne explained to Pol. Seated before a warming fireplace in an anteroom, the agents told the Venniers that they were seeking information on German defenses, especially those on the towering cliff, where there was thought to be a radio station near the Cap d'Antifer lighthouse. (Actually, the "radio station" was a Giant Würzburg, the technological device the spies did not know existed.)

Eager to help, the Venniers proved to be a gold mine of information. Much to their chagrin, they said, a platoon of Germans had taken over the Hôtel Beauminet as living quarters. The platoon's mission was to defend the village. The French couple briefed Charlemagne and Pol on machine-gun positions, guard posts, minefields, barbed-wire barricades, roads, paths, and the number of soldiers manning various positions. But the couple knew nothing about the radio station atop the cliff, for that area had long been forbidden to French civilians.

Pol and Charlemagne left the hotel and headed toward the beach below the cliff. It was a Sunday, and the men had on their best suits. If halted by Germans, the spies hoped to pass as visitors on a leisurely stroll. As they began picking their way along a downhill path to the shoreline, icy gales cut into their faces and caused them to shudder.

Suddenly, a tall, thin German emerged from the doorway of an old villa. Over his shoulder a bolt-action rifle hung by a strap. Pol and Charlemagne's heartbeats quickened. Were they about to be arrested? The Feldgrau's face was expressionless. "Good morning, Fritz," Charlemagne called out cheerfully.

"What do you want here?" the soldier asked evenly.

"Just taking a little stroll," Charlemagne replied in his best German. "My friend here has just come from Paris, and, just imagine, he has never seen the sea, and I would like to show it to him."[1] The garage owner hoped that the quiver in his voice did not betray him. His legs felt as though they were jelly.

Slowly a friendly smile stole across the German's face. Charlemagne continued talking and told the Feldgrau that it was a good thing that the sentry had halted the two Frenchmen or they might have stumbled into a minefield along the beach.

"Ja, Tellerminen!" (Yes, Teller mines!), the German acknowledged.[2]

Pol handed the sentry a cigarette, and the three men smoked and chatted amiably for several minutes. Charlemagne asked if the German would accompany them along the path toward the beach. "All right," the soldier replied, cautioning his new friends to stick to the path for there were mines on either side.

Reaching the beach, the men again lighted cigarettes. Charlemagne looked out at the surf and suggested that this would be a fine place to swim in peacetime but that there were probably underwater obstacles there now. "No obstacles," the German replied. Pol, meanwhile, was gazing casually at the magnificence of the cliffs that towered over him. Near the top he spotted a pair of machine-gun positions, and he noticed that some paths leading up the heights were obstructed by barbed wire and that others were not impeded.

By mid-afternoon, Pol and Charlemagne were back in Le Havre. There they scribbled extensive notes on what they had seen and heard in and around Bruneval. Only when they had finished their reports did the spies realize the enormous tension they had been under, and they consumed a bottle of Calvados to calm jittery nerves. Within eighteen hours their findings would be encoded, radioed to London, decoded, and on the desk of Colonel Passy at de Gaulle's secret service headquarters.[3]

At Lord Mountbatten's Combined Operations, Charlemagne and Pol's eyewitness reports, along with hundreds of air reconnaissance photographs, were studied minutely. The Würzburg stood near the edge of the cliff, in front of an isolated mansion (code-named Lone House) that was thought to be quarters for radar technicians. Four hundred yards to the north, a compound named La Presbytère housed about one hundred Germans. One fact was clear: the Würzburg was protected by fifteen machine-gun posts along the cliff top, so a frontal assault from the sea would be suicidal. The radar site would have to be entered through the "back door."[4]

The raid would indeed be a combined operation. Twelve Whitley bombers, led by Wing Commander Charles Pickard, would drop a force of 119 men of C Company, 2d Parachute Battalion, under 30-year-old Major John D. Frost. The paratroopers were to seize and dismantle the Giant Würzburg and secure the beach below the cliff. A small naval flotilla, under Australian Commander F. N. Cook, would evacuate the paratroopers and, it was hoped, the dismantled Würzburg. A contingent of 32 officers and men of the South Wales Borderers and the Royal Fusiliers would be aboard Cook's vessels to cover with fire the withdrawal of Frost's men down the cliff to the beach.[5]

The operational plan called for three groups of Major Frost's paratroopers, each of about forty men and named after famous British admirals, to conduct separate missions. Nelson group, under Lieutenant Eulan R. D. Charteris, would parachute first and seize Bruneval and the beach. Drake group, led by Lieutenant Peter A. Young, would storm Lone House and capture the Würzburg. Rodney group, under Lieutenant John Timothy, would jump last, and its function would be to hold off the one hundred Germans at La Presbytère.

Someone with technical radar knowledge had to go on the raid, for if the Würzburg could not be dismantled, the scientist would study the device before the raiders withdrew. Professor Reginald Jones and an associate, Derek Garrard, volunteered, but were rejected. They knew too much about British scientific projects to risk their capture. D. H. Priestly, a capable scientist, but one not so deeply involved in secrets, was chosen to land with the naval force. Doing the actual dismantling (and pilfering) of the Würzburg would be RAF Flight-Sergeant C. W. H. Cox, who would parachute in with Major Frost.

Sergeant Cox was an unlikely candidate for the job of perpetrating one of the century's most audacious heists. He was the son of a postman and a former actress and before joining the RAF in 1940 had been a movie projectionist. The closest he had come to violence was when he had shown old Al Capone gangster movies. Prior to the war, Cox had never been on a ship or an airplane, so he had never parachuted until given a crash course for the Bruneval mission.

When Cox had been mysteriously whisked away from his post at a radar station in southern England (without being told he had been selected for one of the war's most daring raids), he was ordered to report for "special duty" to an air commodore. The officer said to the bewildered Cox, "Congratulations for volunteering for this mission." To which the brash sergeant replied, "Blimey, sir, I didn't *volunteer* for anything!" But Cox had the skill Bruneval planners needed: he was one of England's best radar mechanics.

Sergeant Cox had been kept in the dark as to the purpose of the mission. But he was thrilled to learn that for the first time in his life he would be taking "a short trip abroad." He was assigned to a section of Royal Engineers led by 24-year-old Lieutenant Dennis Vernon, who was eager to take a crack at the Germans for the destruction the Luftwaffe had inflicted on his native London.

On the afternoon of February 27, after a series of postponements due to bad weather, the Bruneval operation was launched. Under a brilliant blue sky, Commander Cook's flotilla slipped into the English Channel and set a course for its destination on the far shore, eighty miles distant.

Meanwhile, at Thruxton airfield, Johnny Frost's paratroopers were keyed up and ready to go. Only that day had they learned that their target was Bruneval. From Major Frost on down through the ranks, the raiders whiled away the hours before takeoff by drinking copious amounts of tea, sometimes laced with rum. Frost was beset with a commander's customary last-minute concerns, including security. Surprise was essential. "If the Germans get an inkling of the operation, we shall be doomed!" he remarked to confidants.[6]

Two hours prior to midnight, the parachutists headed for the Whitleys. In high spirits they marched around the perimeter of the airfield behind a piper playing the regimental marches of Scotland. There was time for one last cigarette; then the men, burdened with heavy gear, climbed into the airplanes.

At the last minute Major Frost was called to the telephone. Group Captain Nigel Norman, in charge of the air side of the operation, had alarming news. "France is covered with snow," he stated. "And German antiaircraft defenses along the coast seem to be particularly alert." Frost shared the disclosure with no one. There was nothing that could be done about either snow or German alertness.[7]

One after the other the big aircraft lumbered down the runway and lifted off. It was cold inside the dimly lit metal cabins, so the men wiggled under blankets. Teeth chattered. But the troopers broke out in song: *Come Sit by My Side If You Love Me* and *Annie Laurie*. Two hours after departure, Bruneval was drawing near, so covers were removed from the large hole in the floor of each Whitley. Icy blasts screamed through the openings, as one man in each plane dangled his legs from the hole, waiting for the signal to drop. Others stood up ready to follow the first man out.

Loud cracks split the moonlit sky as ack-ack guns opened fire. The paratroopers squirmed in discomfort, feeling that their bladders were about to burst. They roundly cursed tea and everyone who grew tea leaves.

Suddenly, red lights inside the cabins flashed green, and men started bailing out. On the way down Major Frost recognized landmarks that had become familiar from studying mock-ups of the locale. It was quiet—very quiet. That boded well. Apparently the Germans at Bruneval had not been roused by the roar of the Whitley engines.

Frost landed in a foot of snow and rapidly shucked his parachute. On all sides he could hear thuds as troopers crashed into the ground. Almost in unison, as though they had practiced the drill, the raid leader and the others relieved themselves of the tea they had consumed back at Thruxton. (Later Frost would describe this spontaneous event as "a gesture of defiance.")

It appeared to Frost that his entire force was coming down right on target. But two Whitleys, forced to take evasive action because of ack-ack fire, had deposited Lieutenant Eulan Charteris and nineteen of his men a mile and a quarter south of their drop zone. It was Charteris's Nelson group that was to secure the Bruneval beach where Commander Cook's vessels would arrive. The lieutenant and his men set off at a trot in the direction of Bruneval, and minutes later they had their first encounter with Germans.

Both sides were moving in single file in the same direction, and somehow one German attached himself to the tail of Charteris's column, under the impression that he was still with his own patrol. Betrayed by the outline of his coal-bucket-shaped helmet in the moonlight, the German was silently disposed of by trench knives. As they neared Bruneval, Charteris and his troopers got into a running gunfight with a German patrol, so they skirted the village and continued toward the beach.

Meanwhile, Major Frost, who had dropped inland with Lieutenant Peter Young's Drake group, took a section of men and headed toward the coast and Lone House, which sat

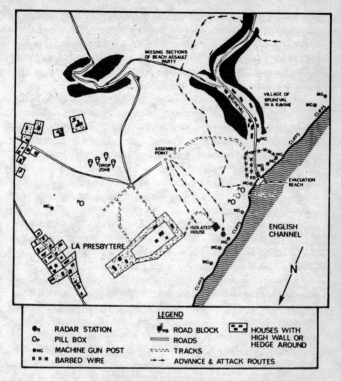

LEGEND

●R RADAR STATION	#RB ROAD BLOCK	▦ HOUSES WITH HIGH WALL OR HEDGE AROUND	
○P PILL BOX	═══ ROADS		
●MG MACHINE GUN POST	┄┄┄ TRACKS		
×∗× BARBED WIRE	▸┄▸ ADVANCE & ATTACK ROUTES		

The Bruneval Raid

—Courtesy Maj. G. G. Norton (Ret.)

ghostlike in the pale rays of the moon. Silently the major and his troopers surrounded the old mansion. There was no sign of movement inside the dark structure. Lone House's front door was shut but unlocked. "What do we do now?" a crouching parachutist called out in a stage whisper. Replied another, "Try ringing the doorbell."

Major Frost blew a whistle (a prearranged signal), and, Sten guns at the ready, the paratroopers bolted through the open door. *"Hände hoch!"* (hands up!), Frost shouted. But the downstairs was deserted. From an upper level could be heard the grating chatter of an automatic weapon. Several raiders dashed upstairs and burst into a room where a lone German, clad in underwear, was firing through an open window at Peter Young's men, who were attacking the Würzburg site. The Feldgrau was cut down by a fusillade of gunfire.

Now Lieutenant Young and his troopers charged the Würzburg, and those Germans on duty there who were not killed took to their heels. One of the raid's objectives was to take prisoners, so a few of Young's men chased a German. In his desperation, the enemy soldier stumbled over the edge of the cliff, and just before plunging four hundred feet to his death, he caught hold of a protruding bush. Climbing back up, weaponless and without hat or outer clothing, the German was collared by his pursuers.

Major Frost left deserted Lone House and hurried to the Würzburg. Off toward the north he could hear firing. Presumably Lieutenant Timothy's Rodney group was engaging the one hundred Germans quartered in La Presbytère.

As Frost and Young's sections took up defensive positions around the site, the imperturbable Flight-Sergeant Cox plunged into the task of dismantling the Würzburg. At the same time the engineer lieutenant, Dennis Vernon, began snapping photographs of the device. The flashbulbs drew fire from La Presbytère, and bullets ricocheted off the Würzburg just below Cox's hands. Picture taking ceased.

By the muted glow of a flashlight, Sergeant Cox had been feverishly dismantling the Würzburg for less than half of the thirty minutes allotted for the task when Major Frost shouted orders to head for the evacuation beach four hundred feet below. Mortar shells were dropping around Lone House and the Würzburg site, and three trucks, presumably filled with German soldiers, were discerned moving toward the scene of the ruckus.

But Sergeant Cox had found that the Würzburg disassembled with surprising ease, and his task had been completed. Various parts of it were rapidly piled into a two-wheeled cart, and Cox, Lieutenant Vernon, and a few others began pulling it across the plateau and toward a path that led down the cliffside.

Negotiating the steep, icy slope was difficult, and the

heavily loaded cart thrashed about. Then Germans holding the beach raked the cliffside with machine-gun fire, pinning down the descending paratroopers. Three bullets tore into Sergeant Major G. Strachan's stomach, and, bleeding profusely, he was dragged to cover by Major Frost.[8]

Moments later a runner crawled up to Frost and gave him alarming news: the Germans had pushed forward from La Presbytère and had taken over Lone House, only a few hundred yards from the pinned-down raiders. With Germans holding the evacuation beach and others closing in from the rear, disaster loomed.

Captain John Ross, a Scot from Dundee and second in command of the operation, and his rear guard, along with ten of the missing Lieutenant Charteris's men, were huddled near the evacuation beach. These men had landed as planned, but Ross's orders were to wait for all of Charteris's group to arrive before attacking German positions along the shoreline. In the moonlight Ross could discern that his comrades on the cliffside were being raked by automatic-weapons fire from the beach.

Ross knew the beach had to be cleared and passed the word to his men to prepare to attack. Then loud shouts pierced the air: *"Cabar Feidh! Cabar Feidh!"*—the battle cry of the Scot Seaforth Highlanders. Lieutenant Charteris and his nineteen men had arrived after a running gun battle with Germans and, shouting at the top of their lungs, were assaulting the enemy-held evacuation beach.

Germans in two pillboxes were quickly wiped out. The defenders fought back violently with machine-gun fire and grenades. Two paratroopers were cut down. One, Corporal Stewart, was a heavy gambler, and his wallet was bulging with currency. Before leaving Thruxton, he had solemnly declared that if he was killed on the raid, he wanted his comrades to split up his money and go on a binge after they returned to England.

Hit in the head by a grenade fragment and bleeding, Stewart lay on the beach and called to the nearest man, Lance-Corporal Freeman, "I've had it. Here, take my wallet." Freeman took the wallet and looked at Stewart's wound. "Oh, it's only a wee bit of a gash!" he told the other Scotsman. "Then gie me back my bloody wallet!" Stewart exclaimed as he got to his feet to rejoin the attack.

A group of paratroopers bolted into an old beachside villa, which was empty except for a badly frightened German orderly. He was on the telephone, talking to a German captain farther inland who was threatening to court-martial the Bruneval area garrison for raising such a racket in the middle of the night and disturbing his sleep.

The evacuation beach was soon secured, but the raiders remained in serious trouble. A lookout reported that several vehicles with headlights blazing were approaching. Most of the raiders, the wounded, and the precious dismantled Würzburg were on the beach. But where was the navy? Signalers told Major Frost that they had tried to make contact by lamp and radio with Commander Cook's ships, presumably lying offshore, but got no reply. There was a light mist out to sea, and visibility was only half a mile.

It appeared to Frost that the raiding party had been left high and dry, that the enemy was closing in. Through Walter Nagel, a German Jew who had volunteered to go on the mission as an interpreter, the major questioned German prisoners as to the location of enemy reserves, but the captives were too frightened to be coherent. After consultation with his officers, Frost issued orders for the parachutists to deploy into defensive positions. The trapped raiders would fight it out to the last man.

Major Frost and his men had great admiration for Walter Nagel, who the raid commander felt was invaluable to the operation. Those on the mission knew that odds were heavy that they would be captured if not killed. If captured, the British paratroopers would have to sit out the war in harsh circumstances. But, they had pondered, what would be the fate of a captured Walter Nagel, a Jew who had fled Nazi Germany and now had the audacity to fight against Hitler's soldiers?

Nagel had been provided with the papers and identity of a British soldier who had disappeared prior to the war. He would later volunteer for another daring raid, one on the German naval bastion at Saint-Nazaire, France, where he would be captured. But the Germans would never discover his true identity.

All the while Commander Cook had been waiting anxiously offshore for the signal to approach the beach. Two German destroyers and a pair of E-boats had sailed past less than a mile from Cook's flotilla. Just after 2:35 A.M. Cook spotted green signals coming from the beach and ordered six landing craft to head for shore. Major Frost had just finished deploying his men for their last-ditch stand when a shout rang out: "The boats are coming in! God bless the bloody navy!"

Aboard the approaching craft were the South Wales Borderers and the Royal Fusiliers, who, following orders, opened a murderous fire against the cliff and to both sides of the evacuation beach. The six craft scraped onto the sand, and the raiders scrambled aboard. Left behind were two dead and six missing (all of whom would be captured). By 3:30 A.M. Major Frost and his paratroopers were aboard Cook's flotilla, which was racing for Pompey (British navy slang for Portsmouth).[9]

D. H. Priestly, the scientist, was aboard the vessel carrying the dismantled Würzburg. In his excitement Priestly began studying the device and concluded that the Germans had had radar "as long or longer than we have." Such a sophisticated device could not have been developed in less than eight to ten years, he told Flight-Sergeant Cox. The man who had pilfered the Würzburg couldn't have cared less—he was curled up on a bunk, violently seasick.

Back in England the next morning, Professor Reginald Jones had components of the Würzburg, one of Germany's most closely guarded secrets, scattered about the floor of a large room and was piecing the device together. Next to him was the German technician captured during the Bruneval raid after he had nearly plunged to his death off the cliff. The enemy soldier was eagerly trying to be helpful, but his technical competence was minimal.

The German seemed bewildered. He told Jones that on his last leave home he had mentioned to his wife that his post at Bruneval was so isolated that the British might raid it and capture him. Now the prisoner speculated to Jones that his wife might be a spy in the pay of the British secret service.

In all respects the Bruneval raid had been a rousing success: the stolen Würzburg provided British scientists with know-how to unlock the secrets of the Kammhuber Line that had been taking such a heavy toll of British bombers. Now British experts knew the extreme limits of wavelengths to which the

Würzburg could be tuned, a vital fact that would aid in developing countermeasures in the ongoing hidden war with German air scientists.[10]

News of the Bruneval raid electrified the British home front and provided a badly needed tonic for sagging civilian morale. Forgotten were the angers and frustrations of only two weeks earlier when the three German battle cruisers escaped from Brest through what *The Times* of London had called "British home waters."[11]

For their part the Germans were furious and embarrassed over having had a secret Würzburg snatched from under their noses. Lord Haw-Haw took to the airways to bitterly denounce Major Johnny Frost and his paratroopers as "a handful of redskins."

At far-off *Wolfsschanze* (Wolf's Lair), the fuehrer's headquarters nestled in a forest in East Prussia, Adolf Hitler flew into a towering rage. His face turned red, and he pounded on the table, demanding that his generals tell him why "the British secret service can make these raids, but the Abwehr cannot." Hitler shouted that Admiral Canaris had formed the commando-type Brandenburg Division for the purpose of raiding Great Britain. Why had it not done so?

The English Channel was but a ditch, the fuehrer stormed, yet it might as well be as wide as Asia for all the intelligence Canaris and his Abwehr were getting out of England. He demanded to know what the Abwehr knew of British radar, and when told that Canaris knew virtually nothing about technical aspects of it, Hitler erupted in another temper tantrum.

The fuehrer seemed able to shrug off the thousands of German youths being slaughtered on the Russian battlegrounds, but he was unable to come to terms with a lone British raid that, in numbers involved and in casualties, in no way compared with the holocaust raging in the East. It was British "impudence" that infuriated Hitler.

Hitler's Eavesdroppers

The sense of triumph in high British circles following the Bruneval raid was tempered by concern. Would the Germans, in their fury, retaliate? If so, in what manner? A parachute or commando-type strike along England's southern coast seemed the most likely form. And located there was the Telecommunications Research Establishment (TRE) at Swanage in Dorset, where nearly all British radar was being developed.

TRE was as vulnerable as had been the Würzburg site at Bruneval: on the water's edge, isolated, fine beaches for attack and escape, and top-secret radar equipment that could be stolen in a raid. Swanage, bustling with skilled workers, was minimally guarded and a choice plum waiting to be plucked by vengeful Germans.

Not long after Major John Frost and his men returned, TRE officials were handed an alarming intelligence report: seventeen trainloads of German paratroopers were converging on Cherbourg, across the Channel from Swanage, to assault TRE. As a result a British regiment was rushed to Swanage, and Royal Engineers placed explosives in secret equipment. TRE scientists, some in their late sixties and early seventies, held long, solemn discussions over what course they should take when the enemy paratroopers struck: flee or stay and fight to the death.

This flurry of near hysteria spurred TRE officials into finding a new home inland, and chosen was a boy's school nestled among the gently rolling hills of Worcestershire. Building the extensive facilities required was time consuming, so it would not be until late May before TRE people would head for Worcestershire by train, vehicle, and bicycle. They would miss the beautiful English Channel seascape of Dorset, but they were aware that the move inland would minimize the chance that they would awaken one night with German paratroopers dropping on them.

At Wolfsschanze two weeks after the Bruneval operation, Adolf Hitler summoned Heinrich Himmler, chief of the Gestapo and SS. The fuehrer was still ranting about the "impudence" of the British and the "incompetency" of his generals for "allowing" the embarrassing theft of the Würzburg. Hitler told the owlish-faced Himmler that he was taking the gathering of technical intelligence from Admiral Canaris's Abwehr and turning it over to the "far more reliable and capable" Nazi Party. Henceforth, the fuehrer decreed, this function would rest with the intelligence branch of the SS, the *Sicherheitsdienst* (SD).

The SD was headed by 37-year-old Reinhard Heydrich, an archfoe of Wilhelm Canaris. Brilliant and with the instincts of a barracuda, the ambitious Heydrich promptly sensed that Canaris had fallen into disfavor with the fuehrer, so now was the time to present Hitler with the plan he had long been developing—absorbing the Abwehr into the SD. Heydrich, of course, would become chief of the one German intelligence agency, and as such he would be the Reich's second most powerful figure.

As cunning and ruthless as he was, Heydrich, the son of an opera singer and an actress, had more than met his match in Wilhelm Canaris. The Abwehr chief, suspecting that Heydrich was partly Jewish, scoured the *Ahnenliste*, the ancestry list kept on everyone in the Nazi Party, for evidence to confirm his suspicions. It was also suspected that Heydrich had homosexual tendencies. Both "traits" would destroy an official in Nazi Germany.

Then Admiral Canaris compiled his findings into a report and sent it for safekeeping to a confidant in Switzerland. In the event anything "untoward" should happen to Canaris or his family, the confidant was told, the secret report on Reinhard Heydrich was to be given to the *New York Times*. The admiral informed Heydrich of what he had done, and the SD chief promptly lost interest in promoting his plan to absorb the Abwehr.

Reinhard's dream of immense power would be short-lived. On May 27, 1942, the SD leader was assassinated by Czechoslovakian patriots.

At Wolfsschanze late on the night of March 6, Adolf Hitler was reading a top-secret report from 58-year-old Wilhelm Ohnesorge, minister of the postal organization, *Deutsche Reichspost*. It concerned the results of telephonic experimentation that had been carried out for a year under such secret conditions that even the fuehrer knew little about the research.

Minister Ohnesorge reported that Reich scientists had developed a technique whereby they could eavesdrop on "scrambled" transatlantic telephone conversations between Allied leaders in London and Washington. The fuehrer stomped his foot in glee over the prospect of learning the word-by-word discussions between President Roosevelt and Prime Minister Churchill.

Roosevelt, from a soundproof room in the basement of the White House, and Churchill, from his underground headquarters at Storey's Gate, had for months been talking freely over the radiotelephone hot line in full confidence that they were fully protected from eavesdroppers.

This security came from a Bell Telephone Company device (known as A-3) that split the frequency band into smaller bands, thereby "mangling" voiced words in transit. Anyone tapping the line would hear only unintelligible gibberish. At the other end of the cable, the words would be unscrambled before reaching the ear of the person there.

Even with the scrambling, extra security measures were taken. President Roosevelt's words went by wire to the overseas switchboard in an AT&T building at 47 Walker Street, New York City. There, in a special security room, technicians constantly altered the transmission from one frequency to another.

As far back as October 1939, German intelligence had been

aware that Churchill and Roosevelt were conferring regularly by scrambler telephone. But in the flood of exuberance over the Wehrmacht's blitzkriegs that overran most of Europe, no one in the Oberkommando der Wehrmacht had any interest in unscrambling a transatlantic radiotelephone line to obtain war secrets.

Finally, in mid-1941, the Deutsche Reichspost adopted the project. (This agency also administered Germany's telephone and telegraph services.) Its own laboratories were engaged in the development of these functions, and Ohnesorge was determined to crack the scrambler on the London-to-Washington radiotelephone. It seemed like an impossible task, as Ohnesorge's engineers had nothing tangible on which to begin research—no blueprints, models, or wiring patterns of Bell Laboratories' A-3 scrambler device.

Despite these seemingly insurmountable obstacles, Deutsche Reichspost engineers and scientists produced a near miracle. In only eight months they created pilot models of both Bell's scrambling and unscrambling devices, built the complex equipment necessary to intercept, record, and unscramble the England–United States conversations, and constructed a monitoring station near Eindhoven, The Netherlands.

No wonder Adolf Hitler danced a jig on March 6 when he learned of this fantastic achievement. And it was a *Nazi* triumph. Only the fuehrer, Heinrich Himmler of the SS, and Foreign Minister Joachim von Ribbentrop received translated intercepts. The generals and admirals—especially Wilhelm Canaris of the Abwehr—would never learn of the operation. It was not just the Churchill-Roosevelt conversations that were being intercepted. Dr. Ohnesorge's operators at Eindhoven were eavesdropping on the transatlantic discussions of Allied leaders in the military, government, and industry.[1]

Ohnesorge's creation was so ingenious and efficient that, from interception to the delivery of translated copies in Berlin, only a few hours elapsed. It probably was the fastest procurement of significant intelligence in the history of secret service operations.[2] In effect, the Eindhoven facility was Nazi Germany's answer to the British Ultra (about which the Germans knew nothing).

* * *

Over one of Germany's powerful Zeesen transmitters, beginning in February 1942, a plump, middle-aged American-born (Atlanta) woman named Jane Anderson had been going great guns four times each week. She was one of Josef Goebbels's prized tub-thumpers, and her harangues were targeted at the shortwave-radio audience in the United States.

Jane Anderson was shrouded in mystery. She had once been a respected journalist and in World War I had covered activities for the London *Daily Express* and *Daily Mail*. She was a correspondent in the Spanish civil war and in America was hailed as "a great champion in the fight against Communism."[3] Anderson (then married to the Marquis Alvarez de Cienfuegos) was accused of spying for the anti-Communist Francisco Franco and was pitched into a Spanish jail for six weeks.

Anderson was released through the intervention of the U.S. government. How she got to Germany remained a mystery. Suddenly she had surfaced on Goebbels's radio. Even though her broadcasts were aimed at America, most of her listeners were in England. The British pinned on her the sobriquet "Lady Haw-Haw."

Now, in March 1942, Lady Haw-Haw was setting her United States audience straight on the reported German food shortages with a luscious visit to a Berlin cocktail bar: "On silver platters were sweets and cookies. I ate Turkish cookies, a delicacy I am very fond of. My friend ordered great goblets full of champagne, into which he put shots of cognac to make it more lively. Sweets, cookies, and champagne! Not bad!"

British propaganda experts rubbed their hands in glee. The following night Lady Haw-Haw's bacchanalian bombast, translated into German, was radioed back to her adopted country, where the *herrenvolk* had begun to feel food pinches. The effect of the turnaround broadcast was considerable. Plain Jane Anderson disappeared from the Nazi airwaves.

As the propaganda-radio duel continued to rage on both sides of the English Channel, a new breed of entrepreneur was emerging in Nazi-occupied and Vichy-controlled France. Theirs was certainly a high-risk venture. Hours were long. Pay was nonexistent. Working conditions were hazardous. They were the outlaw publishers of underground newspapers, high on the list of Gestapo targets.

By spring of 1942, there were numerous clandestine papers being printed and distributed in France, with a total press run of some two hundred thousand weekly. Through hand-to-hand distribution, perhaps two million French men and women read the sheets. In the German zone a resistance group called Libération published a paper of the same name, while another group named Libération Française produced a sheet called *Combat*. In the unoccupied zone a major paper was *Le Franc-Tireur*, while the Communist party put out *L'Humanité*. In addition to these principal sheets, other papers were sponsored by scattered smaller units.

The underground papers were not graphic or journalistic works of art. Yet to French men and women, in whose breasts the flame of resistance was burning ever brighter and who were sickened by the Nazi-controlled press in Paris and Vichy, the outlaw publications were beacons of hope. The papers' news had often already been heard on the French service of BBC, the jokes were copies from old magazines, but the editorials were a force to be reckoned with.

In addition to lifting the morale of French citizens, the editorials slowed down the production of war materials destined for the Reich by appealing to the French worker's patriotism. And they blocked the all-out drive by the puppet regime in Vichy to recruit factory hands to work in Germany.

At this stage of the war, propaganda was more important to the French underground than sabotage or acts of terrorism, for the resisting groups needed recruits, money, and information. Therefore, the activities of the several clandestine organizations centered around their newspapers. The printing of each issue was carried out very quickly and in utmost secrecy to thwart the Gestapo or Vichy State Police. Once the press run was finished, the type was rapidly put back in cases and the plates were melted down. Then the printing shop returned to its normal routine, often printing books and pamphlets for the Germans.

One underground paper was run off the press of a large Paris hotel that was entirely occupied by Germans. Wehrmacht officers idling in the plush lobby paid no attention to the faint rumble of the basement press, for this equipment was used to print the hotel's menus. Eventually the operation was moved for fear that the Germans would recognize that the battered type on their dinner menus was identical to that of the "terrorist" newspaper.

Perhaps the riskiest venture of all by an outlaw publisher was the launching of a sheet called *Unter Uns* (German for Among Ourselves). Its target was the occupying Wehrmacht, and mainly it printed detailed stories of the horrors and agonizing deaths being inflicted on the Feldgrau in Russia. In early March *Unter Uns* published a lengthy account of the British Commando raid at Bruneval, an event that the German-controlled French press had ignored. One week later disaster struck: the two ringleaders of the *Unter Uns* paper were caught red-handed by the Gestapo and gunned down.

Elsewhere in northern France in the middle of March, Squadron-Leader John "Whippy" Nesbitt-Dufort was wrestling with the controls of a Lysander while winging across the blacked-out countryside of northern France. He had taken off from the secret Moon Squadron base at Gibraltar Farm with the mission of dropping off the Joe with him and picking up another. But a thin coat of ice had formed on the Lysander's wings while over the capricious English Channel, causing the plane to steer erratically. As a result, Nesbitt-Dufort became lost, was nearly out of gas, and was gliding downward for a crash landing in a field near Chateroux.

"Hold your hat!" the irrepressible Nesbitt-Dufort called out to his nervous companion moments before the Lysander crunched onto the wet field, skidded for more than fifty yards, thudded into a ditch, and nosed over with its tail pointing upward. Miraculously, perhaps, neither man was hurt, and they scrambled out of the wrecked aircraft. For a few moments Nesbitt-Dufort calmly viewed the Lysander, then exclaimed, "My goodness, I could do with one or six drinks!"[4]

The squadron leader rapidly began preparations for destroying the Lysander. He exploded the SFF (Secret Identification Friend or Foe apparatus, which sent "friendly" signals of distress to British radar stations), then fired a Verey pistol at the fuselage, setting the plane afire. Nesbitt-Dufort and the Joe raced to an empty building to contemplate their next move, believing that the Lysander was cremated. But the plane had been nearly out of fuel, so there was no gasoline to feed the flames; the fire flickered out.

Shortly after dawn a German patrol discovered the wrecked, charred, but largely intact, Lysander. Word was flashed up the chain of command as the Germans had long been hoping to capture one of these little grasshopper planes for study by aeronautical engineers. Down from on high came precise instructions: the Lysander was not to be dismantled, but rather loaded intact onto a large flatbed truck and hauled—with tender care—to a place where it could be examined at leisure.

Acting with typical Teutonic efficiency, a German work crew used a crane to hoist the war prize onto the truck. Knowing the extreme value German commanders placed on the Lysander, the nervous captain in charge of the recovery operation perspired freely as the vehicle began inching across the rough field and onto a dirt road. Great care was exercised to avoid ruts, bumps, and potholes. The guardian of the booty breathed more easily when the truck reached a smooth, hard-surfaced road.

About three miles down the road, the crawling truck neared a level railroad crossing and inched onward. Suddenly the escorting Germans heard a frightening sound—that of a locomotive racing toward the crossing at fifty miles per hour. Moments later the engine smashed broadside into the truck, ripping it and the Lysander into bits.

German commanders were furious over having this prized booty snatched from their grasp and ordered an all-out search for the pilot. In their anxiety to apprehend him, the Gestapo arrested the Curé of Chateroux and charged him with being the RAF flyer and using clerical robes to mask his true identity. But after a score of townsfolk came forward to identify their beloved padre, he was released by the frustrated Gestapo.[5]

Unaware of the slapstick scenario unfolding around his Lysander, Whippy Nesbitt-Dufort was taken in tow by the French resistance, furnished native clothing, and hidden about fifteen miles from the crash site. Five weeks later he contacted England by radio, and a plane was sent to pick him up. Returning to Gibraltar Farm more than a month after he had left, Whippy greeted welcoming comrades with his usual breezy, "What I need is a drink or six!"

Meanwhile, in the vast body of water west of the English Channel, the Battle of the Atlantic had already been raging for twenty-one months by the time 1942 rolled around. Great Britain had been getting the worst of it. In 1940 England lost four million tons of shipping, mainly because of U-boats, and the Germans sent almost the same British tonnage to the bottom in 1941. In all waters, at the rate of more than two merchant vessels per day, German submarines had been sinking ships carrying vital military and civilian supplies to the beleaguered British Isles.

The brutal battle along the North Atlantic trade routes was one of combat and merchant ships, submarines, airplanes, innovative tactics, and intelligence coups. The Kriegsmarine was intercepting and deciphering British convoy ciphers with devastating results, and the British, through Ultra, were reading U-boat coded signals. As the adversaries feinted, bobbed, and weaved—British convoy against U-boat wolf pack—neither side seemed to know for many months that the other side was intercepting and decoding its messages.

Architect of the U-boat onslaught was Grand Admiral Karl Doenitz, *Befehlshaber der Unterseeboote* (Commander of Submarines). On January 12, 1942, the 52-year-old Doenitz launched Operation *Paukenschlag* (Roll of the Drums), which was designed to knock the United States out of the war with Nazi Germany by sinking her ships loaded with troops and supplies that were bound for England. The admiral had selected eleven of his ace U-boat skippers, a resolute breed, to strangle the American east-coast shipping lanes.

Doenitz's U-boats were tough, mobile, and had excellent endurance—Type IXC craft had a range of eleven thousand miles, sufficient to allow them to maraud the Atlantic for several weeks before returning to Saint-Nazaire, France, for maintenance, repair, and provisioning. Along with Brest, Saint-Nazaire was the most heavily fortified German naval base on the entire west coast of Europe.

It was from Saint-Nazaire, a city with a population of fifty thousand, that U-boat wolf packs set out to attack British and

American convoys. Reinforced concrete bunkers, with roofs several yards thick, protected the submarines when they were in Saint-Nazaire, making bombing attacks useless. Aware that an assault on the U-boat base could be made only from the sea, the Kriegsmarine had set up extensive networks of mine and torpedo barriers across the harbor area, studded the docks with ack-ack and coastal guns, established a string of coast-watching posts, and carried out constant ship patrols.

Saint-Nazaire was much more than a haven for U-boats. The special dock, built in peacetime for the French luxury liner *Normandie*, had long haunted the British Admiralty, for it was the only facility along Europe's Atlantic seaboard where the *Tirpitz*, the mightiest battleship operating in European waters, could dock for repairs or to take on provisions. The dock had a dual purpose. Filled with water, it served as a lock; pumped empty, it became a dry dock.

The *Tirpitz* was now hidden in Norwegian fjords, but should she begin prowling the Atlantic shipping lanes, the powerful warship could wreak havoc on British convoys. The admiralty concluded that the only way to prevent the *Tirpitz* from operating in Atlantic waters was to destroy the *Normandie* dock with the largest Commando raid yet. A frontal attack against the formidable Saint-Nazaire defenses would be suicidal, the admiralty knew, unless an intricate hoax was created to hoodwink the Germans and enable the raiders to reach the dock before the defenders realized they were under attack.

U.S. ARMY

U.S. ARMY

Abwehr Chief, Wilhelm Canaris

Field Marshal Erich von Manstein

NATIONAL ARCHIVES

IMPERIAL WAR MUSEUM

Chief of Himmler's SS secret service, Reinhard Heydrich

Nazi Foreign Minister, Joachim von Ribbentrop

WANTED!

FOR MURDER . . . FOR KIDNAPPING . . .
FOR THEFT AND FOR ARSON

One the newspaper full face by habitual smile. Rarely smiles.
Eyes rapidly, and when angered appears like a mask.

ADOLF HITLER
ALIAS

Adolf Schicklegruber,
Adolf Hittler or Hidler

Last heard of in Berlin, September 3, 1939. Aged fifty, height 5ft. 8¼in., dark hair, frequently brushes one lock over left forehead. Blue eyes. Sallow complexion, stout build, weighs about 11st. 3lb. Suffering from acute monomania, with periodic fits of melancholia. Frequently bursts into fears when crossed. Harsh, guttural voice, and has a habit of raising right hand to shoulder level. DANGEROUS !

Profile from a recent photograph. Black moustache. Jowl inclined to fatness. Wide nostrils. Deep-set, suspicious eyes.

FOR MURDER Wanted for the murder of over a thousand of his fellow countrymen on the night of the Blood Bath, June 30, 1934. Wanted for the murder of countless political opponents in concentration camps.

He is believed for the murder of Jews, Germans, Austrians, Czechs, Spaniards and Poles. He is now urgently wanted for homicide against citizens of the British Empire.

Hitler is a gunman who shoots to kill. He acts first and talks afterwards.

No appeals to sentiment can move him. This gangster, surrounded by armed hoodlums, is a natural killer. The reward for his apprehension, dead or alive, is the peace of mankind.

FOR KIDNAPPING Wanted for the kidnapping of Dr. Kurt Schuschnigg, late Chancellor of Austria.

Wanted for the kidnapping of Pastor Niemöller, a heroic martyr who was not afraid to put God before Hitler. Wanted for the attempted kidnapping of Dr. Benes, late President of Czechoslovakia. The kidnapping tendencies of this establishe d criminal are marked and violent. The symptoms before an attempt are threats, blackmail and ultimatums. He offers his victims the alternatives of complete surrender or timeless incarceration in the horrors of concentration camps.

FOR THEFT Wanted for the larceny of eighty millions of Czech gold in March, 1939. Wanted for the armed robbery of material resources of the Czech State. Wanted for the stealing of Memelland. Wanted for robbing mankind of peace, of honesty, and for the attempted assault on civilisation itself. This dangerous lunatic ranks his raids by spurious appeals to honour, to patriotism and to duty. At the moment when his protestations of peace and friendship are at their most vehement, he is most likely to commit his smash and grab.

His tactics are known and easily recognised. But Europe has already been wrecked and plundered by the depredations of this armed thug who smashes in without scruple.

FOR ARSON Wanted as the incendiary who started the Reichstag fire on the night of February 27, 1933. This crime was the key point, and the starting signal for a series of outrages and brutalities that are unsurpassed in the records of criminal degeneracy. As a direct and immediate result of this calculated act of arson, an innocent dupe, Van der Lubbe, was murdered in cold blood. But as an indirect outcome of this carefully-planned offence, Europe itself is ablaze. The fires that this man has kindled cannot be extinguished until he himself is apprehended—dead or alive !

THIS RECKLESS CRIMINAL IS WANTED—DEAD OR ALIVE!

IMPERIAL WAR MUSEUM

Prime Minister Winston Churchill at a demonstration of secret weapons. Holt, Norfolk. Lord Cherwell, Churchill's scientific advisor, is at left and Dr. A. D. Crow, a weapons' scientist, at right.

COURTESY R. V. JONES

Professor Reginald V. Jones

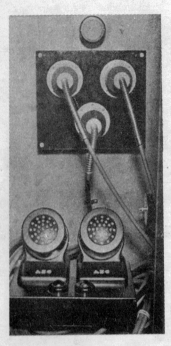

IMPERIAL WAR MUSEUM

NATIONAL ARCHIVES

Above Left: Instant propaganda. Through this installation in Dr. Josef Goebbels' office in Berlin, propaganda could be broadcast through radio stations anywhere in Nazi-occupied Europe. Right: *(Top):* SS Brigadefuehrer Walter Schellenberg. *(Bottom):* SS Reichsfuehrer Heinrich Himmler.

BRITISH AIRBORNE FORCES MUSEUM

"Lone House" on cliffs at Bruneval, quarters for
Würzburg operators

IMPERIAL WAR MUSEUM

British paratroop Major John D. Frost (second from right)
chats with King George during a paratroop mass jump in
1942. Pointing for the Queen is Wing Commander Charles
Pickard who was later killed on a mission.

IMPERIAL WAR MUSEUM

Enigma, the encoding machine considered "unbreakable" by the Germans

IMPERIAL WAR MUSEUM

German radar on English Channel cliff near Arromanches, France

IMPERIAL WAR MUSEUM

Lysander aircraft used by the British to drop off and pick up agents in German-occupied France

BRITISH AIRBORNE FORCES MUSEUM

Royal Air Force photo of St. Nazaire harbor area shortly before the Commando raid

Constance Babington-Smith

Noon Inayat Khan,
code-named Madeleine

Violette Szabo,
code-named Corrine

LtCol A. C. Newman

PHILLIPS PUBLICATIONS

Suitcase radio made in England and known as the Mark II Suitcase Transceiver.

PHILLIPS PUBLICATIONS

The SSR-S-A Transmitter/Receiver radio built in the United States for OSS agents.

IMPERIAL WAR MUSEUM

British soldiers carry an inflated rubber tank used to deceive the Germans.

AUTHOR'S COLLECTION

Identity card carried by "William Martin" in Operation Mincemeat.

COURTESY OF JIM PHILLIPS

Weapons issued to OSS and British SOE agents.

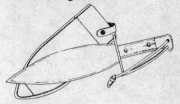

The smatchet was designed for close combat and as a camp knife.

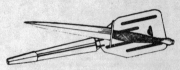

A stiletto with metal pancake flapper scabbard was also for use in close combat.

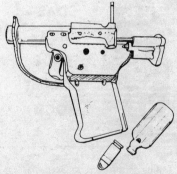

Ten cartridges were carried in hollow handle of single-shot pistol.

COURTESY COLONEL CARLUS C. ALDEN.(RET.)

Nazi propaganda leaflet dropped on Anzio Beachhead.

COURTESY WILLIAM S. STORY

"The Worst is Yet to Come," the calling card pasted on Germans killed by American-Canadian First Special Service Force. Anzio Beachhead.

AUTHOR'S COLLECTION

King George inspects American vessel prior to Normandy invasion. Lieutenant Commander John D. Bulkeley, USN, on his left.

IMPERIAL WAR MUSEUM

Men of the French underground armed with Allied and captured German weapons prepare to launch a hit-and-run strike against the Germans.

U.S. ARMY

Skorzeny soldiers wearing American uniforms being prepared for the firing squad.

NATIONAL ARCHIVES

Otto Skorzeny and Adolf Hitler

USIS

WANTED

SKORZENY

SPY

SABOTEUR   ASSASSIN

Tens of thousands of these circulars were distributed throughout Allied Europe during the Battle of the Bulge.

Adolf Hitler

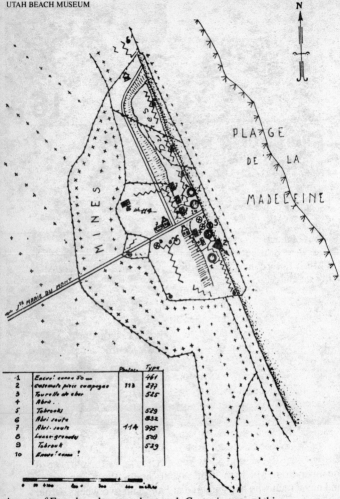

		Photos	Type
1	Encuv! canon 50 m/m		461
2	Cassemate pièce campagne	113	277
3	Tourelle de char		525
4	Abri .		
5	Tobrooks		529
6	Abri soute		832
7	Abri soute	114	995
8	Lance-grenades		529
9	Tobrouk		529
10	Encuv! canon !		

Agents of French underground network *Centurie* mapped this
Atlantic Wall strongpoint at Utah Beach.

Trojan Horse of Saint-Nazaire

In the early afternoon of March 26, 1942, a small armada of vessels slipped out of Falmouth Harbor at the southwestern tip of England and into the English Channel. The sun warmed the bodies and spirits of the 611 men on board, including 44 officers and 224 other ranks of No. 2 Commando, led by 38-year-old, pipe-smoking Lieutenant Colonel A. C. Newman, a building contractor in civilian life.

Immediately after clearing the harbor, Commander R. E. D. Ryder, the naval force leader and in peacetime an Antarctic explorer, gave orders for the vessels to regroup in an arrow-shaped formation, the customary submarine-detection deployment, to mislead snooping German reconnaissance planes. Operation Chariot, a raid to destroy the *Normandie* dock at the German bastion of Saint-Nazaire, had been launched.

Since its inception a month earlier, Chariot had been shrouded in secrecy and intrigue. Only Colonel Newman, Commander Ryder, and a few key officers knew the purpose of the operation. Much to their mystification, the Commandos and naval men who had gathered at Falmouth two weeks earlier had been designated the 10th Anti-Submarine Squadron. In order to explain the extra fuel tanks on the vessels, a whispering campaign had been launched in Falmouth pubs by British agents to indicate that the naval force was going to operate in the Bay of Biscay, far to the south. To avoid interception of radioed messages by German monitoring posts along the French coast, ship-to-ship communications would be limited to visual means.

At Combined Operations an ingenious hoax had been developed in which the 1,090-ton destroyer HMS *Campbeltown* would play the role of a modern-day Trojan horse. Centerpiece of the entire operation, the *Campbeltown* had been the USS *Buchanan*, one of the fifty time-worn destroyers that President Roosevelt had turned over to beleaguered Great Britain. She was an old, untidy crate, but if the audacious raid succeeded, the *Campbeltown*'s fame would become immortal.

Campbeltown's one-time American crew would not have recognized her. She had recently undergone extensive "plastic surgery." Following blueprints (stolen by British spies) of German ships of the *Möweclasse,* workmen had converted the *Campbeltown* from a four-funnel vessel to one resembling a Kriegsmarine submarine chaser. It was hoped that this seaborne Trojan horse could slip into the lair of the enemy, just as the legendary wooden ploy was placed inside the walls of Troy. In addition, her draught was realigned so she could sail through the shallow waters at Saint-Nazaire.

One more touch was added to deceive the Germans: the British flotilla would approach the enemy naval bastion while flying "flags of convenience," meaning large Nazi flags made secretly in London.

The attack plan called for part of Commander Ryder's naval force, having gained total surprise and under cover of darkness, to bolt into Saint-Nazaire harbor. The *Campbeltown*, skippered by bearded Lieutenant Commander S. H. "Sam" Beattie, was to head hell-bent directly for the *Normandie* dock and crash into its gate. The old ship had twenty-four explosive charges, weighing five tons, planted inside and attached to an elaborate system of time fuses. The explosives would detonate after the crew had had time to scramble off the ship.

In the meantime Lieutenant Colonel Newman's Commandos would be storming ashore at three places in Saint-Nazaire harbor to blow up preassigned targets. Two hours would be allotted for the Commandos to do their job, after which the naval force would have to pull out in order to clear the region before daylight brought out Luftwaffe dive-bombers.

As Commander Ryder's flotilla set out on the first leg of the 300-mile circuitous trek to Saint-Nazaire, the men were told their destination. At dusk Nazi flags were hoisted over each ship, and the flotilla sailed on through a routine night. But at 7:06 A.M. a U-boat was spotted idling on the surface 130 miles southwest of Saint-Nazaire. The *Tynedale* headed toward the submarine, but since the destroyer was flying a German flag, the U-boat remained on the surface. At four thousand yards the *Tynedale* opened fire, and the submarine crash-dived. After dropping depth charges, the destroyer sped off to rejoin the flotilla.

The episode brought new worries to Commander Ryder. Surely the U-boat would radio a warning to Saint-Nazaire. He gave serious thought to turning back to avoid a bloody catastrophe, but decided to continue onward.

The gods of war came down on the side of the naval commander. The U-boat had not been damaged, but had remained silent and submerged until noon, and having seen the *Tynedale* racing off toward the southwest (to rejoin the flotilla), the submarine skipper presumed that all the British vessels were heading in that direction. He radioed Saint-Nazaire: "British naval force sailing on a westerly course [away from the port]."

While these events were transpiring, Admiral Karl Doenitz was in Saint-Nazaire inspecting the construction of the heavy concrete submarine pens. He asked the German commander at the port what measures had been taken should the British attack Saint-Nazaire (as they had Bruneval the previous month). The subordinate replied that a defense plan was ready, but he thought such a raid highly unlikely. "Well, I would not be so sure about that," Doenitz exclaimed.[1]

Late that afternoon a new danger to the British convoy arose. French fishing trawlers began appearing on all sides. Would a treacherous Frenchman radio a warning to shore? Two trawlers were boarded and searched, and their crews were removed before the boats were sunk by gunfire. Standing on the deck of the *Tynedale*, the French fishermen were bewildered. Their

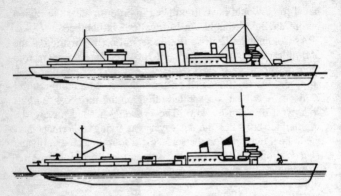

The Campbeltown *before (above) and after her conversion to re-semble a German ship.*

captors spoke English, wore English uniforms, but the flag of Nazi Germany waved in the breeze overhead.

Darkness fell over the naval force as it sailed closer to the German bastion. At midnight gun flashes were detected to the northeast, and the fiery glow of exploding bombs indicated that sixty-five RAF bombers were conducting a diversionary attack. An hour later hundreds of anxious British eyes could discern the dim outline of the Saint-Nazaire shoreline. Now all hands quickly prepared for the dash into the harbor. The Commandos pulled on packs loaded with grenades and explosives and strapped razor-sharp trench knives to their legs. Time fuses were set on the *Campbeltown*.

A few miles away, at his command bunker in Saint-Nazaire, Kriegsmarine Captain Carl C. Mecke was growing suspicious that something extraordinary was in the making, that this was not just another British air raid. Mecke noticed that the bombers were not flying in squadron formation; instead, one or two planes at a time were winging over Saint-Nazaire. Mecke fired off a signal to all defense posts in and around the port: "I don't understand the behavior of the enemy. I suspect parachutists."[2]

Shortly after 1:00 A.M. Mecke received a warning that ships

without lights were sailing up the 6-mile-long Loire River estuary that leads into Saint-Nazaire harbor. He rushed to an observation post, peered through a telescope, and discerned the dark shapes of perhaps fifteen vessels heading in his direction. Mecke ordered a searchlight switched on, then another, and another. Commander Ryder's ships were bathed in iridescence.

Captain Mecke was hesitant to give an order to open fire. One of the intruding vessels (the *Campbeltown*) looked German, but the others didn't, even though all the craft were flying Nazi flags. He directed that a shell be fired across the bow of the leading vessel. Moments later the current German recognition signal—a green flare that split into three red stars—shot into the sky from the challenged ship.

Onward came the British flotilla, under the guns on both sides of the Loire. By 1:30 A.M. it was less than a mile from the *Normandie* dock. Suddenly, all hell broke loose. An enormous roar echoed across the water as every German gun in and around Saint-Nazaire opened fire on Commander Ryder's vessels. British guns fired back as Nazi flags were lowered rapidly and replaced by Union Jacks. Along with British resolve, fraud and deceit had paid off. The raiders had sneaked into the lair of the enemy before being identified as hostile.

Being the largest ship, the *Campbeltown* received most of the attention from German gunners. Shells screamed into the old destroyer, leaving dead and wounded Commandos and navy men sprawled about the decks. Standing calmly on the bridge as machine-gun tracers hissed past, skipper Sam Beattie shouted above the terrific racket, "Full speed ahead!" Now he could see his target, as a score of searchlights had turned Saint-Nazaire harbor into high noon. "Prepare for ramming!" Beattie yelled.

Rocked by shells screaming into her, the *Campbeltown* forged ahead. Now she was 150 yards from the *Normandie* dock . . . 100 yards . . . 50 yards. Then there was a grinding crunch as the sacrificial destroyer slammed into the massive gate. Flying debris, smoke, and flame filled the air. Ten yards of the ship's bow had been ripped open like a tin can, but her fore portion was stuck fast in the dock.

The jarring impact knocked down those aboard. Sam Beattie got to his feet and remarked evenly to officers on the bridge,

"All right, here we are!" He peeked at his watch—1:34 A.M. "Four minutes late," the skipper added in a tone of disappointment.

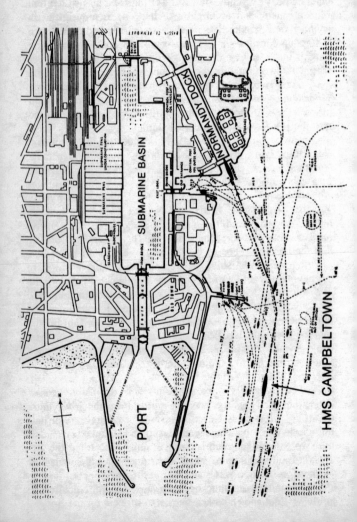

Meanwhile, the motor launches trying to land Commandos had run into a buzz saw. Several of the craft, crammed with troops, were sunk by shellfire, and swimming survivors were killed by heavy machine-gun fire. German fire was so hot that some launches had to turn back, their decks covered with wounded and dead men. Saint-Nazaire harbor had turned into a Dante's Inferno of smoke, fiery streams of tracers, exploding shells, and screams of men struck by bullets or shell fragments.

Many Commandos made it to shore and began blowing up assigned targets under a hail of bullets. At the main pumping station Lieutenant S. W. Chant, although wounded in both knees, climbed up a 40-foot ladder, placed charges in the station's machinery, and shinnied back down. Minutes later, the crucial pumping station was blown to bits. Within thirty minutes of the *Campbeltown*'s crashing into the gate, the Commandos had blown up the machinery and mechanisms of the *Normandie* dock.

Their mission completed, Lieutenant Colonel Newman and his surviving men huddled near the dockside under increasingly heavy German fire, waiting for the motor launches to return. None arrived. Rumor spread that they had all been sunk, but most had been driven off by murderous fire when they tried to come back to pick up the Commandos.

The minutes ticked past. Newman counted his men—there were only fifty of them. It was soon clear that the launches were not coming back, so the Commandos found themselves 225 miles from the nearest British port and surrounded by six thousand Germans in the Saint-Nazaire region. Yet they cracked jokes. "What a beautiful moonlit night," Colonel Newman remarked.

Calmly Newman ordered the Commandos to split into small groups and try to slip or fight their way through Saint-Nazaire and on into open country. Then they should work their way into Spain and from there back to England. "Whatever you do, don't surrender," Newman stated. "But if you must surrender, don't do so until your ammunition is gone."[3]

The Commandos were raked by heavy fire as they tried to get through Saint-Nazaire, and many of them were cut down. It was a hopeless situation. In tiny groups and individually the surviving Englishmen were captured.

At daybreak shots continued to ring out in Saint-Nazaire. Members of the French underground, thinking an Allied invasion was in progress, had taken to the streets and were firing at Germans. The Kriegsmarine port commander, convinced that he was faced with a major uprising of "terrorists," sent for more troops and declared a state of emergency in Saint-Nazaire.

At the badly damaged *Normandie* dock, Lieutenant Commander Beattie's Trojan horse was the subject of intense curiosity. An official party of forty German officers climbed aboard to inspect the martyred vessel. Rumors spread that the *Campbeltown*'s messes and storerooms contained large quantities of cigarettes, whiskey, coffee, and chocolate, and soon scores of German sailors and Feldgrau were swarming onto the ship.

Indeed an abundance of those delicacies were aboard. Along with much valuable equipment that had to be abandoned, they were part of Operation Chariot's deception plan, a ploy to lull the enemy into believing that the *Campbeltown* had crashed into the dock by accident during the shooting melee. The ploy worked to perfection: the German inspection party, unaware that they were inside a Trojan horse, never searched for nor found the five tons of explosives, along with delayed-action fuses, concealed in scattered nooks and crannies.

It was just after 10:00 A.M. At a German headquarters inside Saint-Nazaire, Lieutenant Commander Beattie, unruffled as always, was being interrogated by Kriegsmarine intelligence officers. In response to their questions, the *Campbeltown* skipper merely shrugged his shoulders. The Germans regarded Beattie as an incompetent who, during a raid designed solely to harass the Saint-Nazaire garrison, had gotten excited when the shooting erupted, lost control of his ship, and crashed her through the gate of the *Normandie* dock.

Some fifteen minutes after Beattie's interrogation had begun, an enormous explosion rocked Saint-Nazaire and environs. The delayed-action charges on the Trojan horse had detonated, blowing to pieces the ship, the 130 to 140 Germans on board—and the *Normandie* dock. The Kriegsmarine officers looked at each other in puzzlement. Beattie, expressionless, stared into space.[4]

At 4:32 P.M. on the day following the *Campbeltown* explosion, the Saint-Nazaire region was rocked by another blast. A delayed-action torpedo, fired into a submarine pen during the melee in the harbor, had exploded. While excited Germans were milling around the pen to inspect the damage, a second delayed-action torpedo exploded.

Pandemonium erupted in the dockyard. Panicky French workers tried to storm through the gates to get away from the blasts. German sentries opened fire on them. Now the Germans saw Commandos hiding behind every tree and bush. All around the port they fired on Frenchmen and on their own German workers, who happened to wear uniforms similar to those of the British. When the pandemonium died down, some 250 French workers had been killed.[5] The Germans closed the harbor area for the remainder of the week and launched an extensive search for delayed-action fuses.

Operation Chariot had been a rousing success. The *Normandie* dock had been destroyed and would be denied as a haven for the mighty *Tirpitz*. But the cost had been heavy. Of the 62 British officers and 291 men in the naval force who had sailed from England, 34 officers and 151 ratings had been killed, captured, or were missing. From No. 2 Commando, of the 44 officers and 224 men, 34 officers and 178 other ranks had been left behind, including Lieutenant Colonel Newman. German losses were placed at about 400.[6]

At far-off Wolfsschanze, word of yet another "impudent" British raid, hard on the heels of the Bruneval operation, caused Adolf Hitler to fly into a rage. But not all Germans shared the fuehrer's anger. Two weeks after the Saint-Nazaire raid, the commandant of a prisoner-of-war camp in Germany formed up his British captives and an honor guard of Wehrmacht soldiers. Then the German commandant read out the citation for the Victoria Cross (Britain's highest decoration for valor) that had been awarded to Lieutenant Commander Sam Beattie, skipper of the martyred Trojan horse of Saint-Nazaire.

17

Englandspiel

It was 7:00 P.M. on March 6, 1942. Two cars converged from different directions, heading toward a prearranged rendezvous on the corner of Cyprusstraat and Farenheitsstraat, not far from the heart of The Hague, The Netherlands. The vehicles reached their destinations almost simultaneously. Out of an inconspicuous French car with Dutch license plates stepped a handsome, graying man in civilian clothes—Major Hermann Giskes, the Abwehr chief in Holland. Emerging from a large Mercedes was Obersturmbannfuehrer Josef Schreieder of the SD, Heinrich Himmler's SS security and intelligence branch.

As the two Germans and a few colleagues huddled on the dark, deserted corner, icy blasts from the English Channel blew the falling snow into their faces. They intensely disliked each other, but because of their assignments, they had to collaborate in order to achieve a common goal—the destruction of the British espionage network in The Netherlands. Giskes had code-named his mission *Unternehmen Nordpol* (Operation North Pole). Schreieder's somewhat overlapping function was to organize "reception committees" for Allied agents and supplies parachuted into Holland, and arrest and interrogate the spies.

The overall German counterespionage plan was to "turn" these captured agents, to force them to radio false or misleading messages to their controllers in London. Schreieder called this undertaking *Englandspiel* (English talking game). En-

154

glandspiel would be the counterpart to the British XX-Committee's function.

Major Giskes and Lieutenant Colonel Schreieder found themselves huddled on this frigid corner as a result of the perfidy of a Dutch traitor, George Ridderhof, a sloppy, vulgar creature known to the Abwehr as F2087. Ridderhof, an opium and diamond smuggler by trade, had been arrested in Amsterdam the previous November on a criminal charge of trying to slip diamonds into Belgium. In prison he overheard whispers of a Dutch underground called *Orde Dienst*. He learned that a Captain Van den Berg led one resistance group, and that Van den Berg was in contact with two SOE agents who had recently parachuted into Holland—Hubertus Gerardus Lauwers (known as RLS to the British secret service) and Tijs Taconis.

Ridderhof contacted the Germans, told them what he had learned of Dutch underground activities, and offered to work for the occupiers. Smuggling charges were promptly dropped, and Ridderhof was released from prison. Under the code name George, the traitor switched his allegiance and loyalties (if any) to the Third Reich.

Ridderhof was a godsend to Giskes and Schreieder. Although their *Funk-Überwachungsstelle* (Radio Surveillance Department) had already detected the clandestine radio signals, it had not been able to locate the RLS transmitter. Secretly, Giskes, an officer of high principles who had a job to do, loathed the slovenly, treacherous Ridderhof. But the Abwehr chief in Holland had to admit that the Dutch traitor had been doing exceptional work in his role as a double-agent. He had penetrated Captain Van den Berg's group, gained information on the location of several SOE radio operators, and so impressed Dutch resistance leaders that in February they had asked Ridderhof to take charge of the operation to collect all weapons dropped by parachute in The Netherlands. For his treachery, Abwehr agent F2087 was paid five hundred guilders a month.

Giskes could not understand how Dutch idealists could accept into their inner circles a lout such as F2087. Yet the Abwehr officer knew from playing back messages intercepted by detector vans that RLS radio had sent to London all the data provided by Ridderhof—false information created by Giskes and Schreieder. So in the first week of March, when Ridderhof told the two German officers that now was the time to strike and wipe out the entire network of British spies sent into Holland, they had felt compelled to make the effort.

About twenty minutes after their arrival, Giskes and Schreieder, concealed in the shadow of a building, saw two dim figures trudging toward the corner of Cyprusstraat and Farenheitsstraat. No doubt about it, each German concluded, this was the SOE agent Hubertus Lauwers and a comrade. Ridderhof had assured his masters that it had been Lauwers's habit to pass the corner at this time on the way to a nearby cafe for supper. With RLS was a big former Dutch army lieutenant named Teller, who was not involved in the SOE spy ring and knew no secrets, but had loaned the use of a room in the apartment he shared with his wife for RLS to send his coded messages to Baker Street in London.

Just as Lauwers and Teller started to cross the intersection, a group of German soldiers, who had been concealed in a van parked along the curb, leaped out and overpowered the two men. Then a Mercedes raced up, screeched to a halt, and four Gestapo men clad in dark overcoats and waving pistols leaped out.

Lauwers was handcuffed but not harmed or degraded. Major Giskes himself took RLS by the upper arm and escorted him to the old French car. Such was not the case with Teller. Schreieder's SS men slugged and pounded and kicked him, and the big man kicked back defiantly before he was hurled, half unconscious, into Schreieder's Mercedes.[1]

A few days later Tijs Taconis was arrested in Arnhem and joined Lauwers in Scheviningen prison in a suburb of The Hague. During this same period, all other collaborators in the SOE spy network were rounded up, and Giskes set about putting his "playback" plan into motion. With information provided by Giskes' own double-agents in the British network, Lauwers's secret code was quickly broken. But Lauwers refused to send phony information to London for the Germans.

Major Giskes visited Lauwers's cell and told him that the only way he could escape being executed would be to send London messages for the Germans. "As a soldier I respect your courage," Giskes told the spy, "but I deplore the job London has given you, since it involves arming civilians to shoot us in the back. I shall therefore use every means at my disposal to prevent the delivery of arms to fanatics in this country. For their use can mean only a bloodbath for the Dutch population."[2]

Hubertus Lauwers, a thin-faced, bespectacled man who looked more like a mild-mannered bank clerk or accountant than a spy, agreed to send the messages to London over his own radio. But he had an ace up his sleeve. Before departing England, RLS was given an "identity check" to be used if captured and forced to make transmissions: he was to make a deliberate mistake in every sixteenth letter of each message.

Even though a German technician was seated at his side, Lauwers managed to make these deliberate errors. Incredibly, London failed to pick them up. Forty-eight hours later London radioed Lauwers an important task: prepare a drop zone to receive a new SOE agent plus a large amount of explosives and other sabotage materials. This drop was code-named Operation Brunnenkresse.

During the night of March 27, an RAF bomber flew low over an isolated patch of ground not far from The Hague, and several parachutes floated earthward. Five chutes carried containers of sabotage materials, and the sixth held an SOE agent, Arnoldus Baatsen (code-named Abor). As Baatsen reached the ground and quickly shucked his parachute, he was greeted by a friendly acting Dutchman—George Ridderhof. A convivial conversation ensued during which Abor told the Abwehr agent everything he knew about his forthcoming spy missions.

As Abor began struggling out of his flying suit, several figures—Gestapo men—dashed from the shadows and overpowered him. After daybreak Baker Street in London received a radio message: "Operation Brunnenkresse accomplished without incident. Abor comfortably housed."[3]

Indeed Abor was housed— but hardly comfortably. He was in a cell in a prison in The Hague, confronted by the specter of a hangman's noose.

In Holland there was no shortage of eager traitors. V-Men (*Vertrauensmann*), the Germans called them. Invariably these were despicable scum, the type of greedy blackguards police of all nations have had to endure, just in case the informers would happen to obtain information of value. Most of the V-Men's intelligence consisted of invented tales and idle gossip overheard in cafes.

Colonel Schreieder, the SD chief in Holland, spent more than an hour each morning listening to the tales of a series of these Dutch informers. Schreieder detested them and concluded that they enjoyed the role of traitor, for they were paid but a pittance by the Germans. One informer, 29-year-old Antonius Van der Waals, scurried to Schreieder to reveal the identity of a Dutch "terrorist" who had shot a German soldier on a street in Haarlem. The SD officer asked Van der Waals why he had given him the information.

"Because people who shoot German soldiers are traitors," the informer replied. "Besides," he added softly, "I need the money."[4]

Within hours the assassin was arrested and after undergoing excruciating torture was shot to death.

With the capture of Abor, a quiet interval of several weeks followed in the children's home in Nordwijk where RLS (Lauwers's radio set) was being operated. Why the lack of activity? Had London smelled a rat? It seemed as though RLS had been written off, as Major Giskes had ample proof that the Anglo-Dutch secret service was continuing to build up its network elsewhere in The Netherlands. Now the gods of war came down on the side of the German counterespionage agencies: by sheer happenstance all the radio channels through which Baker Street controlled its spy network in Holland fell into their hands.

Colonel Dr. J. M. Somer, the officer in charge of the Dutch section of SOE and Giskes and Schreieder's direct adversary, parachuted three pairs of agents, each pair with a radio set, into Holland. Two radios were badly damaged on impact with the ground, so the spies linked up and reported to their London controllers over the surviving set, code-named Trumpet.

Suddenly, after the long interval, the RLS set crackled at the Nordwijk children's home. London was on the air with instructions for Lauwers. He was to make radio contact with Trumpet. Within hours Trumpet was seized by the Germans. Then Giskes' men found the body of one of the spies who had been killed on landing when he struck his head against a rock. In it was the signal plan for his radio, and with it the Abwehr opened another channel to London to go with the RLS and Trumpet sets.

From this point onward, the Abwehr and the SD apprehended every spy Colonel Somer sent into Holland. On the night of May 29, a pair of Somer's agents named Van Steen and Parlevliet jumped from a plane and landed in a desolate field near Steenwijk. The two men shucked their chutes and felt a surge of relief when approached by a "reception committee" of the Dutch underground.

For nearly an hour the group stood in the shadows while Van Steen and Parlevliet told their new friends everything they knew about their mission, including their personal code names.

They had with them a plan to sabotage German naval installations in Holland, the new arrivals said, and they were to install a device for communicating with Allied ships steaming off the Dutch coast.

Then silence descended over the little knot of shadowy figures. Van Steen and Parlevliet had nothing left to tell. Suddenly, their "friends" surrounded the two spies and handcuffed them, while Obersturmbannfuehrer Schreieder and several SD men emerged from a clump of bushes. Van Steen and Parlevliet roundly cursed the Dutchmen who had betrayed them as they were hauled, still struggling, to prison.

Three weeks later two more agents, whose mission was to organize the Dutch resistance, came down by parachute, only to be seized by another "reception committee" of Dutch traitors.

Major Giskes could not believe his good fortune. Now he had five channels of communication with Baker Street, along with codes and most of the security checks. New agents were dropped at the rate of two or more each week, and all were intercepted.

In late June a technician told Giskes that Lauwers had added extra letters to the end of his last message, but that London's suspicions had apparently not been aroused. However, the Abwehr officer feared that Lauwers might throw a monkey wrench into his Englandspiel (in which Giskes had been flooding Baker Street with false information), so he decided to put an end to Lauwers's transmissions. London was asked if unnamed "reserve operators" could replace Lauwers, and, to Giskes' astonishment, approval was received without an inquiry as to the reason for the switch.

Giskes put his own men to work operating the "turned" transmitters, a risky procedure. If an SOE spy's "fist" (everyone had an identifiable way of sending dot-and-dash messages) had been recorded in London before his departure and matched with the German "fist" now being used in Holland, Baker Street would know that the agent was dead or in custody and that the messages coming over his set were false ones from the enemy.

By late June Colonel Somer in the SOE Dutch section was ready to launch his most ambitious operation yet—Plan Holland. George L. Jambroes, who before the war taught physics at Utrecht University in The Netherlands and was widely known in the world's scientific community, was chosen to spearhead the clandestine mission.

The Germans had offered Jambroes a goodly sum to work for them as a scientist, but, instead, in December 1941 he escaped to England. There he volunteered for "special duty"— that is, perilous tasks in German-held territory. Now he was being given the most important mission of his life: parachuting into his native Holland to organize a "secret army" whose function would be to sabotage and disrupt the Wehrmacht to pave the way for the Allies' eventual return to the Continent.

In the predawn hours of June 26, Professor Jambroes and a radio operator jumped from a Halifax bomber and parachuted into a field near Steenwijk. Jambroes was met by the customary party of Dutch traitors, and he and his operator were apprehended. Incredibly, Jambroes was carrying in his pocket the entire *uncoded* SOE plan for organizing seventeen sabotage and resistance groups of one hundred men each throughout The Netherlands.

Using the secret ciphers and other material found on Jambroes, Major Giskes began milking the coup for all it was worth. His German operators reported steadily to Baker Street over Jambroes's transmitter on the progress of Operator Kern, the buildup of the seventeen sabotage and resistance groups. Clearly Professor Jambroes (who was actually ensconced in a prison near The Hague) was doing a superb job. His transmitter reported that some fifteen hundred Dutch resistance fighters had been recruited and were undergoing training. But, "Jambroes" signaled London, this secret army would need vast quantities of weapons and supplies.

A few nights later hundreds of containers—weighing more than five tons—of the requested goods dropped from the sky. These and the parachuted cargoes of scores of succeeding supply drops were intercepted by Giskes' Abwehr agents. In all during the coming weeks, 3,000 pistols, 15 tons of explosives, 100 machine guns, 2,000 hand grenades, millions of rounds of ammunition, 75 transmitters, and a wide variety of other equipment were collected by Abwehr agents. This huge arsenal was stored in a building at Wittenborg Palace in Wassennaar (outside The Hague), the headquarters of the occupying Wehrmacht.[5]

Along with the cache of weapons, the Abwehr steadily apprehended SOE agents (most of them Dutch patriots) who were coming down as though on a conveyer belt. On June 30 Giskes' men seized a parachuting spy, Jan Emmer, who had a written order for Tijs Taconis to blow up the powerful German radio transmitter at Kootwijk. The complex was a major German nerve center, for it kept the Kreigsmarine high command in contact with U-boats prowling the Atlantic and monitored Allied air and naval activities over and upon the English Channel and the North Sea by receiving reports from German coast watchers.

Giskes, through his radio channels to London, tried to stall "blowing up" the transmitter. But Baker Street was insistent— it had to be done, and done immediately. Why the great urgency? the Abwehr officer reflected. Were the Allies planning a large military operation in which they would cross the English Channel and strike at Holland, France, or Belgium? Whatever the reason for London's feverish tone, the fact that the British had reopened contact with RLS was highly encouraging to Giskes: his ruse was still working, for Baker Street would not be giving detailed instructions for a crucial mission to agents they knew to be in prison or dead.

After a flurry of signals between The Hague and London, the raid to blow up the Kootwijk transmitter was set for the night of August 8. Tijs Taconis would lead the operation, London was told.

Major Giskes dressed a group of German soldiers in Dutch civilian clothing to resemble resistance fighters, and the "attack" was made on the key communications center. The "underground warriors" pitched a few harmless grenades, then retired from the scene.

Two days later RLS (Lauwers's transmitter) reported to London: "Kootwijk attack a failure. Our men ran into mine-field. Five men missing, Tijs [Taconis] and others safe, including two wounded."

Taconis indeed was "safe" for the time being—in a Gestapo jail cell. After many weeks of imprisonment under the constant threat of execution, the Dutch patriot had become mentally deranged.

Giskes had an account of the Koowijk "raid" published in German-controlled Dutch newspapers, knowing that it would reach Baker Street through neutral countries. Criminal elements, the account stated, had been foiled in an attempt to blow up the Kootwijk transmitter. Equipment left behind, the story pointed out, provided evidence that the British secret service was behind the dastardly deed.

A week later London sent a signal to The Hague praising the courage of those Dutch fighters who had taken part in the Kootwijk attack and stating that Tijs Taconis had been awarded a medal for leading the mission.

If the Abwehr in Holland was to continue to bamboozle Baker Street with false information, there would have to be signs of action by the phony, 1,500-man Dutch secret army, Major Giskes knew. At Utrecht a violent exchange of gunfire broke out in the street between German soldiers and a band of resistance men. The episode was widely reported in the Dutch press. Only Giskes, a few of his officers, and those involved knew that the shoot-out had been staged and that the bullets were blanks.

Near Appeldoorn a large bridge was blown sky high. This incident, too, was highly publicized, but no mention was made that it was an old, abandoned structure—or that the perpetrators were German soldiers disguised as resistance men. At Arnhem and elsewhere around The Netherlands railroad sidetracks no longer in use were destroyed by explosives, and worn-out boxcars were blown to smithereens. The "resistance" received full "credit" in Dutch newspapers. Hermann Giskes saw to that. To unknowing observers it appeared that organized underground groups were raising merry hell with the German war effort all over Holland.

Now Major Giskes, the architect of Operation North Pole, one of warfare's greatest counterespionage coups, began to ponder intently over the subtle duel of wits between the Abwehr and the SD in The Hague and Baker Street in London. He was puzzled. Why had the British secret service, long recognized throughout the world for its cleverness and ingenuity, suddenly become stupid? He speculated over why the veteran, sophisticated men on Baker Street had compliantly fallen into one German trap after the other. Why did they sacrifice such irreplaceable agents as Professor George Jambroes and others? And it was inconceivable to Giskes that the cagey British would parachute an agent into Holland armed with the entire sabotage plan—in *uncoded* form. What was Baker Street trying to get the Germans across the Channel to believe? Giskes had no answers. His job was that of spybuster. Enemy strategic design would have to be determined by *Oberbefehlshaber West* (Commander in Chief, West), 67-year-old Field Marshal Gerd von Rundstedt, known in the Wehrmacht as the Last of the Prussians.[6]

18

French Underground

Behind drawn blinds in a flat at 105 rue Courlaincourt in the Montmartre district of Paris, three solemn-faced men were holding a clandestine conference. Loitering in the front doorway downstairs was a youth and his teenage girlfriend, outwardly engaging in amorous embraces, but actually serving as lookouts to warn those above if the Gestapo were to approach. It was April 4, 1942.

Taking part in the conference were Marcel Berthélot, right-hand man to Colonel Alfred Touny, a founder and leader of a spy ring called the *Organisation Civile et Militaire* (OCM); Gilbert Renault (code name Colonel Rémy), chief of the Confrérie Notre-Dame; and Marcel Girard, a cement salesman who lived in Caen, the historic capital of Normandy.

Forty-one years old and graying, Girard soon learned why he had been called to Paris. Renault explained that de Gaulle's secret service in London had been pressing him to organize a spy network along the Normandy coast, a crucial region since it is directly across the English Channel from Britain. But Rémy's efforts had been in vain, so now he asked Girard to take over the job of organizing an espionage network along the entire Normandy coast, from Le Havre to Saint-Malo.

The burly Girard pondered the proposal long and hard. He was being asked to put his life (and that of his family) on the line and to take on a task of great magnitude. During recent days he had become aware that the Germans had thrown up barriers and established a *Zone Interdite* (Forbidden Zone) that ran inland for several miles along the entire French coastline. What were the occupiers doing along the waterfront that required such drastic and secret actions? That is what Allied leaders in London wanted to know.

Now, in the Paris flat, Girard looked up and said softly, "I'll do it." Shaking hands with Berthélot and Renault, the cement salesman slipped out of the flat and caught a train back to Caen, where he had lived for forty years and was widely known.

Unknown to Girard (or anyone else in the Allied camp), Adolf Hitler had launched what he conceived to be one of the great engineering feats in history. British Commando and paratroop raids at Bruneval, Saint-Nazaire, and elsewhere along the French and Norwegian coasts had driven home to the fuehrer the threat to his stolen empire of invasion from England. Consequently, in mid-March 1942 Hitler had signed Directive 40, decreeing that an *Atlantikwall*, stretching from the snowy fjords of Norway to the Spanish frontier, be constructed with "fanatic speed."

Hitler ordered the building of fifteen thousand concrete and steel structures, immune to bombing and naval gunfire, to protect a continuous, interlocking belt of weapons commanding the major ports and potential landing beaches. This monumental construction project, the German dictator ordained, must be completed no later than May 1, 1943—a mere thirteen months away.

"An impossible task!" fumed Field Marshal Gerd von Rundstedt, Commander in Chief West, at his headquarters in an ornate villa outside Paris. "It would take ten years to complete the project!" The aristocratic von Rundstedt considered the Atlantic Wall to be an enormous waste of energy, time, and materials.

But the fuehrer had spoken, and work got under way. Thousands of slave laborers from all over Europe were being rushed to the coast, where they would toil around the clock building massive fortifications under the direction of the Reich's paramilitary construction agency, the Todt Organization.

From his base in Caen, an ancient city of forty thousand

known for its magnificent cathedral, Marcel Girard (code-named Moreau) roamed the coast of Normandy, using his commercial job as cover. Only his patriotic boss knew that the traveling salesman would never sell one pound of cement. A special permit issued to him through his company permitted Girard to enter towns along the coast to peddle cement, from Ouistreham in Calvados westward to Courseulles, Arromanches, Colleville, Vierville, and Port-en-Bessin, then northward up the eastern shore of the Cherbourg peninsula to Cherbourg.

Girard was under the constant threat of arrest, but he continued to recruit spies—farmers, housewives, train conductors, plumbers, doctors, mechanics, government officials, policemen, secretaries. Girard called his network of instant spies *Centurie*. No one in Centurie would ever have an inkling that one day powerful Allied forces would storm ashore along these Normandy beaches to be named *Omaha, Utah, Sword, Gold,* and *Juno.* Each of Girard's spies would risk his or her life daily solely on faith in the cause of liberation from the Nazi yoke.

One of Girard's early recruits was Eugene Meslin, an engineer who was in charge of the network of streets, roads, and bridges in Calvados. A longtime friend of Girard, Meslin's duties permitted him to penetrate the Zone Interdite at many points along one hundred miles of English Channel coastline. The engineer quickly organized a small group of agents, and its leaders met regularly in the basement of Caen's popular Café des Touristes. The cafe's owner was a staunch member of the resistance, so he allowed Meslin to place a drop box inside the boiler into which spies could put messages. Another drop box was set up in the Hôtel de Rouen opposite the railroad station.

René Duchez, a small, unimpressive-looking painter in his mid-forties, was courier for Meslin's group. Twice a week he collected messages from the drop boxes and took them to Meslin's office, where they were hidden in a cupboard. Duchez's task was a perilous one; a sudden personal search by the Gestapo would catch him red-handed with the incriminating messages.

Duchez had been chosen as a courier even though he was well known to the Caen Gestapo, who considered him to be retarded. The Frenchman had a talent for putting on a convincing portrayal of an idiot seized by epileptic fits. He loved to taunt the Gestapo. If Duchez spotted Gestapo agents in a cafe when he was drinking late at night (which was often), he would stroll casually toward their table, fall to the floor at their feet, jerking and twitching and uttering curious gurgling noises. He would drool large amounts of saliva, and his eyes would bulge until they promised to burst from their sockets. The "fit" would continue for two or three minutes, until the Gestapo men could endure no more and stalked out of the cafe.

As a result of these escapades, the members of Himmler's dreaded secret police in Caen regarded René Duchez as a harmless and repulsive creature, so it was not likely that the Frenchman would be halted and searched while walking or driving with the Centurie messages.

Every ten days another Centurie agent collected the raft of messages hidden in Eugene Meslin's cupboard and rushed them to a secret office in Paris where, along with material gathered from all over northern France, they were placed in sacks and flown to Colonel Passy in London by Lysander.

After six weeks as a spy master, Marcel Girard had grown frustrated. His agents were unable to think of valid reasons for getting into the Forbidden Zone, although a few had reached the Channel coast by the use of superb permit forgeries fashioned by a 38-year-old Caen housewife, Jeanne Vérinaud, who kept the records for Centurie. Consequently, Girard's spies had been able to report mainly on secondary defenses being erected by the Germans far behind the beaches.

In this depressed frame of mind, Girard, on the night of May 13, met René Duchez at the Café des Touristes. Girard was concerned; clearly the courier had been drinking a considerable amount, and when in this condition Duchez took an especial delight in mocking German customers, thereby attracting unwanted attention to himself and to those with him. The Centurie chief glanced around the room. He spotted two men whom he believed to be Gestapo agents, and the bar was filled with carousing German soldiers.

Duchez slipped a large envelope to Girard, and when the latter asked what was inside it, the clever painter put on his idiot face and replied casually, "Oh, it's nothing but a blueprint of the entire Atlantic Wall." Girard felt a chill race up his spine. Duchez was a great joker; was this one of René's skits for taunting the Germans in the room?

"Where did you get it?" Girard whispered, convinced that the enemy soldiers and Gestapo were focusing on him.

"Stole it from the Todt Organization," Duchez replied airily. In a low voice, Girard swore at the grinning Duchez, and he had to fight an overpowering urge to rush out of the bar. The network leader stashed the envelope in his pocket; he didn't dare look at its contents. After an interminable period of time, Girard shook hands with Duchez, who was now putting on his drooling act, and as inconspicuously as possible strolled out of the cafe. His legs felt like jelly, and he expected to hear the shout, "Halt!" at any moment.

Walking through the dark and nearly deserted streets, Girard fought off repeated temptations to look back over his shoulder. "Calm. Be calm," he kept telling himself. At the railroad station he caught a train to Paris, and then five hours later, only when he was inside the apartment he used when "selling cement" in the capital, did Girard dare open Duchez's envelope. If this were another of the free-spirited painter's jokes, Girard pledged to strangle him at the first opportunity.

The Centurie chief began perusing a six-foot-long blueprint, and his heart pounded furiously. The document was stamped in several places with the German equivalent of Top Secret. From across the top of the blueprint in large letters the words *Atlantikwall, Normandy Sector,* leaped out at Girard. What he was looking at was a map of 125 miles of coast, from Le Havre to west of Cherbourg, depicting all planned fortifications— bunkers, gun batteries, machine-gun and flame-thrower positions, ammunition dumps, and command posts. Clearly, René Duchez had pulled off an enormous espionage bonanza.

After daybreak Girard hurried with the map to Colonel Alfred Touny's Paris OCM headquarters, which was disguised as a Red Cross headquarters. Touny inspected the blueprint and could hardly believe his eyes. He directed Girard to have a precise copy made, then rush the original to Colonel Rémy (Gilbert Renault) in Brittany, from where the Confrérie Notre-Dame chief would take it to de Gaulle's secret service headquarters in London.

A week later Marcel Girard returned to Caen. Intensely curious as to how Duchez had stolen the Atlantic Wall map, he sought out the house painter. Over glasses of watery beer in the Café des Touristes, Duchez related his story. A German army engineers' office in Caen had advertised for bids to repaper the premises. Duchez, seizing on the opportunity to prowl around inside a German headquarters, appeared with his sample wallpaper book and was escorted into the office of the German commander, an aging reserve colonel.

The Wehrmacht officer began thumbing through the sample book and marked a few selections that caught his eye. Duchez, trying to be helpful, leaned over the colonel's shoulder and drooled saliva on the expensive, field gray tunic. Then an officer came into the room and laid a stack of blueprints on the commander's desk, hardly taking note of the village idiot. Duchez's sharp eye caught the wording on the top blueprint: Atlantikwall. Minutes later the colonel was called out of the room, leaving the Frenchman alone with the Top Secret map.

Duchez's keen mind was spinning. Here was a once-in-a-lifetime chance. Should he steal the map? Could he get out of the building with the map on his person without being searched? If he did pull off the coup, wouldn't the blueprint be quickly missed and the Gestapo sent in search of the painter? Duchez reached over and lifted the Atlantic Wall map off the stack, then quickly concealed it behind a wall mirror moments before the office door opened and the colonel returned.

A price deal was struck between the two men, and the next morning Duchez appeared and began papering the office of the colonel, who stayed away so as not to impede the work of the Frenchman. Late that afternoon Duchez retrieved the blueprint from behind the mirror, thrust it into an empty wallpaper container, and strolled casually out of the German headquarters with the incriminating document under his arm. Outside two Feldgrau sentries eyed with disgust the grinning, drooling dimwit who bowed and saluted as he brushed on past.

For many days Marcel Girard expected the Germans to react with violence when they discovered that the map had been stolen. But Caen remained outwardly tranquil. RAF photo intelligence revealed that the Wall was being built precisely to specifications, so for unknown reasons the Germans apparently never realized that the blueprint was missing. Or perhaps the elderly colonel who had been victimized by the idiot Duchez decided that, as a matter of self-preservation, he would report to no one that the map had disappeared.

At the same time that the former soldier Marcel Girard was roaming Normandy recruiting Centurie spies, three men knocked on the door of a house in the Norman village of Veules-les-Roses, about fifteen miles from the port of Dieppe. Two of them were Frenchmen, André Lemoin and Raoul Kiffer, both members of de Gaulle's underground. When Madame Jeanette Dumoulins, also a member of the local *réseau* (cell), opened the door, Lemoin and Kiffer introduced the third man as Mr. Evans, a Canadian agent. Actually, Mr. Evans was Captain Heinz Eckert, an Abwehr counterespionage officer who had been sent to Normandy for the specific purpose of penetrating the growing French underground. Lemoin (code-named Moineau) and Kiffer (known as Kiki) were French traitors who had been caught and "turned" by the Abwehr.[1]

A friendly conversation ensued, and Madame Dumoulins told "Mr. Evans" that her husband had escaped to England to join de Gaulle's army there and that a few nights earlier she had heard a *message personnel* over the BBC French service: "Georges will embrace Jeanette." Now she asked Captain Eckert if he knew the time and place of Georges' arrival. Eckert said that he did not know, but that he would contact London to find out.

Then Madame Dumoulins let slip a startling revelation. The leader of the local réseau was in close contact with an anti-Hitler officer of the Todt Organization who held a key post at Dieppe. This German officer, Madame Dumoulins stated, had been furnishing London with requested data on Dieppe's harbor, fortifications, position of gun batteries, and the posting of German units.

Captain Heinz Eckert had unexpectedly hit pay dirt. The message "Georges will embrace Jeanette" no doubt meant that the British were ready to strike at some point along the coast, and the special request for information on Dieppe indicated that Dieppe most likely was the target.

On July 9, 1942, Adolf Hitler, at Wolfsschanze, where he

was directing a massive offensive on the Russian front, issued an appreciation of Allied intentions in the West: "England may be faced with the choice of either mounting a major landing in order to create a second front or of losing Soviet Russia as a political and military factor. It is highly probable that the landings will take place . . . on the Channel coast, in the area between Dieppe and Le Havre."[2]

As a result of his conclusions, the fuehrer, at a time he needed every soldier, airplane, and gun to administer a knockout blow to the reeling Russian army, rushed strong forces to man the Normandy coast against an expected Allied landing.

At Bletchley Park, Ultra had been unbuttoning German messages telling of the troop movements to the West. It confirmed that Operation Overthrow, an LCS campaign that had been in progress since early spring, had achieved its goal; convincing the fuehrer that the Allies would launch a cross-Channel invasion in 1942, thereby taking pressure off the Russian army.

19

Dieppe: Sacrificial Ploy?

A heavy rain was drenching London on the morning of July 8, 1942, as a three-man delegation from Washington, D.C., checked into fashionable Claridge's. U.S. Army Chief of Staff George C. Marshall, Chief of Naval Operations Ernest J. King, and presidential advisor Harry Hopkins had been rushed to England by President Roosevelt to "sell" Winston Churchill and his Chiefs of Staff on the crucial need to launch Operation Sledgehammer without delay.

Sledgehammer had been drawn up under the direction of Major General Dwight D. Eisenhower, chief of the War Plan Division; it called for cross-Channel operations to gain a beachhead on the Cherbourg peninsula in northwestern France that fall, from which full-scale offensives (code-named Roundup) might be launched in 1943. D day for Sledgehammer would be September 15, 1942—barely sixty days away.

President Roosevelt's eagerness to initiate large-scale operations had been triggered by a fear that Russia was on the verge of being knocked out of the war unless the Western Allies opened a "second front" at once. In late May Premier Joseph Stalin had dispatched Foreign Minister Vycheslav Molotov to London to demand that the Grand Alliance (as Churchill called England and the United States) invade Hitler's Europe in 1942. He declared that the Red Army, in the face of massive trip-hammer blows by the Wehrmacht, could not hold out much longer. Churchill recognized the threat: unless the West-

172

ern Allies established a second front at once in order to draw off German divisions from the eastern front, Stalin would seek a separate peace with Germany—just as Lenin had done in 1917 during World War I.

General Alan Brooke, chief of the Imperial General Staff, was not impressed. Tough, shrewd, and a decorated combat leader in two world wars, Brooke knew that the Red Army had suffered enormous casualties, but he was convinced that the Russian situation was not yet that desperate. So Churchill rejected Molotov's plea.

The Soviet foreign minister hurried on to Washington, where his reception was quite different. Roosevelt and General Marshall were deeply alarmed by Molotov's briefing on the plight of the Red Army, and the president informed Stalin's emissary that the Western Allies would launch a cross-Channel invasion of northwestern France in September.

Learning of Roosevelt's promise to the Soviets, Winston Churchill and his advisors were stupefied. Both England and America were hanging on by their eyelids on all world fronts. Only a massive campaign of charades (and the courage of RAF fighter pilots) had kept Hitler from overrunning Great Britain itself. And the Grand Alliance did not have the trained troops, logistical know-how, ships, airplanes, landing craft, and tanks to strike in force at the French coast. Ultra had revealed that there were twenty-five combat-tested German divisions, backed by a formidable array of Luftwaffe squadrons, across the Channel.

"Sheer madness!" General Brooke exploded. "Any cross-Channel attack this year will meet with total disaster!"

Before the Marshall-King-Hopkins "sales delegation" arrived in Great Britain, Churchill and Brooke had agreed that some dramatic event would have to be staged, even though it might result in a debacle, to impress upon an inexperienced American leadership the folly of attempting a full-scale cross-Channel operation in 1942. Better this tragedy, Churchill was said to have believed, in which as many as five thousand Allied troops might be sacrificed, than a premature invasion in which perhaps a half million British and American soldiers, their weapons, and equipment—and the war—would be lost.

Consequently, Operation Rutter (German for a mercenary

horse soldier) was mounted. Rutter would be a reconnaissance in force against Dieppe, an old pirate lair on what was known as the Iron Coast of France. Involved would be 6,058 troops, mainly two brigades of the Canadian 2d Division, supported by a detachment of British Commandos, 50 U.S. Rangers, a flotilla of 252 vessels, and 56 squadrons of RAF fighters—more than existed at the time of the Battle of Britain. Plans for Rutter had been finalized, troop training was in its final stages, and in mid-July commanders were waiting for the "go" signal.

In the meantime, on July 20, the confrontation between the American and British military over Sledgehammer opened at the War Office in London. Hardly had the participants settled in their chairs than heated controversy erupted between General George Marshall and General Alan Brooke. Since their first meeting months earlier, there had been friction between the two strong-willed officers.

The showdown sessions were exhaustive and acrimonious. Marshall, who had been a staff officer in World War I and had never led a unit in combat, argued forcefully for mounting Sledgehammer in sixty days. Brooke plugged Operation Torch, a British plan to open a "second front" by invading French Northwest Africa, fourteen hundred miles south of England, where defenses would be infinitely weaker than those across the Channel. Almost from the first verbal salvo the Americans were on the defensive fighting a losing battle against facts ticked off by General Brooke.

After four days of intense dueling, the British carried the ramparts. Northwest Africa, not northwest France, would be the locale of an Allied blow to relieve the pressure on the Russian army. Churchill and Brooke were jubilant over the American acceptance of Operation Torch, and Rutter was canceled. There was no longer a need for heavy bloodletting to show the green Americans the folly of a cross-Channel assault in 1942.

In Berlin the day after the Grand Alliance powwow concluded, Reichsfuehrer Heinrich Himmler was reading a sheath of verbatim conversations in which Allied leaders in Washington and in London were discussing proceedings at the Sledgehammer versus Torch conference. These discussions had been monitored and translated by the secret German station at

Eindhoven, Holland, that had long been tapping the transatlantic hot-line cable that ran between the White House and Churchill's underground command post at Storey's Gate.

An SS general had noted across the transcripts: "The [London] conference will probably determine where the Second Front is to be established and when." Among the voices identified at Eindhoven were those of Churchill; Lieutenant General Dwight Eisenhower (who would command Torch); U.S. Major General Mark W. Clark, Eisenhower's deputy (who would be chief planner for Torch); and U.S. Lieutenant Commander Harry C. Butcher, naval aide and confidant to Eisenhower.[1]

Early in August Winston Churchill learned that "certain influential American leaders" were boring in on President Roosevelt to convince him that Sledgehammer was still the best course of action. Those "influential leaders" were General Marshall and Secretary of War Henry Stimson. Churchill ordered Rutter to be remounted. How else could he convince Washington that Sledgehammer would be a catastrophe?[2]

Planning for Operation Jubilee (as Rutter was now called) was conducted in a mystifying climate. Nothing was put on paper, including discussions by the Chiefs of Staff, and the First Lord of the Admiralty was kept in the dark about why 252 ships were required. There would be no rehearsals and *no deception plan*. The XX-Committee was ordered *not* to use its stable of double-agents to feed their German controllers with faulty information about the purpose and destination of the shipping assembling in the Channel ports of England.[3]

The Jubilee force was to blow up docks, power stations, fuel dumps, and railheads; to destroy all German coastal defenses; to shoot up the Saint-Aubin airfield a few miles inland; to bring back German invasion barges for study; to steal secret papers from a divisional headquarters; to release French prisoners held in a Dieppe prison; and to escort a scientist on a secret mission to a Freya radar perched on a 300-foot cliff outside Pourville, just west of Dieppe.

The radar mission was laid on at the urgent request of Winston Churchill by the Director General of Signals and Radar, Air Vice Marshal Victor H. Tait. As the Germans had ceased using radio plotting, it was crucial to make the enemy use their standby radio transmitters so that the British could observe them in action. This would necessitate cutting the German telephone communications at a Dieppe radar station.

In the ongoing duel of wits with their German counterparts, British scientists had benefited enormously from studying the Würzburg stolen in the Bruneval raid. Now they wanted to learn details of the Freya, which had a far longer range than the Würzburg, but its accuracy and plotting precision was not known.

Selected as the scientist for the Freya mission was RAF Flight-Sergeant Jack M. Nissenthall, the 24-year-old son of a Jewish tailor who had immigrated to England from Poland before the war. Nissenthall had volunteered for the perilous task, and his background seemed ideal. Tough and well conditioned (he had taken the Commando training course), the sergeant would have to make his way up the mile-long hill to the Freya at Pourville. Presumably, Germans would be firing at him during the entire climb. If he reached the top and the radar-station defenders were killed or driven off, Nissenthall could study the Freya in operation during an air battle that undoubtedly would be raging over Dieppe.

Despite his relatively tender years, Flight-Sergeant Nissenthall had a lengthy background in radar, both before and after the outset of war. Even though he had volunteered for combat duty on enlistment, Nissenthall was assigned to radar stations in Scotland and England because of his expertise. Consequently, he had one flaw in his makeup that caused British authorities deep concern: he knew too many radar secrets. If captured and forced to talk (every man has his breaking point), Nissenthall could provide German scientists with technical information that could swing the radar-duel advantage to Hitler's camp. Such an eventuality was unthinkable and would have to be prevented, no matter how drastic the means.

In his office in rambling old Norris Castle on the Isle of Wight (off England's southern coast), 32-year-old Lieutenant Colonel Charles C. Merritt, commander of the South Saskatchewan Regiment, summoned his A Company leader, Captain Murray Osten. Merritt, a former star football player and practicing attorney in Vancouver, told Osten that "a radar expert" would be attached to Osten's company because the Freya the scientist was to examine was located in A Company's sector. "It's all very hush-hush," Merritt said.

The colonel instructed Osten to provide ten riflemen to "protect" the scientist at all times. "This fellow's not to be captured," Merritt added. "Orders from above."

Captain Osten gave assurances that he would assign his best men to cover the scientist. "I know that," Merritt replied. "But if he is wounded or about to be captured, you will have to deal with him. He knows too much to be taken prisoner. Is that clear?"

Osten was shocked. Indeed it was clear. Higher-ups, through Colonel Merritt, had just given him an order: if a fellow soldier, Jack Nissenthall—the Man Who Knew Too Much—were about to fall into German hands, he was to be killed by his "bodyguards."

At his headquarters in suburban Paris, Field Marshal Gerd von Rundstedt had been piecing together evidence that told him the Allies were about ready to strike a heavy blow at Calais or Dieppe or Cherbourg—probably Dieppe. Abwehr agents had been shadowing the anti-Hitler officer in the Todt Organization who had been unmasked by Captain Heinz Eckert (posing as the Canadian Mr. Evans) in a conversation with Madame Dumoulins at Veules-les-Roses. German monitors intercepted radio messages for the Todt officer instructing him to report on the docks, installations, and gun batteries in and to both sides of Dieppe.

Other clues pointed to Dieppe as the Allied target. The Abwehr had broken codes between London and the French underground, and this achievement led to a loft of homing pigeons at a house outside Dieppe. The birds belonged to a Frenchman who had fled to England and were used by the British secret service to carry messages to London. Abwehr agents shadowed a French courier who had clamped a message to the leg of a pigeon, and the trail led to an SOE radio operator, who was arrested.

Now Field Marshal von Rundstedt launched his own deception operation (code-named Porto II) to mislead spies into reporting to London that the Dieppe area was held by only fourteen hundred low-grade troops. In fact the region was defended by the tough, battle-tested 302d Infantry Division. And Dieppe itself was not held by the lone battalion of inferior troops that Porto II suggested, but rather by a crack regiment of five thousand men backed by artillery. Just inland in reserve were three battalions of infantry, a tank battalion, and an artillery battalion. Only three hours from Dieppe by road was the first-rate 10th Panzer Division.[5]

A principal component of Porto II was the SOE operator near Dieppe who had been betrayed by the carrier pigeons and "turned" by the Abwehr. The Germans forced him to send to London false information on troop strengths and defenses in and around Dieppe. MI-6, which was responsible for collecting intelligence for Jubilee, had been badly hoodwinked by the German charade. It passed word to the assault force that only fourteen hundred low-grade troops were defending the targeted region.[6]

In the Dieppe sector early August had been unusually quiet. But Major General Conrad von Haase, commander of the 302d Division, had the defenses fully manned from high tide each night to sunrise the next morning. On August 9 von Haase ordered a *drohende Gefahr* (threatening danger) alert for twelve nights.

Meanwhile, Jubilee D day was set for August 19. Only a week before that date, on August 12, British secret service agents in disguise had descended on pubs and other public places in the Shoreham area, where large numbers of Jubilee troops were posted. Indiscreet conversation abounded. Canadians were talking loudly of waterproofing their vehicles for an operation. In a curious security lapse, a Royal Navy lieutenant commander left a copy of the Dieppe naval operation in a bar.

In mid-August General von Haase's forces were put on full alert. B-Dienst (wireless monitors) along the French coast had warned that there had been a sudden change in the pattern of wireless traffic across the Channel, then a period of total silence. Such patterns by the British had often meant that a military action was imminent.

The night of August 18 was starlit and calm over the English Channel. It was nearly midnight when Major General John H. Roberts, the 48-year-old commander of the Canadian 2d Division, strolled out onto the deck of the destroyer *Calpe* to breathe in the refreshing sea air. All around him were the ghostly silhouettes of an armada of ships, most crammed with assault troops. Except for some of the Commandos, none of them had ever heard a shot fired in anger.

Tension gripped the troops. Would the Germans be lying in wait along the Iron Coast? A month earlier, before Churchill had canceled the operation, several thousand men had been told that the target was Dieppe. Now the armada was sailing toward that same objective. Could that vast number of men have kept their mouths shut about the target?

A few miles off Dieppe, just before dawn, ships lowered their landing craft and grim-faced Canadians scrambled down rope ladders and into the boats. As the craft neared shore, the Channel was deathly still. Suddenly the tranquillity was shattered. Up and down the Dieppe coast brilliant white flares burst in the gray sky, and one hour later the first assault craft crunched onto the beach and lowered ramps. On the beach in Dieppe town, machine guns and antitank guns concealed in cliffside caves raked the Canadians as they leaped out. Bodies piled up on the ramps. Many soldiers staggered forward only a few yards before they were cut down. Hardly any of the Canadians got past the seawall, so devastating was the heavy fire.

Eighteen Churchill tanks crawled out of LSTs in Dieppe and bogged down in the shingle. Antitank guns poured flat-trajectory fire into the helpless monsters, and within minutes many of the Churchills were twisted, burning pieces of junk, their crews dead or captured.

East and west of Dieppe, Commandos scaled rocky cliffs to try to knock out coastal gun batteries, but they met with withering bursts of fire and were chopped to pieces. Only on the heights at Varengeville, after killing the German defenders to the last man, did one Commando assault team succeed in blowing up a gun battery.

High above the carnage being inflicted on the invaders, the clear blue sky over Dieppe appeared to have gone mad; the greatest duel since the Battle of Britain in 1940 was raging between the RAF and the Luftwaffe.

Just west of Dieppe, at Pourville, Captain Murray Osten and his company of South Saskatchewans had run into a buzz saw

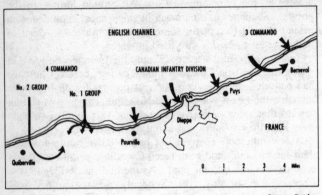

Dieppe Raid

as they tried to scale the towering cliffs to seize the Freya radar station. With them was Jack Nissenthall, who had learned earlier that the two teams of five men each had orders to kill him if they were about to be captured. Bitterly defending the station was the *23 Funkmess* (Radar) *Kompanie Luftgau Nachr*, and Canadian dead and wounded were strewn around the approaches to the position. While Nissenthall lay in a ditch with bullets hissing past like swarms of angry bees, he realized that the Canadians could not dislodge the dug-in and heavily armed Germans. Peeping over the rim of the ditch, the scientist noticed that the defenders were fighting from trenches in front of and to each side of the Freya building, but that the rear appeared to be unguarded. He also spotted a telephone pole with eight wires leading up from Dieppe town, and Nissenthall knew that these led to a control center where details on approaching RAF squadrons were plotted. If he could cut those wires, it would force the Germans to use radio plotting in the heaviest air battle of the war.

Sergeant Nissenthall pulled wire cutters from his pack and began slithering over the bullet-swept terrain toward the unprotected rear of the Freya building. It was a hundred yards away, but Nissenthall had to take a circuitous route to approach the structure from behind. He struggled forward, pouring sweat from the heat and tension. He finally reached his destination without being discovered and snipped the wires. Slithering away, he reached a sunken road and dropped into it, then crawled back to Captain Osten's company. Breathless, Nissenthall slumped to the ground next to one of his bodyguards. Grinning, the man said, "Jack, I had you in my sights all the time." The scientist knew the soldier was sincere. If the scientist had been on the verge of being captured while cutting the wires, the man would have carried out his orders and shot him.

At 11:00 A.M., according to plan, the remnants of the Jubilee force began withdrawing from the bloody beaches of the Iron Coast. Flight-Sergeant Nissenthall, along with the lone survivor of his bodyguards (the rest had been killed or wounded), scrambled down to the smoke-covered shore. But there was no landing craft to evacuate them. Capture appeared imminent. The scientist eyed his "protector"—would he really kill him as ordered? A landing craft appeared on the horizon, emerging through the thick haze, and the young radar expert, along with Sergeant Roy Hawkins, swam out to it. A few hours later the Man Who Knew Too Much was back in England.

Nissenthall's elation over being snatched from the jaws of death was tempered by anguish—he had failed in one part of his mission, inspecting the Freya. So he was startled the next day to be greeted enthusiastically by the officer who had sent him, Vice Marshal Tait. The RAF officer explained that British monitors at the listening station at Brimsdown had picked up much valuable information on the German's Freya precision plotting, and scientists now knew that the enemy would use radio if his land lines failed. This knowledge, Tait explained, would be invaluable in developing jamming techniques. (Nissenthall would help to create the first jammer for Freya radar.) Another round had gone to the British in the endless radar duel of wits.[7]

Despite the radar-snooping success, the Dieppe raid had been a disaster. Sixty percent of those in the assault (3,623 men) were killed, wounded, or captured—pawns in high-level strategic machinations. Of the 4,963 Canadians involved, 68 percent became casualties. For two weeks nearly 500 bodies from the Jubilee force would be washing ashore along twenty miles of the Iron Coast. The RAF had 106 aircraft destroyed, and the British navy lost 551 men plus a warship and 33 landing craft.

German losses were relatively light—391 casualties, 46 airplanes.

At 5:38 P.M. on the day of the raid, Field Marshal Gerd von Rundstedt, from his headquarters in a chateau outside Paris, wired Adolf Hitler a terse report: "No armed Englishman remains on the Continent."[8]

In Washington and in London, Generals Eisenhower and Marshall and other American leaders were shaken by the Dieppe bloodletting. If the ill-fated raid was intended to have been a sacrificial ploy to persuade the American "newcomers to war" to abandon Sledgehammer, the ploy was successful.

Field Marshal Alan Brooke exclaimed, "It is a lesson to the people who are clamoring for the invasion of France [in 1942]!" Those "people" were Marshall, Eisenhower, and Secretary of War Henry Stimson.[9]

Prime Minister Churchill, who was in Cairo when he received word of the catastrophe, wrote his deputy prime minister, Clement Atlee, in London: "My general impression of Jubilee is that the results fully justified the heavy costs."[10]

Because of the machinations surrounding the Dieppe affair, Colonel Oliver "The Fox" Stanley resigned abruptly as Controller of Deception, as the chief of the LCS was called. He had objected vehemently to the Dieppe operation and was said to have told friends that he refused to be associated with a regime that would risk butchering Empire boys for the sake of keeping Russia in the war.[11]

In the wake of the Dieppe debacle, American and British leaders agreed on one point: the road to Berlin would be a long and bloody one.

Atlantic Wall

In early September 1942 German commanders in Saint-Lô, a major road center and Wehrmacht headquarters below the base of the Cherbourg peninsula, were growing increasingly frustrated and angry. Ack-ack protecting Saint-Lô was intense, and many British airmen were being downed, but only a few had been captured. What had become of the rest of them? Clearly the French resistance had organized escape routes, so the Gestapo was brought into the region to smash the clandestine operation.

Twelve miles away at Torigni, nine leaders of the local resistance gathered early each morning to discuss plans in the only place considered relatively immune from the prying eyes of the Gestapo—the rear of an ancient church. Among the group were Father Gauraud, the village priest and chief of the local resistance; Georges Lavelle, who operated a garage in Torigni; and 37-year-old Pierre Touchette, a mentally impaired man who worked as a helper in Lavelle's business.

Father Gauraud, diminutive and soft-spoken, and Lavelle were the only ones who knew that Touchette was neither a Frenchman nor a half-wit. He was a spy, a Canadian, whose real name was George DuPre. In 1940 he had joined the Royal Canadian Air Force, but was told that he was too old to fly. When DuPre's squadron reached England, he was recruited as a spy to be dropped into France. Because he spoke French poorly, his controllers decided that he would masquerade as a man with the mind of an eight-year-old.

Father Gauraud had long shouldered much of the burden of his réseau. Each Friday night he bicycled into the countryside to recover a container of needed items dropped by a British bomber. The réseau's radio transmitter was concealed in a ramshackle barn four miles from Torigni, and four times a week the priest went there to establish contact with London.

At this time the resistance in the Saint-Lô region was concentrating on helping downed British flyers. The Normandy escape routes began in villages farther inland and led to Torigni, and then continued to Saint-Lô. When the weather was right, the RAF evaders were escorted to the coast, where they climbed into fishing trawlers that sneaked out to link up with speedy British launches lying five miles offshore. The escape route was well known to RAF men, who called it the Rat Race of Saint-Lô.[1]

The Torigni underground used boys and girls, who enjoyed the "game" of outwitting the Germans, to bicycle messages to adjacent villages and to Saint-Lô. None of the youngsters knew the identity of réseau members, for the messages and instructions were left at their homes by unknown parties. The couriers were proud of their shiny bicycles, unaware that they were precise French models built in England and dropped by the RAF. These cycles were different from others in only one respect: one handlebar unscrewed to reveal a space just large enough to hold a written message.

In early October a 15-year-old girl courier had just arrived at Saint-Lô when she lost control of her bicycle, and it slid into a parked car, sending her sprawling to the pavement. It was a Gestapo automobile. A German about to enter the vehicle saw that the impact had knocked loose half of the handlebar, and out of it protruded the incriminating message.

Within two days the Gestapo had hauled in three other teenage girls involved in shuttling resistance messages. They were tortured, but did not reveal the names of the underground leaders, for they did not know the names. A week later a truck pulled into a field outside Saint-Lô, and the four girls were dragged out. Their hair was matted with dried blood, and their bodies were covered with cuts, bruises, and cigarette burns. Eyes had been blackened. Rough hands forced them toward an embankment, and as the terrified, weeping youngsters huddled together they were shot to death.[2]

Father Gauraud, who had been under incessant strain for months, and other leaders of the Torigni réseau were devastated by news of the girls' deaths, but they vowed to continue aiding downed British flyers. Now a new means for sending messages would have to be found; the Gestapo would be suspicious of all bicycles.

Pierre Touchette came up with the solution. Four Torigni girls were recruited as couriers, and each was given a dog. They were told to live constantly with the pets, feed them, play with them, sleep with them, stroke them lovingly until girl and dog were inseparable. Meanwhile, craftsmen fashioned round leather collars for the animals.

Soon the new couriers, trailed by their faithful dogs, were walking casually along roads, paths, and through the fields. Often the girls were stopped and searched by the Gestapo, who found nothing incriminating and allowed them to continue onward. All messages reached their destinations—concealed in the dogs' hollow collars.

During the two months following the restoration of the crucial message lifeline between réseau in area towns and villages, thirty-one British airmen were herded along the Rat Race of Saint-Lô to eventual safety.

Shortly before midnight on September 2, *Ober Maat* (Chief Mate) Hans Munte was seated in his office in the Casquets lighthouse on tiny Sark Island. Sark is one of three Channel Islands (the others are Jersey and Guernsey) just to the west of the Cherbourg penninsula that the Germans seized in 1940. Now Munte heard a slight noise that sounded like a door being closed gently. Turning around, Munte felt a surge of terror. Confronting him, with automatic weapons at the ready, were four ferocious-looking, black-faced men—British Commandos.

The raiders hustled the chief mate outside, where he joined his six men who had been rousted out of bed by the Commandos. The purpose of the mission was to take prisoners for interrogation, and, fearing that the Germans might escape in the blackness, the Commandos handcuffed them. Moments later the raiders were fired on, and two of the handcuffed Germans were killed and left behind. All of the Commandos and the surviving captives reached England at 4:00 A.M.

At Wolfsschanze, Adolf Hitler flew into one of his rages over the latest Commando escapade. Word that two Germans had been killed while handcuffed intensified his fury. A few days later the fuehrer issued a drastic order: "All enemy troops taking part in so-called commando raids . . . in uniform or not . . . whether a prisoner or in battle . . . will be destroyed to the last man."[3]

Fourteen hundred miles south of Sark Island's Casquets lighthouse, shortly before dawn on November 8, 1942, Operation Torch, cloaked for months in an intricate web of secrecy, burst like a meteor over the Mediterranean's North African coast. The vanguard of ninety thousand Allied soldiers, later to be augmented by another two hundred thousand, began pouring ashore in a vast arc from Casablanca to Algiers.

Adolf Hitler was awakened on his private train parked outside Munich, where he had gone for a celebration marking the nineteenth anniversary of the Beer Hall Putsch of 1923—Hitler's first attempt at revolution, which collapsed in a gunfight with police. The fuehrer was stupefied by news that the Allies were landing in North Africa.

The fuehrer and the Oberkommando der Wehrmacht had been bamboozled by two deception campaigns, Solo I and Solo II, that had been launched weeks earlier by the spate of British secret agencies under the LCS umbrella. Two huge Torch convoys, one sailing from Great Britain and the other from the United States, could not be "hidden" from the Germans. So a myriad of intricate fabrications, in which turned Abwehr spies controlled by the XX-Committee played a key role, masked the true landing sites in Algeria and French Morocco.

Solo I had conveyed the impression that the Allied troops and ships assembling in Great Britain were preparing to attack Norway or to launch a cross-Channel smash against France (for which Dieppe had provided valuable information on German coastal defenses). The true destination of the convoy coming from the United States was covered largely through a world-wide campaign of *sibs* (from the Latin *sibilare*, to hiss) that suggested this force's target was Dakar on the west coast of Africa.[4]

The British machinations had caught the fuehrer off guard, but he reacted with great speed and foresight, ordering all available combat formations to be rushed to Tunisia (east of the Torch landings) to confront the Allied forces.[5]

The full weight of the shooting war between the Western Allies and the Germans was now centered in the Mediterranean. But Torch was a sideshow on the periphery of Adolf Hitler's empire. Before Nazi Germany could be brought to its knees, powerful Allied forces would have to be assembled in Great Britain and one day storm across the English Channel to engage the Wehrmacht in massive battles on the Continent. So the hidden war of charades continued to be waged on both sides of that embattled moat.

In the fall of 1942, Marcel Girard, leader of the Centurie underground in Normandy, was being pressed constantly by London for more information on the Atlantic Wall. The map stolen earlier by the house painter René Duchez had provided the original specifications, but the Germans were making additions as the coastal complex continued to grow. Consequently, Girard proposed that Centurie create its own detailed master map of the Wall in Normandy, one that would depict the entire coast extending from the Cap de la Hague at the northwest tip of the Cherbourg peninsula all the way to Ouistreham, 125 miles to the east.

Obstacles to the immense mapping project seemed insurmountable, but soon Centurie agents, armed with official German passes—all painstakingly counterfeited by the Caen housewife Jeanne Vérinaud—infiltrated the Forbidden Zone to recruit hundreds of ordinary French men and women living along the coast to serve as the eyes and ears for the map project. They would pass bits and pieces of information on the Atlantic Wall to collecting points in Caen.

Between Cherbourg and Le Havre, the most important harbor was Port-en-Bessin, where the Germans based a minesweeper flotilla and five E-boats. Unknown to each other, ten Centurie agents were snooping out secrets there. One of them was a husky young fisherman, Léon Cardron, who periodically obtained permission from the Germans to take his trawler from the harbor to ply his trade. Cardron became an irritation to the Germans, who considered him far from bright. They had to chase his boat away when it came too close to shore near Longues, where a battery of large-caliber coastal guns was being installed.

On another occasion Cardron's trawler stumbled into the center of an offshore area being surveyed for a minefield. Eventually, the German port commander had had enough of this stupid Frenchman and declined him future fishing permits. But Léon Cardron didn't mind. Using an ancient Kodak camera, Cardron had photographed the entire coast from Arromanches to Port-en-Bessin. The fisherman had no way of knowing that one day invading British forces would build an artificial port (known as Mulberry) off Arromanches or that his pictures would be of great assistance in developing the Mulberry.

Not far from Port-en-Bessin, Centurie agents were unable to penetrate the small port of Luc-sur-Mer. The nervous German commandant had slapped a 7:00 P.M. curfew on civilians. But people did get ill, so the Germans, at his request, issued a special permit to Dr. Jacques Sustendal to travel through the restricted area at all hours to visit patients at their homes. After returning to his office from a house call, the middle-aged physician quickly wrote down everything he had seen of the Atlantic Wall construction and passed his notes along to Centurie collecting points in Caen.

Dr. Sustendal would never know of his contribution to his country's liberation. Late in 1943 he would be caught and shot by the Gestapo.

At Caen, Robert Douin was considered an eccentric, even by townspeople. The prewar director of a fine arts school in Paris, Douin was a sculptor, and since becoming a Centurie agent, he began to show great interest for work on statues perched high in church towers. German sentries paid little attention to the "nut" with the goatee, weird clothing, and hat with its brim pulled down over his eyes who often bicycled into the countryside north of Caen, toward the English Channel.

One day Douin climbed into the tower of Notre-Dame

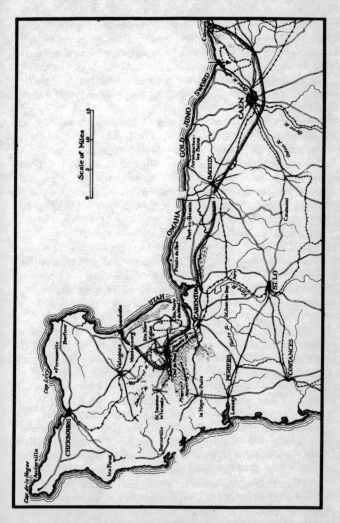

Atlantic Wall Sector Mapped by Centurie

church near Ranville and immediately decided that the statue there needed a great amount of restorative work, for from that height the sculptor could view flat landscape reaching from Caen to the coast at Ouistreham, twelve miles to the north. The entire region was a beehive of German construction activity. Removing his old camera from its case, Douin began snapping pictures of concrete bases for a German gun battery outside Merville, then scrambled down from the tower and rushed back to Caen.

Robert Douin's photos of German defenses reached Allied intelligence in London almost weekly. In late 1943, however, his luck ran out: Douin was caught and executed.

In his Atlantic Wall directive, Hitler had declared, "If we can keep a major port out of the hands of the Allies, we can defeat any attempt to gain a foothold on continental Europe." So the large ports, including Cherbourg, received the highest priorities for materials and manpower. Cherbourg became one of the most closely guarded cities in France.

As Centurie's activities grew, German reprisals became more brutal. Several agents were caught and shot to death by firing squads in public squares. One of these measures permitted Centurie to penetrate Cherbourg, where in peacetime the luxury liners *Queen Elizabeth*, *Normandie*, and *Queen Mary* had discharged their passengers.

Outside Caen a German troop train going from Paris to Cherbourg was blown up, and several soldiers were killed. In reprisal angry German commanders had several hostages shot. In addition the occupiers inaugurated a new procedure to discourage blowing up troop trains. Just before a train departed Paris or Cherbourg, a number of French civilians waiting in the station or passing by were seized and forced onto the train. The hostages traveled first class—in a coach immediately behind the engine. No Centurie agent in his right mind would volunteer as a hostage on a German troop train—except for Gilbert Michel of Caen. In Cherbourg he had to wait for four hours each time for the return train, so, armed with a fake permit crafted by Jeanne Vérinaud, Michel was free to roam the city. Through his regular hostage trips, Michel was able to provide Centurie with a wealth of information for the master map of the Atlantic Wall.

The Germans, too, assisted the mapping project by unwittingly providing information on areas it was impossible for Centurie spies to reach. When the Todt Organization built a new fortification in Cherbourg, it notified the French civilian agency responsible for operating the port. The agents of Centurie surreptitiously traced the German drawings, and within hours the new construction or gun battery was part of the master Atlantic Wall map.

Bits of information on German defenses and troop dispositions along the entire Normandy coast flowed steadily into central collecting points in Caen. Every day after work at his regular job, 23-year-old Robert Thomas, Centurie's cartographer, bicycled around and emptied drop boxes. Thomas's crucial task was to translate this raw data onto precise small maps.

Thomas had faced serious handicaps when launching his work. He had neither the needed basic ordnance maps nor a copying machine. Even obtaining drawing paper seemed impossible. But the youth's father solved the problem. He worked as an inspector in Eugene Meslin's office of roads and bridges and, with Meslin conveniently looking the other way, "borrowed" the required ordnance maps. Working feverishly through several nights, Bob Thomas copied the maps, which were then returned. (During the coming year, Thomas would draw more than four thousand small maps of fortifications and troop dispositions of sections of the Atlantic Wall.)

Every week a courier collected Thomas's maps and a large bundle of notes, diagrams, photos, drawings, and other data and carried them, usually by train, to a dingy suite of rooms in an old building located in a run-down section of Paris. This was Centurie's headquarters for the Battle of the Atlantic Wall. A bespectacled, round-faced young Frenchman named Jacques Piette (code-named Colonel Nobody) directed the operation of the spy network's communications center. Here dedicated checkers daily sifted through a mountain of material collected by spies in Normandy and bundled it for transfer to intelligence agencies across the Channel.

Lysander aircraft, flown by Royal Air Force pilots, landed under a blanket of darkness at predesignated pastures outside Paris. The planes taxied up to signaling flashlights held by

French underground agents, collected the bundles of Centurie Atlantic Wall data and maps, sped down the grassy field, and lifted off for England.

Eventually this mass of data reached a closely guarded and supersecret facility known as the Martian Room, located outside London. There a remarkable master map of 125 miles of the Atlantic Wall, between Cherbourg and Ouistreham, was being pieced together from the thousands of scraps of information gleaned by Centurie agents.

Later the huge map would be updated daily. When the Allies were prepared to strike a mammoth blow across the English Channel against Hitler's Fortress Europe, the Martian Room map would have become an amazingly detailed compilation of German defenses along the Atlantic Wall—even giving the names of officers at each defensive position and how those officers were regarded by men serving under them.

Centurie would pay an enormous price for this achievement. Scores of its men and women would be executed by the Gestapo. But when the Allies crossed the Channel, a general named Dwight Eisenhower would have more data on the Atlantic Wall at his fingertips than would German commanders in France.

21

Spies and Spy Masters

Just before two o'clock on the morning of December 20, 1942, a German bomber winged over fields glistening with frost in Cambridgeshire, and a dark figure leaped out. Burdened with an Afu radio set and £7,000 in a waterproof bag, Abwehr agent Fritz parachuted onto English soil outside Littleport. His mission would be one of the most daring of the war: blowing up the de Havilland aircraft works at Hatfield, a short distance north of London.

After burying his parachute, Fritz hid until daylight, when he caught a train for London. If all went according to plan, once the de Havilland plant was sabotaged, he was to return to his Abwehr base in Paris, probably by way of a neutral ship through Spain or Portugal.

Fritz's tone was optimistic when he contacted his controller in Paris the next day and on succeeding days. He told Paris he had gone to Hatfield several times and crept around at night to case the target. The spy also reported that he had located a quarry near Hatfield where the owner was willing to sell him all the explosives needed. On January 27, 1943, he radioed Paris: "Will attempt sabotage this evening at six o'clock."[1]

Just before dawn Captain Stephan von Grunen, chief of the Abwehr station in Paris, received a signal from Fritz: "Mission successfully accomplished. Powerhouse blown up."

Von Grunen, an experienced secret service officer, was skeptical. How could one man create such enormous damage to what must have been a closely guarded plant? He arranged for two reconnaissance planes to confirm Fritz's triumphant report. Von Grunen was elated by the photographs. They revealed that damage was even more extensive than Fritz had indicated. Huge holes had been blown in the roof of the de Havilland powerhouse, and through the openings could be seen pieces of generators scattered about the premises.

Fritz's daily radio contacts with Paris indicated that British counterespionage agents were hot on his trail. On February 16 he signaled von Grunen: "Am closing transmission. Too dangerous to work."[2] He caught a freighter for Lisbon, and upon arriving at Abwehr headquarters in Paris was hailed as a hero of the Third Reich. That night at a champagne celebration for him at fashionable Maxim's, Fritz regaled admiring German officers with tales of outwitting the British.

Fritz was a double-agent, called Zigzag by the Double-X Committee. He was actually Eddie Chapman, a notorious British criminal whose forte was safecracking. In early 1940 Scotland Yard had been hot on Chapman's heels for a variety of crimes, so he moved to the Channel Islands. There he was thrown in jail for another offense and was released by the Germans when they occupied the Channel Islands in mid-1940. In gratitude Chapman volunteered to spy for the Germans; the Abwehr quickly accepted, for the notorious safecracker no doubt detested his home country and her Scotland Yard, so he would make a dedicated and trusted spy.

Whatever his faults, Eddie Chapman never planned to become a traitor to his country. As soon as he had parachuted into England in December 1942, he had reported to the police. The XX-Committee welcomed the domestic outlaw with open arms, especially after learning that he was to return to the Abwehr camp on the Continent after blowing up the de Havilland plant. That would mean yet another trusted double-agent planted in the heart of the German secret service.

But if Zigzag were to be accepted by the Abwehr when he returned, the de Havilland works would have to be "blown up." Young Major Tar Robertson at the Double-X knew that the Germans would confirm Zigzag's "sabotage" by sending over reconnaissance planes to take photographs. So an elaborate scheme was devised to hoodwink the Abwehr.

For this purpose Major Robertson acquired the services of Major Jasper Maskelyne, who in civilian life was an accomplished magician and illusionist. His mission: create fake bomb damage at the de Havilland plant. Maskelyne and his helpers covered the entire roof of the powerhouse with a relief canvas and painted on it in color the damage that was supposed to have occurred below. Meanwhile, the magician's workshop built papier-mâché dummies that resembled pieces of the sabotaged generator. Those pieces, along with dummy chipped chunks of brick, cracked cement blocks, splintered furniture, and other props, were scattered about the premises. So realistic was the handiwork of Maskelyne and his team of magicians that RAF photos taken the day before the "sabotage" stumped interpreters as to whether the damage was real or faked.[3]

In the meantime RAF and American bombers had been increasing the frequency and weight of their attacks on facilities used by the German war machine in France and the Low Countries, and flyers were being downed in greater numbers than before. Hundreds of ordinary civilians had been risking their lives continually to hide Allied airmen in their homes until the evaders could be escorted along the escape lines to other "safe houses." By late 1942 and early 1943, the Gestapo had grown even more brutal in its efforts to destroy these escape lines.

In Brussels Georges Maréchal, his wife, an Englishwoman, and his 18-year-old daughter Elsie had been hiding escaping British flyers for many months. Pretty and vivacious Elsie's function was to meet Allied airmen arriving in Brussels from elsewhere in Belgium. On reaching the Belgian capital from the provinces, the evaders were taken by an agent named Albert Marchal to St. Joseph's church, where they were met by Elsie and escorted to the Maréchal home on Avenue Voltaire.

On a somber gray morning early in December 1942, Elsie answered a knock at her door and was startled to see the guide, Marchal, standing there with two men dressed as Belgian laborers. Marchal was never to appear at her home. Slightly bewildered, the 27-year-old Marchal explained that the two men with him were RAF flyers who had come from Namur (Belgium) and who in some unknown manner had found him.

Marchal had taken the evaders to St. Joseph's church to be picked up by Elsie, but she had never arrived, so the guide took his charges to the Maréchal home.

The three men were invited into the house, where Elsie and her parents grew increasingly suspicious. The two Englishmen said hardly a word. When one finally did speak, he said the two men wanted to take a walk to get some fresh air. What a strange request, the Maréchals reflected. A walk in the "fresh air" in German-occupied Brussels? Anxieties heightened, but the Maréchals agreed reluctantly, with the understanding that the airmen would return in an hour.

Both "RAF flyers" were Gestapo agents. They rushed to their headquarters, where a trap was quickly conceived to snare as many Belgian "terrorists" as possible at the Maréchal home. Returning to the Avenue Voltaire "safe house," the two masqueraders had just sat down to tea with Mrs. Maréchal when six more Gestapo agents burst through the front door. Three more German secret police concealed themselves outside the house.

When Georges Maréchal and Elsie returned home separately, they were startled to find eight Gestapo men seated comfortably in the living room. All of the Maréchals were hustled off to Gestapo headquarters in the rue de la Traversière in handcuffs. A short time later 25-year-old Victor Michiels, a new escape-line recruit, approached the Maréchal home. He had been sent to see why Elsie had not kept an appointment. Michiels watched the house for thirty minutes, but saw no sign of life. He crossed the street and knocked on the front door. Three figures clutching Lügers leaped from the shadows shouting, "Halt!" Michiels made a run for it, but he had gone only a short distance when four bullets ripped into him. He collapsed in the dark gutter and lay dead in a pool of blood.

At Gestapo headquarters the three Maréchals were herded into an interrogation room, but none would reveal their accomplices in the escape line. As her horrified parents were forced to watch, Elsie was beaten unmercifully. The hamlike fist of a German smashed into her face, causing blood to spurt from her nose and mouth. Both eyes were blackened. She was beaten with clubs and whips and burned by lighted cigarettes. Then the teenager was hurled into a cell at St. Gilles prison; her hair was matted with blood, and her once-pretty face was unrecognizable. Throughout the night inmates could hear Elsie's piercing sobs of pain and anguish. But neither Elsie nor her parents gave away anything to the Gestapo.[4]

In the weeks that followed, the Gestapo struck brutally, not only in Brussels (where one hundred persons were arrested), but all the way to the Spanish border in a coordinated attack to smash the underground escape lines. With the aid of Belgian, Dutch, and French traitors, escape-line leaders by the score fell into German hands; most of those arrested were never heard from again.[5]

Nearly all the great leaders in the escape lines had been rounded up. Their loss, linked with the inevitable distrust the roundup created among escape-line patriots, nearly wrecked the entire escape apparatus. It stumbled, then halted, but was revived again—thanks to the leaders who had escaped the Gestapo dragnet and had remained at their posts.

In April 1943 London began trying to rebuild the shattered escape lines. The Dutch section of SOE radioed their agents in Holland (all of whom were in jail or dead) that several spies under the code name Golf Group were to be dropped. Their mission was to set up new escape routes to Spain and Switzerland.

Major Hermann Giskes, the Abwehr chief in Holland, saw an opportunity to penetrate the real underground escape apparatus. Six weeks after the Golf Group parachuted into the waiting arms of Abwehr agents and SS men, Giskes radioed London over a Golf Group set that a route had been organized as far as Paris. A Dutch agent code-named Arnaud would be the principal escort for downed Allied airmen, Giskes said. "Arnaud" would be one of the Abwehr chief's sergeants, Rudolf Arno.

Arnaud and five other Germans posing as resistance men actually did establish an escape line, and to test its reliability Giskes sent word to London that he (that is, the Golf Group) was dispatching from The Hague two RAF officers who had been hiding there. Unbeknownst to the genuine British flyers, they were being escorted by three Abwehr agents in disguise.

A month later London radioed congratulations to Golf agents after the two unknowing RAF men had reached England by way of Spain. Arnaud's and Golf's credibility skyrocketed in London, and to aid in future escape-route treks, the Dutch section of SOE revealed the locations of three British secret service posts in Paris. But Hermann Giskes made no effort to break up operations at these clandestine stations in the French capital; instead, he arranged to have their lines tapped. As did the XX-Committee, Giskes felt that information obtained from live enemy agents was far more valuable than were dead spies.

Meanwhile, during that spring of 1943, the cloak-and-dagger newcomers from America, the men of the Office of Strategic Services (OSS), and their counterparts, the British secret service, were embroiled in a dispute over sharing espionage responsibility in the war against Nazi Germany. Steeped in a tradition of centuries of clandestine operations and with four years of practical experience under their belts in the current war, the British looked on the OSS officers as fresh and innocent inductees from highbrow finishing schools into the no-holds-barred arena of intelligence. There was considerable merit to the British point of view.

Chief of the OSS in London was tall, handsome David K. E. Bruce, the multimillionaire son of a U.S. senator. Married to steel baron Andrew Mellon's daughter, who was known as the "world's richest woman," the 44-year-old Bruce had been selected for the key London post by the OSS chief in Washington, Major General William J. "Wild Bill" Donovan, a World War I hero.

Blueblood Bruce's first act was to surround himself with other bluebloods. His Number 2 man was a New York investment banker, and his chief of research and analysis was a vice president of the Chase National Bank. Those who weren't wealthy were intellectuals—Ivy League professors, liberal attorneys, scientists. The bluebloods and the intellectuals were received warmly in London's exclusive social clubs, but at OSS headquarters in Grosvenor Square they milled about in bewilderment and confusion. Only a short time ago these Americans had been engaged in tranquil civilian pursuits. Now they found themselves executives in a dark and sinister "business" whose principal assets were fraud, deceit, skullduggery, and periodic mayhem.

In January 1943 Bruce and the chief of SOE, Charles Hambro, had reached an agreement—on paper—that the two allies would cooperate in supporting the European underground. But implementation could not be created overnight, and the seasoned officers at MI-5, MI-6, and SOE found it difficult to treat the Americans as equals in cloak-and-dagger warfare. So the British had been giving lip service to the Americans by periodically handing over suggestions on means for collecting intelligence.

Wild Bill Donovan had grown increasingly irritated over what he considered a condescending attitude by the British toward his OSS greenhorns. He ordered Colonel Bruce to establish OSS's own spy networks on the Continent. Dr. William Maddox, who headed Bruce's Secret Intelligence Branch (SI), was aghast. Maddox had taught international affairs at Princeton and Harvard, a background that hardly qualified him for the rough-and-tumble job of directing clandestine operations in Nazi-occupied Europe. The Ivy League professor fired off a letter to Donovan: "Nothing should be done that would jeopardize the fruitful relationship with MI-6."[6]

The British greeted with a jaundiced eye Donovan's proposal for "competing" spy networks. Undaunted, Donovan, who had been awarded the Congressional Medal of Honor in the First World War, prodded Bruce and Maddox to press even harder for an equal espionage partnership with the British— even if it meant "running competition" with them.

Leading the opposition to full partnership with the OSS was Claude Dansey, the acid-tongued, irascible assistant chief of MI-6. Described by friends as "crusty" and by his British enemies as "that cantankerous old son of a bitch," Dansey was known to be critical of anything American. He nearly broke out with apoplexy when he learned that the OSS upstarts were courting Major André Dewavrin (Colonel Passy), chief of BCRA, de Gaulle's secret service. Dansey had long been working closely with the BCRA and considered that agency his private preserve for obtaining intelligence from the Continent.

For their part the Americans had good reason to romance Colonel Passy. Bruce and Maddox felt that the de Gaulle agency was doing an outstanding job, and they were impressed by the mountains of raw intelligence turned over to the OSS from Passy's spy networks. The fledgling American espionage agency was starving for information from inside Nazi Europe.[7]

Despite his close relationship to Dansey at MI-6, Colonel Passy, for two years, had been at loggerheads with Charles Hambro's SOE. Passy had protested repeatedly over the SOE policy of having its French section, under Colonel Maurice Buckmaster, organize competing spy networks on the Continent. All French espionage activities there should be conducted under one agency, Passy argued. That one agency would be de Gaulle's secret service. But SOE refused to budge, and Buckmaster would send into Europe more than four hundred agents by the war's end.

At his headquarters in Grosvenor Square, David Bruce was convinced that the only way for the late-coming American spy agency to obtain intelligence quickly from German-held territory was to buy it from existing spy networks. In the meantime OSS in London would be working feverishly to infiltrate its own agents into Europe. Consequently, the OSS offered huge sums of money to the French underground in exchange for intelligence—providing that this procedure was approved by de Gaulle's BCRA in London.

Colonel Passy was outraged by the American proposal and curtly rejected it. He argued that French resistance groups "had no right" to accept money from the Americans. The BCRA chief was convinced that the whole thing was a devious plot cooked up in Washington to aid the cause of General Henri Giraud, who was considered Charles de Gaulle's principal rival to lead France after her liberation. Now the Americans became furious. They denied any partisan interest in who would govern France one day and stressed that their only concern was licking Adolf Hitler and the Third Reich.

A violent difference of opinion erupted within the ranks of BCRA's resistance leaders. François de Benouville pointed out that thousands of young Frenchmen, to escape being deported to Germany to work as slave laborers, had fled to the mountains and forests. There they had formed into groups called the Maquis. These freedom fighters could be armed and organized only with the aid of OSS money, de Benouville argued. But Jean Moulin, who was de Gaulle's personal representative to the French resistance, was unmoved. Break off all American contacts, Moulin demanded.[8]

The controversy among French underground factions over accepting American money would continue to simmer. However, the resistance would carry out its duties and look to the day that the Allies would return to the Continent.

Operation Bernhard

In Berlin early in 1943, Major Bernhard Krüger was hard at work directing a Nazi master plot designed to throw England's economy into chaos by counterfeiting currency. The project was code-named Operation Bernhard, and it had been conceived by the former chicken farmer and now Gestapo and SS chief, Heinrich Himmler. (Or at least he had taken credit for it with a delighted Adolf Hitler.)

Youthful, ambitious, hard-driving, Major Krüger had taken over the project in mid-1942. Unable to recruit skilled experts at the Reichsbank and the Reich Printing Office (they were aghast at the thought of printing another nation's notes, even in wartime), the resourceful major rounded up the technicians he needed from the concentration camps. They were transferred to the Sachsenhausen concentration camp outside Berlin, where the counterfeiting plant had been set up in an isolated compound surrounded by armed guards and electrified barbed-wire fences.

The plant would have been the envy of legitimate money printers everywhere. Plates were engraved with painstaking care—the alternative to the craftsmen being the gas chambers. A German manufacturer provided the latest in printing machinery. And perhaps the most notable achievement was the production by a prominent German paper company of high-quality Bank of England paper with its elaborate watermarks.

Under Major Krüger's lash, Operation Bernhard presses

were running at full speed. Some four hundred thousand British notes were being produced each month. Bogus bank notes were being used all over the world to finance German clandestine operations. Many spies would never know that they were being paid off with counterfeit money.

During the first half of 1943, large numbers of the fake notes had been reaching England from Istanbul, Stockholm, Zurich, Madrid, Lisbon, and other neutral cities. London bankers were alarmed by the arrival of batches of one hundred thousand pounds sterling. The Bank of England realized that counterfeiting on such a massive scale had to be conducted by the Nazis, and it became concerned that, with so much bogus money floating around the world, confidence could be lost in the traditionally rock-solid British note, to a point where the Allied war effort could be jeopardized.

Now the financial world was jolted. The Bank of England suddenly announced that it was taking from circulation all of its notes and would replace them with five-pound notes of a new design. The action came just in time, before the British economic system had indeed been wrecked. (After the war, Allied investigators would determine that Major Krüger's operation had produced quality Bank of England notes amounting to 140 million pounds sterling—the equivalent of 564 million dollars.[1]

While the bogus British money was rolling off Nazi presses, President Franklin Roosevelt, Prime Minister Winston Churchill, and their top military leaders met at Hotel Anfa, near Casablanca, on January 13, 1943. Allied armies were steadily squeezing the remnants of the once-vaunted Afrika Korps into a gigantic trap in Tunisia, North Africa. Now the two war partners were seeking to answer the question: Where would their next blow fall?

Debate raged for four days, U.S. Army Chief of Staff George Marshall wanted an assault later that year (1943) across the English Channel. Alan Brooke, chief of the Imperial General Staff, proposed offensive operations in the Mediterranean. Finally the Americans capitulated. The next major strike would be against Axis-held Sicily in 1943, "with the target date to be the period of the favorable July moon." It would be code-named Operation Husky.

When Axis armies in Tunisia surrendered in May, it was obvious to the high command on both sides that Sicily was the next logical target. Located northeast of Tunisia, Sicily is a mountainous, triangular-shaped island the size of the state of New Hampshire. It had long been regarded as a stepping stone to continental Europe. So the Allies were confronted with a monumental problem: what could be done to hoodwink Hitler into believing that the Anglo-American blow would hit elsewhere than the *obvious* target, Sicily? It was decided that the stratagem would be that since Sicily was too obvious a target, the Allies would strike instead at either the island of Sardinia, due north of Tunisia, as a springboard for a thrust into southern France, or Greece, to the east, as a base to drive toward Germany through the Balkans.

In London the brilliant—and devious—minds on the XX-Committee concocted an ingenious plan code-named Operation Trojan Horse to cloak Allied intentions. Its thrust was an improvisation of a ploy as old as warfare—planting false papers where the enemy would "accidentally" discover them and then react to his own disadvantage. The main ingredient of Trojan Horse was code-named Mincemeat.

Mincemeat began with a London search for the body of a man in his thirties who had died recently of pneumonia, so that he would have water in his lungs. If a German postmortem were later to be performed on the corpse, he would appear to have drowned. The coroner of London provided the required cadaver, which was in a funeral home just around the corner from MI-6 headquarters.[2]

The corpse was packed in dry ice and carried by vehicle to XX-Committee headquarters, where it was clad in the uniform of a Royal Marine officer. Papers planted on him identified the officer as Captain (Acting Major) William Martin, serial number 09560. Now Major Martin had to be given a personality. In his pockets were placed an overdraft from his bank, a bill for a ring (he had just become engaged), and two "love letters" from his fiancée—all of the papers had been painstakingly forged. Also jammed into his pockets were carefully dated theater ticket stubs and receipted bills.

These props were designed to give credence to the fictitious Major Martin. The key ingredients of the stratagem were documents the Royal Marine officer would carry in a briefcase, the most significant one being a falsified personal letter from Vice Chief of the Imperial General Staff Archibald Nye to British General Harold Alexander, Eisenhower's deputy for Operation Husky.

On April 19 Major Martin set out from England in the submarine *Seraph*. Shortly before dawn on April 30, the *Seraph* surfaced offshore from Huelva, Spain, in the Gulf of Cadiz. The corpse was removed from the dry-ice container and cast overboard, the apparent victim of an airplane crash at sea. Huelva had been selected as the site of the ploy because the XX-Committee knew that an Abwehr agent based there was in collusion with pro-German Spanish authorities and could be counted on to make a detailed report to Berlin.

Major Martin's floating body was spotted by fishermen who hauled it aboard their little boat and took it ashore. The Royal Marine officer obviously had been a courier, for a dispatch case was fastened to the body by a chain. Spanish officials took charge of the body and quickly notified the German resident spy. While a Spanish physician examined the cadaver and reported that the man had died by drowning after an air crash, the Abwehr agent rapidly photocopied the dispatch-case documents.

On June 4 *The Times* of London published a death notice about Major William Martin, Royal Marines, who had died in an airplane crash. At the same time the Abwehr in Berlin was meticulously testing the photographed documents for authenticity. They were declared to be genuine.

Told that conclusive evidence pointed to Greece or Sardinia as sites for the Allied invasion being mounted in North Africa, Adolf Hitler promptly began shifting forces to strengthen Sardinia and the Balkans, including pulling out troops from the Russian front, where he desperately needed every soldier.

In the meantime Abwehr chief Wilhelm Canaris, the Schwarze Kapelle conspiracy leader, tipped off the Allies in London that Hitler had swallowed the Mincemeat bait—hook, line, and swastika.

As the July 9 D day for the Sicily invasion neared, Field Marshal Albert Kesselring, Mediterranean commander and one of the most capable of Wehrmacht generals, was aware that the

Germans could be taken by surprise, that the Anglo-Americans might strike somewhere other than Sardinia or the Balkans. In that event a scapegoat would be needed, and Kesselring was too cagey an old warrior to allow that title to be bestowed upon him by Hitler. Consequently, the field marshal radioed Berlin the detailed disposition of German and Italian forces in Sicily and elsewhere in the wide Mediterranean. If there were blame to be attached to some future military disaster, Kesselring intended to make certain that the German high command was aware of circumstances in advance so that the fuehrer's wrath could be distributed among many.

Kesselring's lengthy message, transmitted in the Enigma code, considered by Hitler and other Wehrmacht leaders to be "unbreakable," was intercepted by Ultra, translated, and placed on General Eisenhower's desk almost at the same time it reached the intended recipient, Field Marshal Wilhelm Keitel, in Berlin.

Eisenhower was stunned. Allied intelligence had thought that the invaders would be confronted by only the demoralized, ill-equipped, and poorly led Italian army, but the Ultra intercept revealed that the Germans had recently slipped two first-rate panzer divisions across the two-mile-wide Strait of Messina into Sicily. The most alarming aspect of Kesselring's report was that the battle-tested Hermann Goering Panzer Division was in position only a short distance inland from where the elite U.S. 82d Airborne Division spearhead was to jump.

Under 35-year-old Colonel James M. "Slim Jim" Gavin, the thirty-four hundred American paratroopers would be highly vulnerable to armored assault in the early hours of the attack. Carrying only the personal weapons with which they would bail out, the parachutists would be without tanks or antitank guns. A determined assault by the Hermann Goering Division could wipe out the parachute force and allow enemy panzers to rush onward to the beaches to rake American seaborne forces with point-blank fire as they came ashore. In such an eventuality the entire invasion of Sicily could result in a bloody debacle.

General Eisenhower was confronted with one of the most anguishing decisions of his career. He knew that Colonel

Gavin's paratroopers would be better prepared to handle German panzers if they were aware in advance that the thick-plated monsters were in the vicinity of the drop zone. But paratroopers behind enemy lines were likely candidates for capture, and German interrogators would soon learn that the Americans had known of the presence of the Hermann Goering Division.

This top-secret information, Wehrmacht intelligence would conclude, could have been obtained from either a traitor in the German high command or the interception and deciphering of top-secret German messages. In either case the Third Reich would abandon Enigma, thereby denying the Allies the enormous military advantage of knowing enemy intentions and dispositions in advance.

After consultation with staff officers and field commanders who were in on the Ultra secret, General Eisenhower reached a decision. Even if Colonel Gavin and his paratroopers were wiped out, even if the entire invasion were to result in a bloody catastrophe, the precious secret of Ultra would have to be safeguarded.

Just before midnight on July 8, Colonel Gavin and his men bailed out over Sicily, totally unaware that scores of German tanks were lurking inland in the darkness. Later Gavin and a portion of his regiment tangled with the Hermann Goering panzers on a bleak elevation known as Biazza Ridge. Supported by the big guns of navy warships offshore and by a battery of 155-millimeter Long Toms, the men of the 82d Airborne drove the panzers from the battlefield after a savage fight. American and British seaborne forces poured ashore, and the Allies overran Sicily in a lightning, 38-day campaign.[3]

The secret of Ultra was still safe.

Meanwhile, the relentless undercover cat-and-mouse game between British and German radar/radio scientists continued to rage. No longer were the Allies on the defensive over England; rather, the rapidly growing Royal Air Force and U.S. Army Air Corps bomber streams were making a greater wreck of the Greater Reich.

On the night of July 26, 1943, a mighty force of 791 RAF bombers was winging toward its target, the major port of

Hamburg. At a designated point each of the bombers began releasing a batch of two thousand aluminum-foil strips at one-minute intervals. The strips (known to the British as Window and to the Americans as Chaff) were a new weapon of electronic warfare.

British scientists, led by Dr. Robert Cockburn and Dr. Joan Curran, had been working for more than a year to perfect the ECM (electronic countermeasure). They had found that if strips of foil were dropped from a bomber stream in large quantities, they could devastate German radar defenses. Window (or Chaff) would black out enemy radar screens, snarl direction-finding equipment, and create so many false "echoes" that confused operators would gain the impression that not hundreds, but many thousands, of bombers were attacking.

With the approach of the Hamburg bomber force, German radar defenses were thrown into chaos. Frantic radar operators thought that more than twelve thousand British planes were involved. Radar-controlled searchlights leaped wildly about the black sky, and antiaircraft guns directed by radar filled the night with bursting shells aimed at false echoes, not at genuine bombers. Luftwaffe night fighters, which relied on radar to lead them to the intruding aircraft, chased about the air in confusion. Twelve RAF bombers were lost in the raid—a percentage rate far below normal losses in similar missions.

On the morning of July 7, 1943, a black-bodied Heinkel was winging through a murky sky bound from Peenemünde on the Baltic Sea to Adolf Hitler's battle headquarters, Wolf's Lair, in East Prussia, behind the Russian front. On board were 31-year-old Dr. Wernher von Braun, Colonel Walter Dornberger, and Dr. Ernest Steinhoff. These men were the guiding lights at a supersecret rocket experimental station at bleak Peenemünde. They had been summoned by the fuehrer on a matter that could decide the outcome of World War II—and conceivably enthrone Hitler as absolute master of civilization.

Wernher von Braun was hardworking, dilegent—and a genius. In 1934, at the age of 22, he had presented his doctoral thesis to the University of Berlin. Its title: "Constructural, theoretical, and experimental contributions to the problem of rockets with liquid propulsion." He was awarded a doctor's degree without the examiners even seeing his thesis: it had been confiscated by the Wehrmacht. The Army Weapons Office then put von Braun to work on revolutionary rocket development.

Over the years an intense rivalry had raged at Peenemünde, located on the tiny island of Usedom off the coast of northern Germany. On one side of the island, the Luftwaffe was developing a pilotless aircraft packed with explosives that would become known to the Allies as a buzzbomb, while next door the army was experimenting with high-altitude rockets (or missiles). Both weapons were designed to inflict horrendous destruction on targets a long distance away. The buzzbomb eventually was designated the V-1 and the rocket the V-2 (V for *Vergeltungswaffe*—vengeance weapon).

By early 1943 both Peenemünde adversaries—Luftwaffe and army—were going full blast in the race to develop their weapons first. At the same time they continued to spy on each other to see how advanced their rivals were. It was crucial that each develop its V weapon first, for Hitler had not yet made up his mind which would be given the highest priority. Consequently, Luftwaffe and army rejoiced when the other's experiment would fail.

The feverish Peenemünde activities were cloaked with an intense secrecy that would later be matched only by the United States' Manhattan Project—the development of another revolutionary weapon, the nuclear bomb. Colonel Dornberger, commander at Peenemünde, was convinced that the British and Americans had not gotten wind of the experimental base.

Arriving at Wolf's Lair, von Braun, Dornberger, and Steinhoff had to cool their heels for twenty-four hours; the fuehrer was too busy to see them. In fact, he had been so occupied in warding off the Russian hordes that he had never found time to visit Peenemünde. So the three scientists had brought with them a color film of a perfect rocket takeoff and scale models with which to conduct a briefing.

Along with Hitler, a glittering lineup of Nazi brass gathered in the Wolf's Lair theater: armaments minister Albert Speer, Field Marshal Wilhelm Keitel, General Alfred Jodl, and General Walter Buhle. Shot with Teutonic expertise, the film was a dramatic presentation of a long, shiny missile being wheeled onto a launching pad, followed by its magnificent ascent, trailing a fiery plume, until it disappeared into a bank of billowing white clouds. The Wehrmacht bigwigs gawked as though mesmerized, while von Braun delivered a running commentary.

The film ended. Silently, the viewers sat in the darkness. In the mind of each, no doubt, was the vision of sprawling London leveled to a charred, pulverized wasteland. Then Hitler leaped to his feet, grabbed Colonel Dornberger and Dr. von Braun by their hands and pumped them vigorously, in an uncharacteristic display of emotion.

"I thank you," the fuehrer said. "Why was it I could not believe in the success of your work? If I had had these rockets in 1939, we should never have had this war. . . . Europe and the world will be too small from now on to contain a war. With such weapons humanity will be unable to endure it!"[4]

After the Peenemünde team had departed, Hitler conferred alone with armaments expert Albert Speer. The fuehrer was still vibrant with excitement. Speer was told that, effective immediately, the V weapons were to receive the highest priorities in manpower, materials, and whatever else was required.

"This is the decisive weapon of the war," Hitler exclaimed.[5]

The fuehrer's euphoria would have been tempered had he known that British intelligence had begun receiving fragments of information that the Nazis were up to something big at isolated Peenemünde. Polish intelligence officers in London had received from the underground in Poland, by way of Switzerland, dramatic material disclosing the nature of the Peenemünde experiments. Included were rough drawings of the Peenemünde layout, of the pilotless flying bombs, of the missiles.

At about the same time, Pierre Ginter, a Luxembourg citizen working at Peenemünde as a night telephone operator, in some manner stole plans for the secret V weapons. (The Germans considered the Luxembourg workers to be *Reichsdeutschen*— pure German by birth.) Permitted to go home on a short leave, Ginter turned the purloined plans over to the underground cell *Famille Martin* in northern France, and they were slipped out of the country and into England.

Based on these documents and other rumblings from the European underground, and at the urging of the American Photo Interpretation Unit (PIU), British photo reconnaissance planes swept over Peenemünde (as well as the rest of the north German coastline so as not to arouse suspicions). The Americans had good reason to be alarmed. Their intelligence had uncovered frightening (and accurate) information: the Germans were developing missiles capable of reaching New York and Washington. Forty-eight hours later the photographs reached the desk of Constance Babington-Smith at the British Central Intelligence Unit (CIU) in the sleepy village of Medmenham, some thirty miles west of London. The function of the CIU was to interpret aerial photographs.

An attractive brunette, Babington-Smith was regarded as an expert among experts at photo interpretation, so photos requiring rapid and accurate analysis were piled on her desk. Now her sharp eyes, peering through a powerful magnifying glass at the Peenemünde prints, picked out a dark, elongated shape, like that of a railway ramp. New photographs came in, and this time there was a small white blob at the tip of the dark shape. After lengthy consultation with colleagues, it was concluded that this was some sort of an aircraft—at the time the CIU people did not know they had detected what would later be called a buzzbomb.

Bits and pieces of evidence concerning mysterious Peenemünde continued to pour into London intelligence offices. It appeared almost conclusive that the Germans had missiles of enormous destructive power and long range and that Hitler had already set a date for deluging London with his V weapons. Only a few technical problems had postponed the launchings.

Winston Churchill, early in July, agreed that Peenemünde had to be bombed. RAF Air Chief Marshal Arthur "Bomber" Harris was ordered to make the strike as soon as weather permitted. The crucial mission was given one of the highest priorities of the war.

On the morning of August 17, Marshal Harris flashed the word to his alerted squadrons: they would attack that night. The bomber force would consist of 433 heavies (Lancasters, Stirlings, and Halifaxes) and 65 Pathfinders. *Hydra* was the code name given to the operation.

As part of the deception for the Peenemünde bombing, eight fast Mosquito bombers were sent over Berlin as a decoy. At about 11:00 P.M. the Mosquitoes began dropping Window, flares, and bombs over Berlin to give the impression that they were the main force. German air defenses had been thrown into mass confusion. General Josef Kammhuber in Holland, commander of the Luftwaffe's Twelfth Air Corps, had been cut off from his airfields dotting northern Germany. Mysteriously, Kammhuber's main radar and communications center at Arnhem, where two Luftwaffe technicians were British spies, had suddenly ceased operating.

It was known that a large Allied bomber force was approaching Germany, but no one had a way of determining its destination. Finally the order went out: "All night fighters head for Berlin!" Two hundred of them rushed to the capital and chased around the black sky in search of the enemy bombers that weren't there. For nearly two hours more than ninety German ack-ack batteries fired shells into the air, but the eight decoy Mosquitoes had done their mischief and were long gone.

Meanwhile, youthful Group Captain John Searby was in a bomber circling high over Peenemünde, directing his force to the target. They came in three waves and were opposed by some thirty Luftwaffe night fighters that had been attracted by the bomb flashes and fires. Finally the roar of the engines faded away. Some 1,600 tons of bombs had exploded on the key German missile-development site, as well as 280 tons of incendiaries. The RAF lost forty bombers at Peenemünde, and one Mosquito was shot down over Berlin. But had it not been for the Mosquito hoax and Window that caused mass confusion within German radar defenses, this total could have been far more.

At dawn heartsick Wernher von Braun and Colonel Walter Dornberger climbed into a light aircraft to assess the damage from the air. It was difficult to determine from there how long it would take to get back into operation. The entire area was pockmarked with craters—utter devastation. One factor perplexed the two Germans: the V-1 (buzzbomb) side of the island had virtually been untouched. It was of no consolation to them that the British had considered their own operation more important than that of their hated Luftwaffe rivals.

In the wake of the Peenemünde disaster, the Luftwaffe chief of staff, General Hans Jeschonnek, was blistered over the telephone by Hermann Goering for the incredible air defense mix-ups. The fat Reichsmarschall charged Jeschonnek with conducting himself "like a recruit." Two hours later, at 9:00 A.M., General Jeschonnek, a capable and courageous officer, was found dead on the floor of his Berlin office, a pistol in his hand. Nearby was a note: "I cannot work with Goering any more. Long live the Fuehrer."[6]

At Wolf's Lair on August 22, a grim-faced Adolf Hitler was discussing the Peenemünde disaster with Albert Speer, SS chief Heinrich Himmler, and Himmler's protégé, 40-year-old SS General Hans Kammler, a scientist who had the qualifications his boss demanded—intelligence and utter ruthlessness. Himmler, forever lusting for greater personal power, had a simple proposal for the fuehrer: the missile program had been threatened because someone betrayed Peenemünde; therefore, the entire rocket organization should be put in his hands.

The intense conference continued into the night. Hitler finally reached a number of decisions. Everything connected with the missile development would indeed be handed over to Himmler and his SS, and missile production would be moved to locales out of reach of Allied bombers. Firing experiments would be conducted in central Poland; development activities would move into caves inside Austria; and missiles would be produced in mammoth underground factories in Germany's Harz Mountains. The V-2 side of Peenemünde would be rebuilt and thoroughly camouflaged.

Meanwhile, the "flying bomb" development had not been touched by Allied bombers. So work proceeded at a feverish pace to launch these awesome weapons against England late in 1943.

Battles on the Airwaves

In late August 1943—the beginning of the fifth year of the war—"invasion fever" reached epidemic proportions on both sides of the English Channel. In southern England there was a rash of troop movement toward Dover, only twenty-one miles across the Channel from the Pas de Calais. Scores of vessels were massed in ports. Air squadrons crisscrossed the land on urgent business. Invasion hints popped up in newspapers and over BBC. Leaves were suddenly canceled, and coastal resorts were ordered closed. Military wireless traffic mushroomed. Invasion talk was heard constantly in pubs.

Across the Channel the French underground began blowing up railroad lines, power plants, and German headquarters. Scores—perhaps hundreds—of Feldgrau were murdered. All along the coasts of France, Belgium, and The Netherlands, folks greeted each other with a whispered, "They're coming!"

But no cross-Channel invasion would take place in 1943; there were fewer offensive troops in Great Britain now than there had been at the time of Dieppe a year earlier. All of the shadowy tumult was the culmination of a master deception campaign code-named Operation Starkey. Launched in the spring of 1943, the stratagem was designed to mask Allied weakness in Great Britain, to lure the Luftwaffe into a battle of attrition with the RAF and the U.S. Army Air Corps and to suggest that preparations were under way for a cross-Channel assault that fall, thereby preventing Hitler from shifting divisions from the West to the Russian front, where they were sorely needed.

British secret agencies were confronted with their greatest deception challenge: simulating a cross-Channel invasion in 1943 when the German high command must have known that most Allied troop strength and shipping were congregated in the Mediterranean.[1]

Masterminding Starkey from LCS's bombproof bunker at Storey's Gate was Colonel John H. Bevan, the Controller of Deception. A wealthy London banker and grandson of the founder of Barclay's Bank, Bevan had succeeded Oliver "The Fox" Stanley, who had resigned abruptly at the time of the Dieppe raid. Bevan was reserved, a very quiet man with a brilliant intellect. He possessed an essential trait for a master spy: an unbridled passion for anonymity.

So crucial had become the hidden war of charades that Colonel Bevan held enormous power (some said equal to that of the prime minister). He enjoyed the full confidence of Winston Churchill and President Roosevelt, both of whom thrived on being involved in the intricate, tangled web of wartime fraud and deceit. As chief of LCS, Bevan had the authority to require any British government department to conform to the dictates of deception stratagems created by LCS or its secret agencies. Through the Pentagon's Joint Security Control (JSC), cooperation was obtained from U.S. government branches.

Colonel Bevan and other Starkey planners had been concerned that French resistance fighters, stirred up by subtle machinations, might believe that the Allied invasion really was imminent, rise up in force, reveal their identities to the Gestapo, and be wiped out. But London had decided that a rash of underground mayhem would be more useful, for the Germans would be watching for this preinvasion symptom. So a blizzard of coded signals went out to the French resistance. It was hoped that the underground violence would stop short of all-out warfare.

D day for the Starkey "invasion" was set for September 9, 1943, a fact made known to German intelligence through a "careless slip" by a British wireless operator. Allied media were encouraged covertly to speculate that *the* invasion was at hand. To thicken the "invasion climate," Allied planes pounded the Pas de Calais area with 2,936 raids in a three-week period.[2]

At his headquarters outside Paris, Field Marshal Gerd von Rundstedt refused to take the Starkey bait. He told his staff, "The movements [by the Allies] are rather too obvious; it is evident that they are bluffing."[3]

On the eve of "D day," the U.S. Eighth Air Force struck German targets along the French coast with 1,208 bombers to support the Starkey illusion. But the Luftwaffe remained on the ground. That same day the Germans flew only six reconnaissance flights over England—where presumably a massive force was coiled and ready to strike.

Starkey had collapsed like a punctured balloon. In fact, the operation may have dramatized to Hitler the Allied weakness in England. During the last half of 1943, the fuehrer pulled out twenty-seven of the thirty-six divisions in the West to fight on other fronts, including Italy, which was being threatened with invasion by Anglo-American armies fresh from invading Sicily.

As London had feared, the uprising of the French resistance tipped its hand prematurely. Striking with great precision and savagery, the Gestapo arrested and executed hundreds of men and women of the underground, and the dragnet destroyed spy networks that had been created arduously over a period of three years. In Caen, Marcel Girard, the cement salesman and chief of Centurie in Normandy, was pursued by the Gestapo and had to go into hiding in Paris. Robert Thomas, the Centurie draftsman who had drawn more than four thousand maps of sections of the Atlantic Wall, also had to flee for his life.

Shaken but undaunted by the bloody Gestapo reprisals, the French underground in northern France carried on with its task. On the hot afternoon of August 12, 1943, an agent of the *Réseau Agir* (Network for Action) was sipping wine in a cafe in the Seine River port of Rouen when he overheard two building contractors discussing mysterious construction being carried on by the Germans. The agent reported the conversation to the chief of Réseau Agir, 45-year-old Michel Hollard.

Hollard, small and stocky, had become a spy on his own initiative when the booted German legions marched into Paris in mid-1940. He quit his job as an industrial designer and obtained a position as a salesman for charcoal-burning gas generators for automobiles. This job permitted him to roam France and later would explain his presence near the Swiss border, which by mid-1943 he had crossed forty-three times with high-grade intelligence. Members of his network had pinpointed secret German airfields, stolen a plan for a U-boat base at Boulogne, located coastal batteries, and reported on German divisions that were constantly shuttling in and out of northern France.

Now, on the basis of the report from the Rouen cafe, Hollard was amazed at the amount of concrete involved in the German construction job. Clad entirely in black, Hollard strolled into the Rouen employment office the following day and announced that he represented a religious organization interested in the spiritual uplifting of laboring men. Clutching a Bible, he asked if there happened to be any building projects taking place in the area. "Why, yes," he was told. "There's one at Auffay [twenty miles from Rouen]."

Two hours later the spy chief was at Auffay—wearing workman's clothes. Strolling around, he stumbled onto a large clearing where a few hundred laborers were pouring concrete. Hollard grabbed a wheelbarrow, filled it with bricks, and pitched in. No one stopped him. Most of the laborers were foreign, but one who could speak French told Hollard they were building garages. Hollard's curiosity deepened. Garages, in the middle of a forest twenty miles from the nearest city?

Hollard's eye was attracted to a 50-yard strip of concrete with a guideline of string. This appeared to be some sort of a ramp. Furtively, he removed his compass and found that the ramp was aimed at London. Aware only that a mysterious "crash" project was being built by the Germans, Hollard rushed a report to England. It exploded like a bomb in the highest councils of the government and military.

What Michel Hollard did not know was that Allied leaders were deeply worried over repeated clues that "flying bombs" were about to be rained on London. Drop everything else, get more details, Hollard was told. The réseau leader and four of his men began crisscrossing the Channel coastline on bicycles, and they discovered in less than one month sixty more mystery ramps. They kept pedaling and by mid-November had detected forty more, all located in a band thirty miles deep, and all aimed at London.

What were these strange ramps? Hollard was ordered to find out. The réseau leader placed a volunteer (André) with the labor force, and he was assigned to a desk job in the Bois Carré, where more strange construction was taking place. A week later Hollard's spy reported to his chief that the German in charge at the site kept a master plan in an outside pocket of his gray-green overcoat—and he wore the garment at all times, even in his office. André noticed that the only time the German removed the overcoat was at about 9:00 A.M., when he left to heed the call of nature.

For a week André timed the absences. They lasted between three and five minutes. On the eighth day the project manager shed his coat and left to perform his morning ritual. Like a jungle cat, André stole into the German's office, removed the master plan, and made a rapid tracing. Just as the Frenchman had replaced the blueprint in the overcoat and left the room, the German returned—unaware that he had just been the victim of a monumental intelligence coup.

Two days later Michel Hollard, evading the German patrols that roamed the region, slipped across the Swiss border. One mistake would mean his death. He was dressed like a woodcutter, carried an ax in one hand, and had a sack of potatoes slung over a shoulder. Hidden among the potatoes was the blueprint tracing of the German mystery site.[4]

Within forty-eight hours André's handiwork reached London. Allied leaders were shaken; here was a drawing of one of the scores of V-1 launching pads from which Hitler planned to demolish London. The V-1 was a pilotless aircraft containing explosives equivalent to a 4,000-pound blockbuster bomb. Built by Volkswagen, the V-1 traveled at 440 miles per hour, faster than any Allied fighter plane. Its engine would be timed to cut off over a target, after which it would plummet to earth and explode.

In late 1943 the Allies launched a mammoth bombing campaign against the buzzbomb sites. The bombers ran into an enormous curtain of flak, and the Luftwaffe rose to challenge the intruders. Allied airmen paid a heavy price in lives (including Lieutenant Joseph P. Kennedy, Jr., brother of a future president of the United States, whose bomber exploded). But the bombers did so much damage to V-1 sites that Hitler was forced to postpone the planned buzzbomb blitz of London scheduled for late 1943, when it might have seriously disrupted the plans for the Allied invasion of Normandy set to strike in June 1944.[5]

After his launching-ramp coup, Hollard had been urged to remain in Switzerland and rest from his three-year ordeal of being constantly on the run from the Gestapo. But Hollard returned to France, and a few months later he was captured in a cafe by the Gestapo. Even though he was tortured, Hollard refused to talk, and since no incriminating evidence could be linked to him, he was thrown into a German concentration camp instead of being shot. (Broken physically, Hollard would survive the war and receive high decorations from the British and French governments.)

On August 18, 1943, the American-British Combined Chiefs of Staff held a stormy session in Quebec. They hoped to continue the momentum from the Sicily victory, but differed on the locale of the next blow. Again General George Marshall wanted to mass forces in Great Britain for a smash across the English Channel, and General Alan Brooke argued forcefully to hop the Strait of Messina into Italy. Again the British prevailed.

General Bernard Montgomery's British Eighth Army would leapfrog from Sicily onto the toe of mainland Italy under cover of darkness on September 3 to draw off German forces from in front of Lieutenant General Mark W. Clark's U.S. Fifth Army, which would storm ashore six days later, on September 9, at the Gulf of Salerno, far up the western coast.

While the massive Allied invasion fleet lurked in the inky blackness ten miles offshore just before midnight on September 8, a 60-foot British PT boat, carrying forty-six men of the veteran U.S. 509th Parachute Infantry Battalion, was edging toward a dark beach on Ventotene Island. The paratroopers were on a secret mission, one that could help assure a successful dawn assault in the Gulf of Salerno.

Perched a few miles off the port of Gaeta, Ventotene held a

German radar installation, which could track Allied vessels and aircraft involved in the Salerno invasion (code-named Operation Avalanche). Ventotene was heavily forested, the radar site was well camouflaged, and its precise location was not known, so the installation could not be taken out by bombing. Under 25-year-old Lieutenant Charles C. W. Howland, of Tallapoosa, Georgia, the paratrooper raiding force had been handed the job of destroying the radar.[6]

Intense secrecy had surrounded planning for the mission. Only Lieutenant Howland knew the target; the paratroopers were told only that they were to knock out a key German facility. Ventotene had never been mentioned.

"It will sure as hell be a hairy mission," was all that Howland had revealed.

For the Ventotene raid, Howland divided his force into two platoons. One was led by Lieutenant Kenneth R. Shaker, a former soldier of fortune who had fought as a teenage private in the Spanish civil war, and the other was commanded by Lieutenant Wilbur B. McClintock.

Now the paratroopers, shoehorned into the small British PT boat along with their personal weapons, bazookas, machine guns, explosives, and land mines, clutched their weapons tightly as they peered through the darkness. The engines had been muffled so as not to alert German sentries. The only sounds were the gentle rustling of birds fluttering through the trees along the shoreline and the soft hum of the engines. Looming ominously in front of them was the dark and eerie outline of German-held Ventotene Island.

A soft thud was felt as the PT boat brushed against a rickety old dock, which appeared to be deserted. The troopers exhaled a collective sigh of relief: had German gunners been hidden along the shore, they would have cut the parachutists to ribbons and blasted the boat out of the water by now.

One by one, as noiselessly as possible, the airborne men began slipping out of the boat and taking up firing positions along the beach. Howland kept the men there for ten minutes while everyone strained to hear or see some indication of an enemy presence. There was only the sound of crickets chirping. Scrambling to their feet, the paratroopers formed into a column and began stealing inland in search of the radar site.

The troopers passed through a sleeping village and halted before the shadowy contours of a high hill.

As the Americans paused briefly, a figure suddenly emerged from the darkness. He was wearing civilian clothes and identified himself as a professor who had been banished from the Italian mainland because of his opposition to the Mussolini government. Lieutenant Howland and the others eyed the elderly man suspiciously and became more leery of the stranger when he volunteered the information that he was a friend of the German major who commanded the radar station on top of the hill looming before the Americans.

In reply to Howland's question, the Italian said he did not know how many Germans were guarding the radar. He said he wished to avoid bloodshed, so he agreed to lead the paratroopers up a concealed path to the radar site and to act as an intermediary to try to arrange a German surrender.

Still suspicious of the professor's motives, Howland ordered Lieutenant Shaker to take his platoon up the hill behind the Italian. "Watch the son of a bitch!" was Howland's parting admonition to his platoon leader. With the Italian up front, the file of paratroopers climbed up the steep hill. About seventy-five yards from the top, the guide raised his hand, and the column halted.

"I suggest that you and your men remain here," the professor said to Shaker. "I'll go on to the radar site. They know me and will let me in. I'll talk to the German major and see what can be done."

Shaker was concerned that the Italian might be more interested in warning his "friend" of the American presence than he was of securing his surrender. "Okay, you can go ahead," the lieutenant replied, "but if anything goes wrong, we're not only coming after the Krauts, but you too," Shaker warned, patting his Tommy gun for emphasis.

The Italian went on up the hill and was swallowed up by the blackness. Shaker deployed his platoon. Five minutes passed. Then ten minutes. Thirty minutes. The lieutenant passed the word: "Prepare to attack!" There was a rustling of equipment as the men moved into the path to charge the radar site. It could be a bloody fight; the Germans were probably entrenched and could far outnumber the paratroopers.

Then the shadowy figure of the Italian professor emerged from the darkness. "What the hell took you so long?" Shaker barked.

Unruffled, the Italian replied, "The major is greatly concerned about his honor. I told him what you had told me, that you had an entire regiment of paratroopers surrounding the hill and a large fleet offshore ready to bombard the radar site at your command."

Shaker's "regiment" consisted of forty-six paratroopers and the "fleet" was one British PT boat.

"The major thought about his situation," the professor continued, "and he decided the sensible thing was to surrender his men and the radar station." Pausing briefly, the Italian added that the German commander would surrender only to an officer with the rank of colonel or above.

Fast-thinking Ken Shaker told the Italian, "Tell the son of a bitch that I'm a full colonel, and if he does not surrender immediately, we're going to blow his goddamned radar and him clear off the hill!"

Shaker knew that the Italian had seen his lieutenant's bar, but he was banking on the fact that the professor probably did not know one American rank insignia from another. In this, Ken Shaker would prove to be correct. The Italian went back up the hill.

Ten minutes later a huge explosion at the top of the hill sent geysers of orange flame shooting into the black sky. Huddled a short distance down the hill, the paratroopers felt like cheering—the Germans had done the Americans' job for them by blowing up their own radar station.

Then out of the darkness Lieutenant Shaker and his twenty-two paratroopers saw a line of shadowy figures, hands on their heads, marching down the path toward them. The German major and his 114-man force were surrendering. When the courtly Italian professor politely introduced the German commander to "Colonel" Shaker, the Wehrmacht officer stared in disbelief at the bar on the American's shirt collar and knew that he had been hoodwinked.

"Where is the rest of your regiment?" the major demanded haughtily.

"Oh, they're down the hill," Lieutenant Shaker replied breezily. "But we're a little understrength—there're only forty-six of us."

By 3:00 a.m. on D day at Salerno, the German radar station had been blown up and Ventotene was in American hands. The landings came off as scheduled, and despite moderately heavy casualties, General Mark Clark's Fifth Army carved out a solid bridgehead by sundown. For the first time strong Allied forces had returned to Hitler's *Festung Europa* (Fortress Europe).

Meanwhile, in the skies over Europe the war of the airwaves did not relax for a minute. Seeking new wavelengths that were not jammed by the British, the Germans regularly replaced or modified their electronic communications equipment. But shortly afterward British scientists would develop a way to jam the new wavelength. One of these jammers was code-named Airborne Cigar, an instrument so light it could be placed in bombers. It proved to be so successful that the Germans had to install a high-powered transmitter to "talk" their night-fighter pilots to approaching bombers.

In turn, the British set up a high-powered transmitter of their own on the same frequency as that of the Germans. Soon "ghost voices" began confusing the German ground controllers. Code-named Operation Corona, the new technique was tried for the first time on the night of October 22/23, 1943, in an RAF raid on Kassel. The ghost voices began issuing instructions contrary to those given by German ground controllers. The Luftwaffe pilots quickly caught on that the British were doing something to snarl their communications.

A frustrated German ground controller finally called out, "Beware of another voice." He warned the Luftwaffe pilots, "Don't be led astray by the enemy." Then the ground controller grew angry and loosed an angry blast of curses.

"The Englishman is swearing," came the German-speaking ghost voice from the RAF.

"No, no!" the German shouted. "It's not the Englishman who is swearing. It's me!"

"Don't let them confuse you," the RAF voice warned. "It's the Englishman swearing."

Now the confounded Luftwaffe pilots grew angry and began

shouting curses at each other, at the German ground controller, and at the ghost voice—whichever was the ghost voice. Meanwhile, the city of Kassel was pulverized by a cascade of RAF bombs.[7]

On the final day of 1943, General Dwight Eisenhower, supreme commander of Allied forces in the Mediterranean, flew to Washington, D.C., for strategy conferences with Chief of Staff George Marshall. Eisenhower, who just over two years earlier had been an obscure staff colonel in Texas, had been appointed commander of London-based SHAEF (Supreme Headquarters, Allied Expeditionary Force): he would direct Operation Overlord, the invasion of Hitler's Fortress Europe.

The 54-year-old general's journey to Washington had been cloaked in intense secrecy; he had simply vanished from North Africa, and German intelligence had been trying desperately to locate him. On the morning of January 14, 1944, the mystery was solved. When Abwehr Major Hermann Sandel, a reserve officer in his forties, arrived at his office on Sophien Terrace in Hamburg, he was handed an unsigned message:

"Hoerte, dass Eisenhower am 16, Januar in England eintreffen wird." (Heard that Eisenhower will arrive in England on January 16.)

The sender of the signal was A.3725, Sandel's best spy in England, the young Dutch draftsman, Hans Hansen. This was the Dutchman's 935th message to Hamburg since the summer of 1940, when he had parachuted near Salisbury. Miraculously, perhaps, A.3725 had avoided capture and remained at large.

Hansen had learned of Eisenhower's arrival even as the general was inside his private railroad coach, Bayonet, which was carrying him through thick fog from Prestwick airport in Scotland to SHAEF headquarters on Grosvenor Square in London. A.3725 had radioed the news forty-eight hours before the official Allied announcement was due.

Good old A.3725. He had come through again. Major Sandel put the important signal on the *G-Schreiber*, the direct-line cipher teletype for distribution to Group 1 at "Belinda," the secret Abwehr post in a Berlin suburb.

Though the Abwehr was not aware of it, Hans Hansen had been captured and "turned" shortly after landing in 1940. The

XX-Committee had given him the code name Tate. The signal to his Hamburg controller that Eisenhower had reached London was calculated to strengthen Tate's credibility with the Abwehr. What harm could result from it? Two days later the Oberkommando der Wehrmacht and the entire world would be let in on the "secret," anyhow.

From the moment that Eisenhower stepped off the Bayonet in London, Overlord began to dominate every aspect of the war against Hitler. Within a few days of taking over, the chain-smoking, affable general with the mule-skinner's vocabulary was staggering under the tremendous burden. Overlord would be one of the largest and most complex military operations of its kind ever launched. Neptune, the assault phase, was in itself an enormous undertaking; its printed plan was nearly five inches thick. Even the typed list of American units—1,403 of them—came to thirty-one pages. On D day alone the equivalent of 350 trainloads of troops—200,000 fighting men—and 19,000 vehicles would be hurled against Normandy. These eight sea and airborne divisions would reach France from 6,500 ships, 1,100 transport airplanes, and 792 gliders. In support would be 10,042 bombers and fighters and more than 1,150 warships. Despite this powerful strike force, Neptune would be a highly dangerous endeavor—almost a gamble. (Major General Walter B. Smith, Eisenhower's chief of staff, would later confide to Washington: "This operation has only a fifty-fifty chance to succeed.") Hitler's legions, barricaded behind the concrete ramparts of the Atlantic Wall, had the means to inflict a bloody disaster, unless the fuehrer could be coerced into dispersing his forces so that he would be taken by surprise on D day. But how could Hitler be hoodwinked? How do you hide an invasion? The invasion date would be determined by the weather, moon, and Channel tides. And in an operation of the magnitude of Overlord, geographical considerations would limit the number of locales where the Allies could land. The Germans knew these factors as well as the Allies did.

Less than a week after his arrival in London, General Eisenhower met at Norfolk House with British Major General Frederick Morgan, architect of the original Overlord plan, and Colonel Noel Wild, an expert in clandestine and unorthodox warfare. Wild, also a Briton, was chief of SHAEF's Committee on Special Means (CSM), also known as Ops B, the panel responsible for implementing Overlord deception stratagems.

The two British officers briefed the supreme commander on Plan Bodyguard, the master stratagem designed to mystify and mislead Hitler on Allied intentions in northwest Europe in 1944. Bodyguard was incredibly intricate; it as divided into thirty-nine subordinate plans, which in turn were broken down into scores of deception schemes. If Bodyguard failed, the entire course of the war would be altered.

Invasion Deceptions

At his underground command bunker in the Paris suburb of Saint-Germain-en-Laye on February 2, 1944, old Field Marshal Gerd von Rundstedt tapped on a large wall map and told his staff, "If I were [the Allied commander], the Pas de Calais is exactly where I would attack."[1]

Von Rundstedt's view coincided with that of the fuehrer and nearly all German generals. Although German defenses and troop formations were stronger in the Pas de Calais than anywhere else along the Atlantic Wall, it was believed that the Allies would accept that risk in order to land closer to the crucial Ruhr industrial region and to the heart of the Third Reich—Berlin.

Since the Pas de Calais was such a logical locale for the landing, Operation Fortitude, a major component of Plan Bodyguard, was set in motion to convince the German high command that the coast across from Britain's famed White Cliffs of Dover would indeed be the invasion site. The centerpiece of Fortitude was Quicksilver, the fabrication of an entire army group that was to appear to consist of more than a million men. This phantom force would be "stationed" in southeastern England, across from the Pas de Calais. Known as the First United States Army Group (FUSAG), this fictitious unit's mission was to keep the powerful German Fifteenth Army in place at the Pas de Calais on D day, while Allied troops stormed ashore in Normandy, 160 miles to the west.

Quicksilver had its beginnings in the United States late in November 1943. J. Edgar Hoover, chief of the Federal Bureau of Investigation, had "turned" an Abwehr spy whom Hoover gave the name Albert van Loop (his real name was Walter Koehler). The Dutch national's radio and ciphers had been taken from him, and while he was held in custody, an FBI agent began radio contact with the Abwehr post in Hamburg in van Loop's name.

In the weeks that followed, "van Loop" radioed a steady stream of information to Hamburg, a careful blend of truth and fiction. Abwehr officers were delighted to learn from him that he had obtained a job as a night clerk in a New York hotel. This position was especially advantageous, for the U.S. Army used the hotel to lodge officers bound for overseas shipment, the spy reported. As a result, "van Loop" learned of all troopship sailings, and from the officers he obtained their divisions and destinations.

"Albert van Loop" would send more than 121 messages to Hamburg (that is, his FBI double would), and soon German intelligence began to create a *Feinbild* (a picture of the enemy) in England. By early 1944 tens of thousands of "live" GIs were pouring into Atlantic ports—and so were large numbers of phantom soldiers of FUSAG. But the wily Germans would not be fooled by phantom divisions alone—there would have to be a whirlwind of activity and invasion preparations in the FUSAG area.

FUSAG became an elaborate deception on an enormous scale. Gifted movie-set designers from Shepperton Studios were called in, and they supplied the fictitious force with landing craft, tanks, artillery, and trucks—all of inflatable rubber. Lumber, wire, and canvas hospitals and warehouses sprang to life. Hundreds of canvas-and-wood landing craft that floated on oil drums nestled in harbors. Some phony facilities were deliberately poorly camouflaged in order to allow detection by snooping Luftwaffe photo airplanes.

Craftsmen from Shepperton Studios built a huge dock and a large oil-storage complex near Dover. Stretching for several miles along the Channel, the facility would support the phantom FUSAG. But there was not a drop of oil anywhere. The entire project was constructed of fiberboard, wood, painted canvas, and pieces of old sewer pipe taken from bombed cities.

This construction feat was hailed by the high and mighty. King George and British General Bernard L. Montgomery (who would lead Allied ground forces in Neptune) paid visits to the project. Despite his heavy schedule, General Eisenhower found time to attend a dinner honoring the engineers and construction foremen that was held at the White Cliffs Hotel in Dover. All of this official attention was publicized in the British press.

Meanwhile, the air over southeastern England crackled with a flood of bogus radio messages that were passed back and forth between nonexistent command posts. On occasion a "careless" wireless operator would send a message in the clear. All of this immense amount of radio traffic (generated by a signals battalion) was closely monitored by the Germans across the Strait of Dover.

A crucial requirement for the Quicksilver stratagem to inject authenticity into FUSAG was a real "live" commander. That commander was at hand—Lieutenant General George S. Patton, Jr. Not only was Patton in England, but the Germans regarded the high-strung armored genius as America's most-gifted and audacious combat commander and therefore a logical choice to lead the assault against the Atlantic Wall. Patton was the key to pinpointing Allied intentions for the *Grossinvasion,* the German high command was convinced.

Tall, trim, devout, and at the same time profane, General Patton held mixed feelings about his Overlord assignment. On the one hand, he was despondent because he would not be leading assault elements ashore. On the other hand, the 59-year-old general relished the role of intrigue to which he had been assigned. "I'm a goddamned natural-born ham!" he told aides.

Patton played his role to the hilt, dashing to and fro around England while presumably preparing to lead Army Group Patton against the Nazis. With his ramrod-straight posture; lacquered helmet liner; a total of fifteen stars gleaming from his headgear, shirt collar, and shoulders; boots polished to a high gloss; an ivory-handled revolver on one hip; and roaring profane commands to all, Patton would have been difficult for even the most myopic and dull-witted German spy to miss.

Shortly before the invasion date, newly-promoted Brigadier General James Gavin, who had led the parachute assault on Sicily in 1943 and had been congratulated warmly on the battlefield by General Patton, strolled into the lobby of London's fashionable Claridge's hotel. Through a sea of humanity, Gavin spotted Patton heading toward the front door. "Hello, Gavin," Patton called out in his high-pitched voice. "How in the goddamned hell are you?"

The two men shook hands and engaged in brief conversation. All eyes in the lobby were on the famous four-star general. Finally, Patton continued on toward the door, then turned and called out loudly, "See you in the Pas de Calais, Gavin!" Unaware of the Patton masquerade, officers in the lobby cringed over this shocking security violation. George Patton never could keep his mouth shut.[2]

While Patton was racing madly around Great Britain, "playing Sarah Bernhardt," as he quipped in reference to the legendary stage actress, General Hans Cramer, the last commander of the Afrika Korps, was confined to a prisoner-of-war camp in Wales. He had been captured in Tunisia when the Axis collapsed a year earlier, and by late May 1944 he was in failing health. Depsite the looming invasion, British authorities decided to repatriate Cramer to Germany through a program administered by the Swedish Red Cross.

Accompanied by two British officers (who were agents of the Double-X Committee), General Cramer was driven from Wales to London. The route took the German officer directly through the assembly areas for the invasion in southwestern and southern England, and Cramer's eyes bulged as he saw the massive buildup of troops, tanks, warplanes, armor and artillery. The talkative British escorts, friendly types, carelessly let slip that they were driving through the Dover region of southeastern England, where Patton's phony army group was supposed to be coiling to spring across the Channel at the Pas de Calais. Since British road signposts had been removed and the names of towns and railroad stations had been obliterated in 1940 in preparation for the German invasion, Cramer had no way of knowing otherwise.

Reaching London, the former Afrika Korps leader was introduced to George Patton, who was identified as "the commanding general of FUSAG." Patton hosted a dinner for the German general and invited several U.S. corps and division commanders. Mixed in with their conversation were fleeting remarks about the Pas de Calais.

Soon General Cramer sailed on the Swedish ship *Gripsholm* and landed at a German port. He rushed to Berlin where he reported to the army high command on what he had seen and had heard in England in recent days. Cramer was promptly sent to Berchtesgaden where he told the same story to Adolf Hitler: the Allies had massed a powerful force under General Patton across from the Pas de Calais.

It had apparently been a master coup by the Double-X. How could the fuehrer and his high command conceivably distrust the word of a German general who had seen it all with his own eyes?

(After the war, Reich Marshal Hermann Goering told Allied interrogators that Cramer had arrived back in Germany from England with "a defeatist attitude.")

Meanwhile, the devious men of the XX-Committee had put their "musicians" to work. In the jargon of the shadowy espionage world, an "orchestra" of its double-agents began sending "authentic information" on the Allied buildup in England to their controllers in Hamburg. The "first violins" would be Garbo, considered by the Abwehr to be their ace spy in Great Britain; Treasure, a Frenchwoman; Brutus, a Pole; and Tricycle, the Yugoslav businessman Popov. Others— "second violins"—would be utilized to a lesser degree in the Quicksilver deception.

The phantom Army Group Patton hoax was crowned with success when *Fremde Heere West* (Foreign Armies West), the German army's intelligence evaluation branch on March 20 rushed out a signal to top Wehrmacht commanders: "It has now been established that General Patton, who is highly regarded for his proficiency, is now in England." Obviously Patton would spearhead the looming invasion of the Pas de Calais.

At the same time Quicksilver was unfolding, a similar scenario was being acted out on the eastern coast of Scotland, some 350 miles to the north. This deception was code-named Operation Skye, and it created a fictitious British Fourth Army that was preparing to invade Norway. Skye was intended to pin down the twenty-seven Nazi divisions in the Scandinavian countries before and during D day. The projected leader of the Fourth Army was an officer well known by the Germans, General Andrew "Bulgy" Thorne, who had been military attaché in Berlin. But running the bogus Fourth Army on a day-to-day basis from his headquarters in Edinburgh Castle was 52-year-old Colonel R. M. "Rory" MacLeod, who had been seriously wounded and highly decorated in the First World War.

Colonel MacLeod's phantom force consisted of nearly three hundred thousand men; they were equipped with a vast array of tanks, trucks, artillery, and even gliders—all constructed of inflatable rubber. It was not long before German monitors picked up the heavy flow of wireless traffic and learned of the Fourth Army. Luftwaffe photo reconnaissance planes confirmed the apparent existence of a large force in the Edinburgh area. But all of this could be just another devious British trick. Eyewitness reports from the ground were needed. The XX-Committee provided that confirmation. A pair of "turned" Abwehr agents, Mutt and Jeff, who had long been in custody, but were thought by the Germans to be living undercover in Scotland, radioed to Hamburg detailed reports on the bustling activity in the Edinburgh region. Mutt and Jeff even described Fourth Army's nonexistent shoulder insignia.

In the meantime Allied leaders in London were deeply concerned with a Nazi threat even more potentially disastrous than the V-1 and V-2. Intelligence had learned the frightening news that Hitler's scientists were in the final stages of developing a revolutionary weapon of enormous destructive capability, one that would become known as an atomic bomb. Only a handful of top-level American and British leaders were aware that a covert and deadly race had been in progress for many months to see which side would come up first with an atomic bomb—the winner could rule the world. The hush-hush Manhattan Project had been going full speed in the United States since 1942.

The Germans had ordered the Norwegian electrochemical plant, Norsk Hydro (the largest of its kind in the world) to produce "heavy water," an ingredient needed for creating the atomic bomb. Paralyzing Norsk Hydro and destroying its supply of heavy water had held the highest priority with the British. The plant was perched on the brink of a 1,000-foot gorge, ringed by mountains, so a pinpoint attack by RAF bombers had been ruled out.

In late 1942 British intelligence had learned from Einar Skinnarland, a member of the Norwegian resistance who had obtained a job at Norsk Hydro that heavy-water production was increasing rapidly and that stocks of it were being shipped each month to the Kaiser Wilhelm Institut, where atomic experiments had been taking place since 1940. Lord Mountbatten's Combined Operations was ordered to launch a commando assault immediately.

Combined Operations, accustomed to suicide exploits, regarded the Norsk Hydro raid as one of the toughest. Four Norsemen, all skilled skiers, were dropped to form a reception committee for an assault by British airborne troops. Coming down one hundred miles from their target, it took the Norsemen fifteen days of incredible suffering in subzero weather to reach the plant. Two gliders filled with British troops took off from England and crashed against craggy, steep mountains in Norway, victims of unpredictable wind currents.

Undaunted, Combined Operations dropped six more Norsemen by parachute, and the newcomers hooked up with the four countrymen who had jumped into Norway a month earlier and Einar Skinnarland, who had joined them from his post at Norsk Hydro. Burdened with sensitive explosives, nine of the Norsemen, on the night of February 27, 1943, began clawing their way up the 1,000-foot, perpendicular, ice-covered rock face of the gorge. Wind blasts threatened to plunge them to their deaths.

While some of the commandos stood guard outside, others slipped inside the giant plant, and after overpowering a few guards, they fastened charges to pipes, tanks, and machinery—wherever explosives would cause the most damage. One man checked the 30-second fuse and lit it; all the commandos raced outside. There was an enormous explosion, dull sounding behind the thick concrete walls, but rocking the ground beneath them. More than one thousand pounds of priceless heavy water gushed onto the floor and down the sewers.

Sirens blared. Germans dashed about outside the plant. The Gestapo went door to door in the nearby village seeking the "terrorists." An entire division of troops was rushed to the scene to join in a manhunt for the culprits. The "terrorists," meanwhile, had scattered. Several on skis headed for the Swedish border; others went into hiding to continue with underground activities. Einar Skinnarland resumed his job reporting to England on Norsk Hydro activities. Not a single Norwegian commando was caught, although all had suffered enormously from exposure to the arctic weather.

In late 1943 Skinnarland, always anticipating arrest at any moment, radioed London that the sabotage damage had been repaired and that heavy-water production had resumed. Within forty-eight hours heavy bombers of the U.S. Eighth Air Force demolished the factory's power station. Early in February 1944 Skinnarland radioed an urgent message: the Germans were moving all of Norsk Hydro's heavy-water equipment and its entire supply to an underground factory in Germany. The ferryboat *Hydro* was to carry freight cars with these heavy-water stocks across Lake Tinnsjo. "Request permission to sink ferry," the Norseman stated. The prompt reply: "Permission granted."

Masquerading as a Norsk Hydro employee and carrying forged papers, a member of the Norwegian underground made an exploratory crossing of Lake Tinnsjo to determine where the *Hyro* should sink in order to make salvage impossible. A few nights later, in late February, men of the resistance sneaked aboard the *Hydro* after it had been loaded with the heavy-water freight cars and was ready to sail. They placed time charges in the bilges, then stealthily fled.

At mid-morning *Hydro* was plowing through the choppy waves of Lake Tinnsjo. Suddenly the ferry was rocked by huge explosions; it halted briefly, then plunged to the bottom in the deepest part of the lake. Buried with the ferry and the Third Reich's stock of heavy water was Adolf Hitler's dream of ruling the world through the power of atomic bombs.

* * *

It was a chilly day early in March as Jacques Bertin, a young member of the French aristocracy with the exalted title *Comte de la Hautière,* was pedaling his battered old bicycle northward along the eastern coast of the Cherbourg peninsula. Six feet two, blond and handsome, the count had urgent business to attend to in the bustling, German-occupied port of Cherbourg. He had something else also—a price on his head, put there by the Gestapo.

For nearly two years the aristocrat, whose code name was Jacques Moulines, had been a man without a home. He was constantly on the go, always in danger of being trapped, seldom sleeping in the same house two nights in a row. Moulines was in charge of operations on the Cherbourg peninsula for Centurie, and he had more than eleven hundred agents working for him.

Moulines, a carefree pilot in peacetime, was wearing his customary old leather flight jacket. Of all the Centurie organizers, Moulines's task was the most difficult—and perilous. Cherbourg and vicinity were saturated with fortifications, and there were nearly thirty-nine thousand German troops in the region. Security was intense.

If the Germans were vigilant, the count was doubly so—for his life depended upon it. On entering a bistro, Moulines had to loiter inconspicuously until he learned if local residents were ordering alcoholic beverages that day. On arbitrary occasions, the Gestapo, seeking to identify outsiders, would suddenly forbid cafes and bistros to serve alcoholic beverages, a fact known to natives of the community, but not to outsiders. Bartenders, under threat of arrest, were forced to report anyone who ordered wine or beer.

Moulines always entered Cherbourg wheeling his bicycle because on certain irregular days the German authorities would suddenly prohibit riding two-wheeled vehicles (pushing a bicycle was acceptable). Entering a cafe to eat, the count had to glance furtively about to see if locals were ordering meat; on some days the Gestapo ordered meat withheld.

Admiring agents swore Moulines was devoid of nerves. One night, while German soldiers in the front room drank boisterously throughout the night, he slept soundly on a cot in the back room of a dingy Cherbourg bistro, a rough drawing of a German gun position in his pocket. One factor kept him from the slow, agonizing death of dangling by a piano-wire noose: despite relentless efforts for two years to trap the underground "terrorist" named Jacques Moulines, the Germans had not the slightest clue as to his description or true identity. Certainly a playboy member of the French aristocracy would not possess the gumption for such a hazardous and demanding venture.

Dashing Jacques Moulines had no way of knowing that Cherbourg would be the key to the success or failure of Overlord. Unless the Allies could seize a major port quickly after landing, the troops ashore could wither on the vine and be cut to pieces as a result of a lack of supplies and reinforcements. Adolf Hitler recognized that fact: he had proclaimed all major ports along the Atlantic Wall to be fortresses and required their commanders to sign oaths that they would fight to "the last man and the last bullet."

Unknown to the imaginative orchestrators of Quicksilver and Skye, the deception stratagems received a boost from a German officer, Colonel Alexis Baron von Roenne, chief of Fremde Heere West (FHW). It was his job to ferret out the Allied order of battle in Great Britain. If von Roenne was successful, Hitler and his commanders could discern the locale of the Allies' landing.

Baron von Roenne had an impeccable military record, and he had been personally decorated by the fuehrer with the *Deutsches Kruez* (German Cross). But von Roenne had grown increasingly disillusioned with Hitler and his Berlin clique and had joined the conspiratorial Schwarze Kapelle. Then in February 1944 he found himself ensnarled in a power struggle between German intelligence agencies.

It had been the practice of von Roenne's FHW to pass its intelligence evaluations to the Sicherheitsdienst (SD), the security arm of the SS. FHW and SD for months had been involved in a bitter conflict to prove to the fuehrer that each was the more capable agency. Confident that they were better qualified to analyze incoming information than was von Roenne's FHW, the SD invariably cut in half FHW's estimates of the number of Allied divisions in Britain. Hitler thought that the estimates reaching his desk had come from von Roenne, whose evaluations he held in high regard. But the reports were von Roenne's Allied strength estimates *cut in half* by the SD.[3]

Acting on the halved estimates, the fuehrer in early 1944 was withdrawing divisions from the West for employment on the Russian front. This turn of events deeply disturbed von Roenne, who thought that the Atlantic Wall should be strengthened. Although a Schwarze Kapelle conspirator, the baron was dedicated to inflicting heavy casualties on the Western Allies so that when Hitler was arrested (or executed), Schwarze Kapelle leaders would have leverage in seeking a negotiated peace with the United States and Great Britain.

Colonel von Roenne decided to take a drastic course of action (one that would cost him his life). Knowing that the SD would halve the estimates in FHW reports, von Roenne began grossly exaggerating Allied strength in Britain. When his figures reached the fuehrer, after having been cut in half by the SD, the resulting numbers would reflect an accurate assessment.

Late in April von Roenne submitted a false report that stated the Allies had eighty-five to ninety conventional divisions and seven airborne divisions available for the invasion. (Actually, there were thirty-two infantry and armored divisions and three airborne divisions.) Then an unanticipated event occurred: the SD, for unknown reasons, put its mark of approval on the greatly exaggerated estimate of ninety-seven divisions. The report was forwarded to Hitler who, thinking it had come from von Roenne, accepted the information as fact. Thus the feud between German intelligence agencies had fostered the myth of General Patton's ghost army and General Thorne's phantom Fourth Army.[4]

When Clark's U.S. Fifth Army had stormed ashore at Salerno the previous September, it had rapidly captured the major port of Naples, then had become bogged down. On January 22, 1944, in order to break the stalemate, elements of Fifth Army made an amphibious "end run" around German lines and splashed onto the beaches at the old pirate's lair of Anzio, sixty miles up the coast from Naples and twenty-five miles south of Rome. Reacting with typical alacrity, Field Marshal Albert Kesselring ringed the Anzio beachhead, and one hundred thousand Allied troops were hemmed in with their backs to the sea.

Six weeks later, on March 9, at about 10:00 P.M., four figures carrying a small boat and explosives slipped through the darkness near the village of Fossa Incastro, thirteen miles south of Rome. The men were highly trained saboteurs of the Gestapo who had been assigned an important mission—sneak behind Allied lines and murder the Allies' two top commanders in Italy, British General Harold Alexander and U.S. General Mark Clark.

The Gestapo murder plan was for the assassination team of Italian Fascists to sail seven miles south along the Tyrrhenian coast to the Anzio beachhead and sneak ashore near the mouth of the Moletta River, behind Allied lines and only a half mile from British positions on the left flank. From that point the "hit men" were to work their way inland to advanced Allied headquarters on the beachhead, and after determining that both Generals Clark and Alexander were inside, they were to blow up the building—and the two Allied commanders with it.

The hit men should have little trouble reaching the Allied headquarters on Anzio, the Gestapo felt, as all were Romans who knew the region well and, if halted, they could pass themselves off as residents. Provisions had been made for the Gestapo in Rome to radio to the assassins on the beachhead when Clark and Alexander, who was the Allied commander in Italy, were both at the Anzio beachhead headquarters (information presumably to be obtained from German spies).

As the assassination team shoved off from dark Fossa Incastro, a young one-armed man named Michelle Coppola, despite his physical handicap, insisted on steering the small boat. The others did not protest: Coppola was highly regarded by his Gestapo masters in Rome and was recognized by them as a zealous agent with a deep hatred for the Americans and the British.

Curiously, Coppola, instead of hugging the shoreline as planned, steered the craft in a sweeping arc, almost as if he were trying to be spotted by Allied vessels known to be patrolling the region. His three comrades had grown uneasy. Had it not been for Coppola's stupidity in steering the boat off course, the hit team would have been ashore by now.

The boat burrowed on through the black waters. "When are we going to land?" the others asked Coppola with increasing frequency.

"Soon," was the repeated reply. "Very soon."

Now the others had grown mutinous. This idiotic, one-armed Coppola was lost and would get them all captured and executed, they muttered to each other.

Coppola was aware of the increasing anger and concern. He reached into a pile of ammunition, grabbed a grenade, pulled the pin, and told his startled comrades that he was an Allied agent, loyal to the King of England, and that he intended to head for shore and turn himself—and the other three—over to the Allies.

Coppola had long been working for British intelligence in the Rome underground and had connived his way into the confidence of the Gestapo, so much so that he was one of their most-trusted agents.

Furious and frightened over the turn of events, the three assassins, cursing and snarling, began edging toward the one-armed man. Coppola brandished the live grenade and in a firm voice called out: "One more step and I'll blow us all to hell!"

As the others muttered threats, Coppola laid the grenade beside the tiller and steered the boat toward shore and up onto the beach at the designated spot near the mouth of the Moletta River. Laying his pistol beside him (the other three men had already been ordered to pitch their weapons overboard), Coppola hurled the grenade into the distance, where it detonated with a roar that echoed across the black landscape. As if on cue—and that was precisely what the grenade blast was—several shadowy figures, carrying rifles and wearing the pie-plate helmets of British soldiers, emerged from the darkness and took Coppola's three companions into custody.

For two weeks Allied intelligence had been aware of the Gestapo plot to murder Generals Alexander and Clark. After learning of the scheme, Michelle Coppola had insisted that he be allowed to join in the mission. The he slipped away from the Gestapo on a pretext and told an underground leader of the plan. In turn, the underground alerted Fifth Army headquarters by a secret-radio communication. For several weeks after the aborted murder mission, the Gestapo in Rome was in a quandary, trying to determine what had happened to the hit team—it had simply vanished.[5]

25

Buzzbombs

When Adolf Hitler had made the decision to rebuild Peenemünde after it had been heavily pounded by the RAF the
previous August, the Germans implemented a cunning hoax.
While new construction was in full swing and successfully
camouflaged, the bomb craters from the raid were left untouched. As expected, RAF photos indicated Peenemünde had
been abandoned, so bombers would not return for nine months.

In any event the Peenemünde bombing, which had concentrated on the "missile half" of the island, had come too late.
V-1's (buzzbombs) were rolling off the production lines at the
Volkswagen plant in Fallersleben in the Third Reich. Plans
were to produce fifty thousand of the pilotless aircraft that
exploded with the impact of a 4,000-pound blockbuster and
could attain speeds of 440 miles per hour, faster than any
Allied fighter plane could fly.

By May 1944 the Germans had drawn up a schedule for
launching the "secret weapon" onslaught against England:

Grosses Wecken (Massive Reveille), two hours before
dawn, a deluge of 300 buzzbombs.

Salut (Salute), at noon, 100 V-1's.

Grosser Zapfenstreich (Grand Tattoo), just after nightfall,
concentrated fire as rapidly as possible.

It was a few minutes past 4:00 A.M. on June 13 when an elderly member of the Royal Observer Corps in Kent viewed a strange object streaking through the dark sky toward London. Its dim contours resembled those of an airplane, but its exhaust was belching reddish orange flame, and it gave off a sputtering sound. Onward the object raced, and a few minutes later its present timer cut off the motor; it crashed into the village of Swanscombe, some eighteen miles from its intended target, the Tower Bridge in London. The buzzbomb explosion rocked the region, hurling terrified villagers out of their beds. England was under attack by lethal robots—"doodlebugs," the Britishers would come to call them.

Code-named Target 42 by the Germans, sprawling London lived in constant fear and chaos in the days and weeks ahead. Hundreds of buzzbombs rained down on the capital, killing and wounding thousands of civilians. Thousands more were homeless, and the threat of an epidemic due to smashed water lines and sewers increased official worries. An evacuation program for children, some women, the elderly, and the sick was rapidly organized. The mass exodus from Target 42 into the countryside resulted in a severe strain on British railways and slowed the vital flow of ammunition, weapons, and supplies to the fighting men in Normandy.

As the days rolled past and the carnage in London increased, there were hushed whispers in dark corners of British government buildings that unless something was done about the flying bombs, England might be forced to seek a negotiated peace. Allied Supreme Commander Eisenhower, as a result, had to make a crucial decision: a large portion of the powerful Anglo-American heavy-bomber force would be diverted from support of the Normandy fighting and begin pounding V-1 launching sites along the Pas de Calais. This crisis-bombing operation was code-named Crossbow.

More than two thousand antiaircraft guns were rushed to the south coast of England. Home Secretary Herbert Morrison "demanded" that the Allies invade the Pas de Calais to capture the launching pads. By early July three hundred thousand London houses and thousands of other buildings had been destroyed. Tens of thousands of civilians had been killed or wounded.

In desperation—as national survival hung in the balance—Prime Minister Churchill, on July 13, proposed the all-out use of poison gas against the German homeland to "shorten the war." Churchill then began promoting another scheme to halt the buzzbomb terror: he would select one hundred small, undefended German towns, and Royal Air Force bombers would wipe them out, one at a time, "until Herr Hitler calls off his dogs."

Launching bacteriological warfare against the Third Reich's home front, with all its hideous consequences, was seriously considered. British scientists had earlier developed a top-secret bacteriological agent against which there was no known remedy. Using the agent as a retaliatory weapon against Germany was finally ruled out—large enough quantities would not be available for at least one year.

Great pressures were brought on General Eisenhower to scrap long-standing tactical plans to defeat Germany and to cancel Operation Dragoon, a forthcoming landing in southern France set for August, and instead to invade the Pas de Calais. A fateful decision was reached. Frightful as was the carnage, Hitler's vengeance weapon was not greatly affecting the prosecution of the war. So London would have to endure, and an all-out effort would be made to break out of the Normandy bridgehead at the earliest possible time and overrun the launching sites along the Pas de Calais.

In the meantime savage fighting had been raging among the hedgerows of Normandy. The British on the left were trying to capture the key road junction of Caen, while the Americans on the right were attacking toward the major port of Cherbourg. Hitler long before had designated the port to be a fortress, one to be defended to "the last man and the last bullet." Without a major port, both Hitler and the Allied high command knew, the invasion could fail.

Camouflaged under spreading apple trees at Lieutenant General Omar N. Bradley's U.S. First Army headquarters in an orchard behind Omaha Beach was a curious-looking truck of British make. A rigid antenna reached twenty-six feet into the sky from the center of the vehicle's roof. Uniformed personnel regularly rushed to and from the mystery truck, most of them wearing the blue of Britain's Royal Air Force, a handful of the Royal Corps of Signals.

The British servicemen were pleasant to the Americans at the First Army headquarters—but tight-lipped and casually aloof. Seldom would they pause to chat with their cousins from across the Atlantic. The English truck and its activities were so shrouded in a thick cloak of intrigue that its presence in the midst of an American army command post was a source of unrelenting interest and speculation.

Mystified and frustrated, the Americans began calling the truck's servicemen "The Secret Limeys." The Americans would have been even more puzzled had they known the name of the unit's base in England—Station X—with which The Secret Limeys were in wireless contact on a round-the-clock basis.

Only a handful of top commanders and intelligence officers in First Army were aware that the truck and its British staff were known as a SLU (Special Liaison Unit) and that its function was to furnish General Bradley with a continual flow of details on the German command structure and the strength, location, and morale of enemy units, often down to battalion and even company levels. A similar SLU was operating in General Montgomery's British sector on the left flank of the bridgehead.

Station X was the supersecret Ultra center at Bletchley Park, north of London. After decoding intercepted German messages, Station X encoded them again and transmitted them to the SLU units in the field. SLU officers, sworn to secrecy under pain of a long prison sentence for violation of security, would decode the Station X messages and personally take them to the commanding general of his designated staff officer.

Now, at the SLU truck in General Bradley's apple orchard on the evening of June 19, the Royal Air Force officer in charge noted that a message was coming in from Station X marked with the symbol for utmost urgency—ZZZZZ. When issued at Bletchley Park, each decrypt was marked from Z to ZZZZZ, a system that would leave no doubt in the mind of the other officer in the field as to the degree of its urgency.

The RAF officer clasped the ZZZZZ signal in one hand and slipped out of the truck. He lifted one of his flying boots and glanced at the sole, then repeated the procedure with the other boot. He could not risk the off chance that bits and pieces of ultrasecret material in the wireless truck had stuck to the bottom of his boots, to be shaken loose and found by unauthorized parties.

Reaching General Bradley's tent, the RAF officer entered and handed the decoded message from Station X to the First Army commander. Bradley studied the message as the Britisher stood by silently. Without a word the general (who was known affectionately to American reporters as Omar the Tentmaker) handed the signal back to the SLU man. No one was permitted to retain copies of the SLU messages. In accordance with standard procedure, the RAF officer returned to his truck with the secret signal and destroyed it.

As a result of reading the Station X message, Omar Bradley knew precisely of German plans. The signal had been from Field Marshal Erwin Rommel to General Kurt von Schlieben, defender of Cherbourg, and contained the terse order: "Launch Operation Heinrich tonight."

From earlier Ultra intercepts, Bradley knew that Operation Heinrich was the code name for the withdrawal of German forces into prepared fortifications ringing Cherbourg. Word was passed on to Major General J. Lawton "Lightning Joe" Collins, U.S. VII Corps commander, whose three divisions had been designated to seize Cherbourg. "The German is pulling back tonight," the peppery Collins told his commanders. "Get right on their heels, starting at dawn!"

By July 1—D day plus 24—mighty Cherbourg had fallen, and the last armed German on the Cherbourg peninsula had been killed or rounded up. In London, SHAEF breathed more easily. With a major port in Allied hands, the invaders were on the Continent to stay.

In the first seven weeks of Overlord, the Americans suffered 133,326 casualties (34,133 dead), and the combined British and Canadian losses were 83,825 men (16,138 killed). But how much larger would these figures have been had it not been for the intricate, devious, often brutal Plan Bodyguard that masked the date and locale of the invasion, to say nothing of Ultra and all the other stratagems employed earlier in the war? While the German Seventh Army in Normandy was being cut

to pieces, the much stronger Fifteenth Army sat idly behind the
Atlantic Wall along the Pas de Calais for seven weeks, waiting
for the sledgehammer blow from General George Patton's
phantom army group.

Seven weeks after D day General Eisenhower and SHAEF
were desperate. Hundreds of thousands of Allied soldiers were
bottled up in a thin strip along the Normandy landing beaches.
Their repeated efforts to break out had been beaten back by
Germans obeying Adolf Hitler's order not to yield a foot of
ground.

Now the Allied high command was betting all its chips on
Operation Cobra, a plan to break out of the bridgehead.
Through a wide array of deception stratagems, the Germans
were hoodwinked into believing that a breakout would be
spearheaded by General Bernard Montgomery's British force
at Caen, on the eastern sector. Most of the available panzers
were rushed to Montgomery's front.

On July 24, however, three thousand American and British
planes pounded a strip of ground only three miles wide and a
mile deep along the Saint-Lô-Périers road in General Bradley's
sector on the west flank. Through the gap American armored
spearheads plunged southward deep behind the lines of the
German Fifth and Seventh Panzer armies.

Early on the morning of July 28, Field Marshal Hans
Guenther von Kluge, who had just replaced Erwin Rommel as
commander of the battlefront (Rommel had been seriously
wounded when his speeding staff car was strafed), was on the
phone to General Alfred Jodl at Wolf's Lair. The leaking
German dam in Normandy had cracked wide open under the
gigantic tidal wave of American bombs, shells, and bullets.

"Herr Jodl," von Kluge cried, "everything here is *eine
Riesensauerei* (one hell of a mess)!"

At last Adolf Hitler had become convinced that Patton's
army across from the Pas de Calais was a hoax. Nearly eight
weeks after D day, the fuehrer authorized von Kluge to pull a
few divisions from the Fifteenth Army to help halt the
rampaging American spearheads. But it was too little and too
late. U.S. armored flying columns behind the Normandy front
now cut eastward and then turned north to link up with General
Montgomery's British and Canadian forces south of Caen, near

Falaise, snapping shut a gigantic trap on one hundred thousand Germans—a disaster for the Third Reich unrivaled since Stalingrad.

Again, intricate Allied deceptions—along with the courage and blood of American, British, French, and Canadian fighting men—had paid off on the battlefield. Even before the final Nazi soldier was killed or captured in the enormous steel pocket, American tanks were racing eastward and approaching a glittering prize—Paris.

Meanwhile, a few hundred miles south of the Nazi-held French capital, U.S. Army Captain Aaron Bank, leader of a three-man Allied guerrilla and sabotage team known as a Jedburgh, parachuted into the Massif Central, just west of the Rhône Valley, prior to Operation Dragoon, the invasion of southern France. D day was set for August 15. Grand strategy called for the invading Allied force to drive northward up the Rhône Valley and link up with the forces breaking out of Normandy.

Aaron Bank, five feet eight, wiry and tough, was in his late thirties, a bit advanced in years for such demanding and strenuous cloak-and-dagger activities in the midst of German forces. The two members of his Jed team were a French lieutenant whose *nom de guerre* was Henri and a French radio operator known only as Jean. None of the French Jeds used their real names, since their families were in France.

Prior to D day in Normandy, the Allied brain trust had known that there were some sixty French underground *réseaux* (circuits). But if they were to be fully effective, the resistance groups would have to be heavily reinforced with parachute drops of weapons, ammunition, and supplies. Allied soldiers of great judgment, courage, leadership qualities, and skill in guerrilla tactics would have to jump into France to supervise these drops and to train and direct the fighting of the underground warriors (known as Maquis) in accordance with Allied operations.

As a result of these needs in the shadow war behind German lines, the Jedburgh teams were created. (Jedburgh was an area in Scotland where the Scots, several centuries ago, conducted guerrilla warfare against the British.) Captain Bank, who spoke

French and German fluently, was a member of Wild Bill Donovan's OSS, while all French Jeds belonged to General de Gaulle's secret service branch, the *Bureau Central de Renseignement et d'Action* (BCRA).

Bank's Jed team had flown to southern France from Algiers, in North Africa, and, after bailing out, hooked up with the resistance leader of the southern sector, who went by the name of Commandant Raymond. Shortly after the Jeds arrived, they were taken to a "safe house" in a small village near where Bank planned to set up his command post. Commandant Raymond assured Bank that there was no danger that the Germans would discover them there.

The OSS man and his two comrades fell into exhausted sleep in a room on the ground floor. They slept in their underwear and with boots on—just in case. During the night, the Jeds were jolted awake. Someone in the house was yelling, *"Les Boches! Les Boches!"* (Germans! Germans!). Grabbing uniforms and weapons, the Jeds leaped out the window and followed Commandant Raymond along a path leading into a forest. Bank had forgotten that he was wearing only his underwear until Raymond quipped, "Captain, you're out of uniform!"

Minutes after the guerrillas had fled, the Germans broke into the house—apparently they had been tipped off by a French informer. After daybreak the Jeds' precious radio, which had been hidden within a basement coal pile, was retrieved.

In the days that followed, Aaron Bank and his Jeds led Maquis bands in the ambush of German convoys, attacked enemy posts and installations, and organized and formed reception committees for the recovery of arms and explosives from the drop zones. Then one day, through an informant, Bank learned that the Gestapo had built up a dossier on him and Henri, classifying the two Jeds as the region's "leading terrorists." Commandant Raymond's pride had been bruised— the Gestapo had labeled him "only" as an underground leader, not as a terrorist.

Early in August Captain Bank stayed close to his command post, waiting for the invasion alert. He and his comrades were deeply concerned: Operation Dragoon was possibly the war's worst-kept secret. Certainly the Germans knew that the invasion was about to strike. Finally the anticipated alert reached Bank. The coded message outlined the mission of the Jed team and its Maquis comrades: when the Germans started retreating northward up the Rhône Valley, Bank's guerrillas were to keep them from using secondary roads, to force them to remain on main roads, where they could be cut to pieces by swarms of American fighter-bombers and devastated by 155-millimeter Long Toms.

Bank organized his guerrillas into a paramilitary regiment of three battalions, a task easily accomplished as most of the Maquis were former soldiers. All three battalions were then deployed in blocking positions. A few days later Captain Bank and his guerrillas, far inland, cheered raucously as they heard the distant rumble of big navy guns and the dull thud of bombs: the Allies were storming ashore along the fabled French Riviera.

At his command post in far-off East Prussia, Adolf Hitler could also hear, figuratively, the Riviera guns. He knew that the Wehrmacht force of more than one hundred thousand men in southern France was in immediate danger of being cut off from Germany by the Allied spearheads from Normandy that were racing hell-bent across northern France toward the Reich. Reluctantly, the fuehrer ordered the Wehrmacht in southern France to pull back the several hundred miles to the Siegfried Line on the Reich border.

During the German retreat up the Rhône Valley, Captain Bank, Napoleonlike, directed operations of his three guerrilla battalions from a command post in the telephone exchange in the town of Alès. Fleeing German units and convoys were pinpointed with incredible accuracy. Motorcycle couriers from Maquis reconnaissance teams regularly sped up to Bank's CP with urgent intelligence messages. With the entire regional telephone system at his disposal (there was no longer fear from Gestapo wiretappers, as they were also fleeing), Bank was able to give instant orders over the telephone to his widely spread guerrillas.[1]

Bank's personal situation was not without peril. The main roads leading northward passed through Alès, and the OSS officer could look outside and see long columns of German infantry, vehicles, and a few tanks moving past under his window. Seeking frantically to escape from the gauntlet of bombs and bullets from swarming *Jabos* (as the Germans called Allied fighter-bombers) and the deluge of shells from Long Toms, the Germans occasionally tried to reach the mountains to either side. Forewarned by telephone from Aaron Bank's CP, the guerrillas set ambushes and inflicted heavy casualties on the enemy, driving them back into the Rhône Valley.

Despite the loss of large numbers of men, equipment, rolling stock, and guns, remnants of the southern France army, exhausted, dispirited, and bedraggled, finally stumbled into the protective ramparts of the Siegfried Line—there to fight another day.

Patrols from the Riviera invaders and those of the Normandy breakout force linked up below Paris, and all Allied armies in France pressed eastward abreast toward the Third Reich. All along the line the Wehrmacht in the West was fleeing in disarray. It had suffered horrendous losses since D day in Normandy: 400,000 men killed, wounded, or captured; 3,500 aircraft; 1,300 tanks; 500 assault guns; 1,500 pieces of artillery; and 20,000 vehicles lost or destroyed. SHAEF was euphoric. Allied victory seemed but a few weeks, perhaps days, away.[2]

The one man who counted, however, Adolf Hitler, was not yet ready to concede defeat—he was about to spring another awesome secret weapon on the Allies.

26

Specter of the V-2

In late August and early September 1944, war-weary Londoners were breathing sighs of relief. Rampaging Allied armies on the Continent had overrun most of the buzzbomb sites along the English Channel coast in France, so the long nightmare of sudden death from flying robots seemed to be over. Unknown to these millions of civilians, near panic was gripping a handful of top British authorities and scientists: they knew that London was about to be struck by a rain of V-2 missiles, Hitler's terrifying new secret weapon.

Prime Minister Winston Churchill and his cabinet held grim sessions over the latest threat to Great Britain's existence. One haunting specter dominated discussions: there was no defense against the missile barrage with which Adolf Hitler intended to smash London into a charred pile of rubble and force the Allies to seek a negotiated peace.

As a result of an epic espionage coup by the underground of Poland, British scientists knew that the V-2 was shaped like a fat cigar, was forty-seven feet long (as tall as a 6-story building when erect on its launching pad), and carried a 1-ton warhead capable of leveling an entire block of buildings. The huge missile could attain a height of ninety miles and such enormous speed (990 miles per hour) that those on the receiving end would not hear it approaching. Graphite rudders in the tail steered the rocket, and the missile maintained radio contact with the ground by a built-in transmitter.

Air attacks against V-2 launching sites would be futile. Unlike the large ramps needed to catapult buzzbombs, the missiles required only small concrete slabs with portable metal devices sitting on them. It was known that the V-2 launching sites were in Holland, but the sites were camouflaged and invisible from the air. To further thwart Allied detection, the Germans planned to fire a few V-2's, then move quickly to another site, so even the handful of Allied spies remaining in Holland would not be able to pinpoint the next missile-launching site.

As far back as November 1943, British intelligence had been aware that mysterious and feverish activities were going on in and adjacent to the remote village of Blizna in Poland. Blizna had been cleared of its residents, and German army men and civilians began arriving in droves. Barracks were hastily thrown up and camouflaged. Ack-ack guns and searchlights were rushed in and ringed the site. Almost at once the Polish underground began sending reports to London.

Then a railroad spur connecting Blizna with the outside world was rapidly constructed, and within hours tightly sealed freight trains carrying unknown cargoes arrived each day. An airfield was scraped out of the black terrain, and a steady flow of planes landed and took off. The Germans took no pains to mask the name they had given to the site—*Artillerie-Zielfeld Blizna* (Blizna Artillery Training Ground)—their secret testing ground for V-2 missiles.

Early in 1944 Polish agents who had been snooping about the outer fringes of the district for several weeks suddenly heard a loud boom and looked up to see a strange and huge projectile, trailing a fiery plume, leap skyward from the center of the forest. A few days later an underground member, using a small, cheap camera, succeeded in taking a picture of another one of the projectiles as it swooshed upward past the tree-line. The clandestine photo was rushed to London, where it was greeted by British intelligence with deep concern.

Bits and pieces of alarming information from the Polish underground continued to filter into London. One daring agent, noticing a German train (whose cars were marked "dry goods") halted at a siding outside the closely guarded testing grounds, sneaked up to one open car and saw that it contained some sort of long object covered by tarpaulins. Glancing around nervously, the agent threw back one corner of the tarp and saw a huge projectile shaped like the fuselage of an airplane.

Then in May 1944, just as Allied armies marshaled in England were about ready to cross the English Channel and storm the Normandy beaches, yet another Polish underground member pulled off a startling espionage bonanza. Somehow he had managed to draw a detailed and perfectly scaled map of the entire Blizna missile-testing area. This, too, was rushed to London.

Now an alarmed British intelligence sent an urgent request to Polish underground headquarters in Warsaw: could the Poles send parts of an intact rocket? It was an outrageous request—the British might just as well have asked the Poles to smuggle them parts of Adolf Hitler's headquarters at Wolf's Lair. Then an extraordinarily fortuitous event occurred—a V-2 missile that had gone awry in flight plunged into the swampy bank of the Bug River and failed to explode. Its nose was buried deep in mud, but the projectile was largely intact. The rocket was spotted by a farmer living nearby, and he excitedly reported it to a member of the underground.

Two resistance men rushed to the site and photographed the V-2. It was risky business, for already German patrols were literally beating the bushes in a frantic effort to locate the missile. The partisans covered the projectile with brush and foliage.

A few nights later a few resistance men came to the Bug River bank on a strange mission: to steal key parts of a 47-foot missile. Constantly in fear of detection by Germans, the Poles worked feverishly through most of the night and finally, with the aid of three teams of husky, snorting plow horses, the men pulled their coveted prize out of the sticky morass of mud. The engine and steering mechanism were removed, laboriously loaded onto carts, and trundled across the rough fields to a nearby barn, where they were hidden.

In the morning a team of Warsaw scientists disguised as laborers arrived at the barn, took many photographs and measurements of the components, made drawings, then dismantled the parts into hundreds of pieces, large and small.

Covered by loads of potatoes, the V-2 components were sneaked into Warsaw underground headquarters in two wheezing and coughing old trucks. It had been a sobering experience for the drivers, who had been halted at three different German roadblocks. While the resistance men sat motionless, their hearts pounding furiously, the enemy soldiers had studied their potato cargoes, then permitted the trucks to continue.

In London the Polish Section of the SOE (Special Operations Executive) was electrified by the intelligence bonanza and set into motion a plan to smuggle the key components out of Warsaw and back to England. It would be a difficult and perilous task, the SOE knew, but the effort had to be made. Code name for the operation was Wildhorn III.

At about 10:00 P.M. on July 25, a lumbering C-47 transport plane (called a Dakota by the British) lifted off from Brindisi airfield in Italy and set a course for an abandoned airfield in Poland. Its pilot was Flight Lieutenant Stanley G. Culliford, a New Zealander, and the copilot was a Pole, Flight Lieutenant Kazimierz Szrajer. The two officers and their British crew held no illusions that their secret mission would be a "milk run," as airmen labeled routine flights. The C-47 was to land directly in the center of territory crowded with German units retreating westward under pressure of the advancing Russian army.[1]

It was just past midnight at the dark airstrip, once used by the Polish air force, when a band of armed partisans heard the faint engine hum of an approaching plane. The men were tense. That day German units had moved into villages in the area; one enemy force was bivouacked only a half mile away. Off in the distance could be heard the muffled boom of artillery, for the fighting front was not far away.

Now the aircraft circled overhead, and the partisans (who had been notified by radio that it was coming) recognized the dim silhouette as that of a C-47 transport plane. Lieutenant Culliford began coming in for a landing when suddenly the dark meadow burst into brightness—the pilot had turned on his headlights. The partisans cringed: if the roar of the engines did not alert the Germans in the district, no doubt this blast of iridescence would.

The plane rolled to a stop, and shadowy figures stole silently from surrounding woods. They were pulling carts carrying several large containers that had served as oxygen drums. In the drums were the key V-2 components. The cargo was loaded onto the plane, and four Polish scientists scrambled aboard. Culliford revved the engine for the takeoff—but the plane refused to budge. Something had gone wrong.

Lieutenant Culliford dashed back from the cockpit and called out in a stage whisper for everyone to get out. The crew hastily inspected the wheels and began shoveling dirt away from them. Then everyone piled into the aircraft once more. Again the raucous revving of engines. Again the plane refused to move. Everyone out, the pilot ordered.

The tension was nearly unbearable. Passengers and crew jumped back onto the landing strip. Now the wheels had sunk into the mud. Visions of Gestapo torture chambers danced before their eyes—at any moment the Germans, attracted by the loud turmoil, might race up.

Gather up sticks was the order. Dark figures dashed about. The sticks were lodged under the wheels, and everyone reboarded the aircraft. It was not easy, getting in and out in the blackness, for each passenger was burdened with suitcases and boxes holding intelligence documents and other materials. Once more the harsh revving of the engines. This time it seemed louder than ever. The C-47 shuddered violently—and remained stuck. Everyone out!

In desperation Lieutenant Culliford switched on the headlights to allow crewmen to see the wheels more clearly. This brought a renewed surge of cold fear into the hearts of the passengers. The wheels had sunk deeper into the mud, and Culliford gave the order to blow up the craft.

With heavy hearts the partisans and scientists watched silently. All that painstaking work. All that peril. Had it been in vain now that they were so close to success? As the crew placed the explosives, a few partisans began digging frantically around the wheels with their hands. They clawed, and clawed some more. Blood trickled down their palms. Other partisans ran to a fence and brought back several wooden slats, which were wedged under the wheels. The Poles begged Culliford to try to take off one final time. Everyone got back into the plane.

Now the abused engines grew obstinate. They coughed and sputtered and groaned. Suddenly the engines turned over and roared loudly. The C-47 pulled loose from its vise of sticky mud, rolled down the runway, and lifted into the air. A flood of cheers rocked the plane. Glancing back, crewmen saw a string of vehicle headlights moving toward the airstrip.

Forty-eight hours later the C-47 landed in England, and British scientists began studying the V-2 components. Earlier they had theorized from available information that they could alter a flying missile's course by radio waves, but they soon learned that this would be impossible, because the steering mechanism did not react to radio machinations.

Great Britain was in mortal danger.

Running the entire V-2 operation, on which the Third Reich's survival might well depend, was SS Reichsfuehrer Heinrich Himmler's protégé, young SS General Dr. Hans Kammler, a man cut from the same cloth as his mentor. Hitler no longer trusted his army generals, so Kammler did not report to the Oberkommando der Wehrmacht (high command), but directly to Himmler, who kept the fuehrer briefed.

General Kammler was no fool. He knew that the buzzbomb sites along the English Channel in France had been erected in sparsely populated areas, so the Allies had sent over large bombing fleets to plaster the sites, without fear of massacring countless numbers of civilians. Now Kammler had his V-2 sites set up in the heart of Holland urban centers, including The Hague, a city with a population of about four hundred thousand, and its suburb of Wassenaar. If the Allies tried to carpet-bomb missile-launching sites (in the hope that an occasional bomb might hit a target), they would slaughter thousands of Dutch civilians.

Just prior to 7:00 P.M. on September 8, while many Londoners were eating dinner, a terrific explosion rocked the suburb of Chiswick. It sounded like a thunderclap, but the sky was clear. Terrified citizens dashed for basements, unaware that Adolf Hitler's first V-2 missile had arrived. The blast demolished nineteen Chiswick houses and gouged out a 30-foot-deep crater in the ground. Scores of dead and injured were dug out of the ruins. More missiles rained down on London. British authorities quickly clamped a muzzle on any mention of the V-2's, and it would be more than two months before the British public learned details of the ghastly new weapon.

In desperation the Allied brain trust decided to pinpoint-bomb the V-2 sites, but where were these invisible sites? Four teams of Dutch agents were parachuted into Holland in mid-September to ferret out missile-launching pads, storage depots, and fuel tanks; then they were to radio their findings to London. Two of the teams prowled Holland for several weeks, but were able only to report on the general locales the Germans were using to launch missiles. *Boucle,* code name of a Belgian underground circuit, penetrated Reich territory and sent word to London that some V-2's were being launched from Bonn, on the Rhine River.[2]

Sporadic efforts to knock out the elusive and invisible V-2-launching sites by pinpoint bombings did nothing to halt or even diminish the death and destruction being heaped upon London. Heavy pressure was exerted on Supreme Commander Eisenhower to scrap strategic plans that called for Allied armies to storm across the Rhine River on a broad front and drive on into the heart of the Third Reich, leaving Holland in the backwash of war and in German hands.

Forty-eight hours after the first V-2 exploded in Chiswick, Field Marshal Bernard Montgomery (he had been promoted on September 1) called on Eisenhower to present a bold plan of action: his Army Group would make a lunge deep into Holland, cross the Rhine River at Arnhem, and then dash on toward Berlin. The operation (code-named Market-Garden) would also wipe out the V-2 menace, Monty stressed.

General Eisenhower was astonished by the audacity of the plan. Customarily cautious and methodical in battle, Montgomery now proposed a daring parachute drop and glider landing by an entire airborne army, the largest of its kind in history. The U.S. 82d and 101st Airborne Divisions, the British 1st Airborne Division, and the Polish 1st Parachute Brigade would seize a number of key bridges over the multitude of waterways that crisscrossed Holland. They would lay down "airborne carpets" from Eindhoven (near the British frontlines) up through Nijmegen and on to Arnhem—a narrow javelin thrust sixty miles deep into German-controlled territory.

Along this corridor, tanks and Tommies of Lieutenant

General Brian Horrocks's XXX Corps were to dash at full speed all the way to Arnhem, where the crucial objective of Market-Garden, the bridge over the Rhine (known in this region as the Neder Rijn) was to be captured and held by Red Devils of the British 1st Airborne Division.

Bernard Montgomery never drank, smoked, or cursed, and he was in bed each night by 10:00 P.M. Nor had he ever gambled. Now the peppery little field marshal was proposing one of the war's greatest gambles. However, Eisenhower, who also had one eye on the secret missile sites, bought Montgomery's plan.[3]

Now Allied intelligence broke down, possibly because of the fact that energetic Abwehr Major Hermann Giskes' Operation North Pole had virtually wiped out the Dutch underground. Montgomery believed that he was facing only a ragtag, decimated, and demoralized Wehrmacht in Holland. Actually two crack SS panzer divisions, full of fight, were concealed in the forests and villages around Arnhem and its key bridge.

At 2:30 P.M. on Sunday, September 17, the vanguard of three Allied airborne divisions and a brigade, packed into twenty-eight hundred transport planes and sixteen hundred gliders, began bailing out and crash-landing along the 60-mile corridor. Almost at once the missile assault on London virtually ceased, as General Kammler, reacting swiftly to the sudden threat against his launching sites, pulled back his V-2's to population centers to the north and east.

For ten days bitter fighting raged, but Operation Market-Garden ended in failure for the Allies. Horrocks's ground troops had been halted a short distance below the crucial bridge at Arnhem, which had been captured and held for four days and nights by a battalion of Lieutenant Colonel John Frost's Red Berets. (Frost had led the February 1942 parachute raid on Bruneval, France, in which the German radar was stolen.) Colonel Frost had been seriously wounded in the savage fight for the Arnhem bridge, and he and the remnants of his battalion, reduced to some 100 men, were taken prisoners. About one-third of the 34,876 Allied airborne soldiers who fought between Eindhoven and Arnhem had been killed, wounded, or captured.[4]

Battered London's respite from missile carnage was short-lived. As soon as the Wehrmacht had halted Operation Market-Garden, General Kammler rushed his V-2's back into the heart of The Hague, and the next day explosions again were rocking the British capital. Now Hitler gave orders to divide the missile targets between London and Antwerp, the finest port in northwest Europe, through which was pouring most of the supplies for the Allied armies.

At the same time, thirty-five hundred miles from exploding V-2's, a group of Americans was considering ways to undermine the fuehrer.

Cowboys and Choirboys

By the fall of 1944, the U.S. Office of Strategic Services (OSS) had begun to come of age. When General "Wild Bill" Donovan had created the cloak-and-dagger agency four years earlier, it had consisted of himself and seven assistants. His task had been mind-boggling: within months he was to create a global secret service that would try to catch up to those of Germany and other European powers whose clandestine organizations had been in existence for a few centuries. With the help of their British tutors, OSS men learned fast, and the agency mushroomed to all corners of the world, especially into Europe.

Early on, British spy masters had urged Donovan to recruit mainly men and women in their forties and fifties, for they presumably would possess sounder judgment. But such conservative advice did not suit Wild Bill. For his agents—who were to spy, conduct sabotage, and gather information behind enemy lines—the OSS chief preferred younger men (and a few women) whom he described as "hell-raisers who are calculatingly reckless, of disciplined daring and trained for aggressive action." In the OSS these field agents were called Cowboys, because of their wild exploits.

Also, Donovan did collect large numbers of mild-mannered "gray hairs," who were assigned to Dr. Stanley Lovell's Research and Development Division—inventors, scientists, historians, geographers, psychologists, linguists, political scientists, and anthropologists. They came to be known as the Choirboys. Their job was to conduct studies and to dream up unorthodox and devious plots, weapons, and schemes to undermine and befuddle the enemy. One of their infernal devices, developed for use by agents in the field, looked like a common candle, but when the candle had burned down about one-third, the high explosive in the remainder detonated. Another R&D invention was a flashless, nearly silent pistol–machine gun.

The Morale Operations Divisions (MO) consisted mainly of skilled professionals in the mass communications field—journalists, Hollywood screenwriters, advertising and public relations experts, and authors. They cranked out "black"—or covert—propaganda, and their work had so infuriated the Nazis that propaganda chief Josef Goebbels sneeringly lampooned them as "fifty professors, twenty monkeys, ten goats, and twelve guinea pigs."

Among the black-propaganda ploys designed to subvert German morale was the distribution within the Third Reich of phony "German" newspapers containing praise for the fuehrer (to add authenticity) intermingled with hints that Hitler's thousand-year Reich was doomed. Using names culled from German newspapers smuggled out of the country, the OSS black-propaganda experts mailed fake "official" death notices to the families of Wehrmacht soldiers known to be at the fighting fronts.

There was no bottom to MO's bag of tricks. It had become adept at spreading frightening rumors throughout Germany. One rumor that gained widespread currency in the Reich was that the Allies had developed a bomb that sucked oxygen out of the air and caused massive—and agonizing—deaths by suffocation. A tiny outbreak of bubonic plague in German-occupied Rotterdam inspired another MO hoax, the planting of a rumor that the outbreak had been triggered by a new Allied secret weapon—a germ-carrying rocket.

One macabre scheme was implemented by OSS agents while a bloody, seesaw battle was in progress. They planted fake newspaper clippings in the uniforms of dead German soldiers, then cut each corpse's wrists and throat to make it appear the man had reached the end of his tether and had committed

suicide. If Germans found the corpse, they would be likely to
read the phony clipping. It was a pronouncement from SS chief
Heinrich Himmler that any German wife of child-bearing age
who had not had a baby during the previous two years would
have to report for duty to an SS "breeding farm."

By October 1944, in Bern, Switzerland, Allen Dulles, who
was fond of tweed jackets and bow ties, wore rimless spectacles, and was seldom caught without his briar pipe—a stereotype of Hollywood's version of a kindly college professor—for
four years now had been going through the motions of being a
special legal assistant to the American ambassador. In reality
Dulles was the OSS master spy in Europe. As a result of his
presence in neutral Switzerland, adjacent to the Reich border,
Bern had become a hotbed of espionage.

Despite his deceptively mild appearance, Dulles was tough-
minded and cagey. During World War I Dulles had been
stationed in that picturesque city, doing the same job he was
doing a war later—collecting intelligence from inside Germany. In the earlier conflict, however, he had ostensibly been
an employee of the U.S. State Department.

Since his arrival in Bern in 1940, Allen Dulles had enjoyed
phenomenal success in penetrating into the heart of the Reich's
high command and government, mainly through the shrewd
recruitment of Germans who were secretly anti-Hitler. Yet the
OSS station chief's greatest intelligence bonanza, a mild-
mannered, obscure Berlin bureaucrat, Fritz Kolbe, fell unexpectedly into his lap.

Kolbe had been with the German foreign service since the
mid-1920s. His reputation was that of a civil servant who
plugged along without complaint on humdrum administrative
details. His perseverance paid off, and in the early 1940s Kolbe
was appointed assistant to Karl Ritter, Foreign Minister
Joachim von Ribbentrop's liaison to the Reich's military high
command. It was a position of great trust, for Kolbe's job was
to sift through the hundreds of cables that poured into the
Foreign Office each day from Reich diplomatic and military
posts around the world, then place the important ones on the
desk of his boss, Ritter. In this seemingly minor and routine

job, Fritz Kolbe may have known as much about what was going on in the Nazi world as any man alive.

Kolbe had long been anti-Nazi. But in August 1943, convinced that Hitler was racing Germany down the road to ruin, the diminutive bureaucrat decided to take action. He wangled an assignment as a diplomatic courier to Bern and there arranged to meet a British Embassy official. Kolbe, nervous by nature, fussed and fidgeted, and the British official grew suspicious. Even when Kolbe pulled from his pocket a batch of top-secret cables, the Englishman said sternly, "I don't believe you!"

Fritz Kolbe, plunged into gloom by the curt rejection, went to see Allen Dulles's aide, Gerald Mayer, whose cover was that of an employee for the Office of War Information. Mayer, who spoke fluent German, was stupefied when he read three top-secret cables. Mayer took the pilfered cables to his boss, but Dulles was cautious. This could be a Nazi trick to infiltrate the OSS. But Kolbe might be authentic, so a meeting was arranged that night at Dulles's apartment at 23 Herrengasse.

Gerald Mayer was present, and he introduced Dulles as "my assistant, Mr. Douglas." This time Fritz Kolbe was determined not to be rejected. He got down on his hands and knees, opened his briefcase, pulled out nearly two hundred top-secret cables and other documents, and spread them out on the living-room floor. Dulles, who had had a lifetime of shocks and surprises in the turbulent and unpredictable world of global intrigue, could not mask his astonishment.

"Where did you get these?" the OSS boss finally asked.

"I smuggled them out of the Foreign Office a few at a time, strapped to my legs," Kolbe replied softly.

The two "Office of War Information officials"—Dulles and Mayer—spent the night examining the documents. They appeared to be authentic. But as a hedge against the German being a sly double-agent, Dulles asked OSS headquarters in Washington for an investigation of Fritz Kolbe's background. Back came the word: "He is genuine."

Kolbe promptly became an OSS spy and was assigned the code name George Wood. By the end of the war, the man that the British attaché had rejected smuggled out of Germany and to Bern more than sixteen hundred top-secret Foreign Office cables. Allen Dulles would describe him as "an intelligence officer's dream, undoubtedly one of the best [spies] any intelligence service ever had."[1]

Three thousand miles from where Wild Bill Donovan and his operatives were scheming, Colonel David Bruce, the courtly OSS station chief in London, and his top men were working with the British SOE to concoct a plan to murder Hitler. The fuehrer would be gunned down during a daring raid on his headquarters. Captured German generals being held in England were interrogated in an effort to obtain detailed information on Hitler's personal routine, his headquarters layout and security arrangements, and the habits of his entourage.

After plans for the raid had been finalized, British and American leaders began having second thoughts. At this stage of the war (October 1944), with Germany hanging on by its fingertips, would the murder of Hitler be in the Allies' best interest? It would be a suicide mission, so should a large number of American and British paratroopers and Commandos be sacrificed when everyone in London knew that the war was as good as over? Besides, Ultra in Bletchley Park was still revealing all German plans and most troop movements and dispositions, and Hitler's successor might junk Enigma and turn to another communications vehicle. So why risk shutting off Ultra's enormous military advantage? The raid to murder the fuehrer was quietly abandoned.

On a dark night in September 1944, a former German trade union official, Jupp Kapius, parachuted into the Ruhr, the Reich's industrial heartland in which the sinews of war were being turned out. Kapius (code-named Downend) was an agent in the OSS Labor Division, which had been set up and directed by George Pratt, general counsel for the National Labor Relations Board, and by Major Arthur Goldberg, a Chicago labor lawyer (who would later become a Supreme Court justice).

Downend's mission was an especially hazardous one. As a German national, his fate if captured by the Gestapo would be even more horrendous than would be the agony and torment of non-German spies. Undaunted, Downend set to work. Within a few weeks he organized a number of cells of factory workers, who furnished him with crucial information on German war production. Downend instructed his war-plant agents to encourage work slow-downs, even sabotage, in their factories.

OSS leaders in London were astonished over the gold mine of intelligence culled by their master labor spy. Downend, constantly facing sudden arrest, radioed back data on bomb damage and on occasion furnished German plans for rebuilding destroyed factories.[2]

After the bloody nose inflicted on the Allies in Operation Market-Garden, Adolf Hitler had succeeded in stabilizing the Western Front. All that fall and on into the winter, the adversaries, pounded by torrential rains, engaged in a brutal slugging match: Walcheren Island (to clear sea approaches to Antwerp), Aachen, the Huertgen Forest, the Roer dams, the Saar Basin, and the Vosges Mountains. Allied casualties were heavy, and the gains were measured in yards. But SHAEF was gripped by heady optimism, convinced that the Reich was about to disintegrate.

Adolf Hitler was fully aware that powerful American, British, and French armies were massed at the front that stretched for five hundred miles along the German border, from Holland to the Swiss frontier. And he knew that the Allies were preparing to launch one final full-blooded offensive that would smash into the heart of the Reich and end the war.

Time. That was what Hitler needed. Time to turn out new secret *Wunderwaffen* (wonder weapons), which could snatch final victory from the jaws of defeat. Time to produce hundreds of his revolutionary Messerschmitt ME-262 jet fighter planes, which would render obsolete the Allies' huge propeller-driven air armadas and sweep them from the skies. A few of the jets were already operational over the Western Front, and the fuehrer rejoiced in a report that a single jet had shot down thirty-seven Anglo-American bombers.

Inside the enormous labyrinth of tunnels and caves (codenamed Dora) in the rugged Harz Mountains of central Germany, thousands of slave laborers under the direction of German technicians were toiling around the clock under inhuman conditions to turn out the jets, which were far faster and more maneuverable than anything the Allies could put in the sky.

Also nearly ready to go into production was a jet-powered, futuristic "flying wing" (code-named Horten) that looked like a huge bat in flight. It could attain a speed of six hundred miles per hour and reach a height of forty thousand feet.

The fuehrer would have taken enormous comfort had he known that the Nazi jet threat and the prospect of hundreds, perhaps thousands, more to be built was "scaring hell" out of the Allied air barons.

At a remote locale in Austria, German technicians were testing the rocket-propelled Natter, a startling new concept for a fighter plane that would be used to defend Fatherland skies. Natter was of simple construction and had a radically new operational technique. Looking much like a buzzbomb (only the Natter was manned), it was catapulted straight up from a launching apparatus and could fly 660 miles per hour. But it had a maximum range of only thirty-six miles, so the pilot was to fire the twenty-four rockets in the nose at enemy bombers, then detach the forward section, ejecting himself. Pilot and engine would then land by separate parachutes, and both would be used again in another Natter.[3]

After having been tossed in jail by Heinrich Himmler and released by Adolf Hitler, Wernher von Braun and fellow scientists were working feverishly on a multistage missile (code-named V-3) that could put a satellite into orbit—or hit New York City, Washington, Philadelphia, and other cities on the American east coast. The fuehrer rubbed his hands in glee over the prospect. But von Braun would need more time.

Under General Walter Dornberger other scientists were developing a remote-controlled rocket that could be guided to its target and destroy Allied bombers over Germany. Also in the works was a new type of submarine that, it was hoped, would be able to travel underwater halfway around the world without surfacing or refueling, a revolutionary weapon that could play havoc with American and British warships and merchant vessels. All this would take time.

Because of these looming Wunderwaffen and his deep-rooted conviction (backed by many historical precedents) that the brittle and squabbling Allied alliance would yet fall apart,

Adolf Hitler found grounds for optimism. But if there was to be a salvation—even ultimate victory—for the Third Reich, the fuehrer's hard-pressed generals and their weary troops would have to buy the needed time on the battlefield.

"The Most Dangerous
Man in Europe"

It was December 12, 1944, a cold, bleak, and rainy day. Milling about ancient Ziegenberg Castle in west Germany near Frankfurt were sixty-one German field marshals and generals from the Western Front. A day earlier each had received a mysterious order to report, alone, to Ziegenberg. This caused deep apprehension, for in recent months Adolf Hitler had had several generals shot. Only Field Marshals Gerd von Rundstedt and Walther Model knew the true reason for the strange proceedings, and they had been forced to sign statements pledging total secrecy—under pain of being summarily shot for violating their oaths.

The anxiety of the generals was heightened when black-uniformed SS troopers took away their sidearms and briefcases (ideal for carrying bombs). Then the commanders were herded out the front door of Ziegenberg Castle. They filed past a cordon of Gestapo agents and climbed aboard an old bus—much like a gang of hardened criminals being moved from one prison to another.

The bus drove in circles about the countryside for an hour, then pulled up in front of a huge concrete bunker a mile outside Ziegenberg. Many on board recognized it as *Adlerhorst* (Eagle's Nest), Adolf Hitler's command bunker in the West. A junior SS officer ordered the commanders to leave the bus, and they walked through two files of SS and Gestapo men into Adlerhorst, where they were escorted into a large conference room and told to take seats. Hard wooden chairs had been arranged in rows, like those in children's schoolrooms. Fifteen minutes later the fuehrer strode into the room.

To those who had long known him, Hitler's haggard appearance came as a shock. He seemed to be a broken man, with an unhealthy color and trembling hands—a man suddenly grown old at age fifty-five.

As a hush fell over the room, Hitler began talking about great victories of his Teutonic idol, Frederick the Great, and of the glories of the Nazi Party. He rambled on for an hour. The commanders had heard all this before, but each appeared to listen intently. All the while the sharp-eyed SS troopers and Gestapo agents standing around the room stared at the field marshals and generals. None dared to fidget in his hard chair or even to reach for a handkerchief to mop his perspiring brow for fear that the gesture would be interpreted as going for a concealed pistol.

Suddenly the fuehrer paused. Now breathing the fire of bygone glory days he exclaimed, "I have made a momentous decision. I will take the offensive in the West!" Pointing to a huge wall map, Hitler said, "I will strike the enemy here—in the Ardennes."

Accustomed to a two-year diet of defeats and bad news, the Wehrmacht commanders were thunderstruck. Take the offensive? With what? Few were aware that for two months Hitler had secretly been hording two powerful panzer armies with which to strike the overconfident Americans.

Adolf Hitler's final roll of the dice for victory in the West would depend upon surprise. Surprise was crucial. And it would be obtained through an ingenious deception, one that would keep the Allies ignorant of the fact that two panzer armies were being infiltrated into the Ardennes—a feat equivalent to moving, undetected, the entire population, with all the automobiles and trucks, of Cincinnati, Ohio, or Liverpool, England.

Even the locale of the attack had been selected to surprise the Allies. Sparsely populated, hilly, heavily wooded, and surfeited with deep gorges, the Ardennes had few roads capable of supporting tanks and vehicles. In winter these difficulties would be compounded. This 75-mile-long sector of Belgium and Luxembourg had become known as the Ghost Front. Both sides used the Ghost Front to "blood" new units and to rest those exhausted by battle. Seldom was a shot fired in this sector. For three months there had been something of an unspoken agreement between the two adversaries: "You don't shoot at us, and we won't shoot at you."

Even the code name of Hitler's operation—*Wacht am Rhein* (Watch on the Rhine)—was tailored to surprise the Allies by giving the impression that the Germans were preparing for a last-ditch stand at that historic water barrier to the Third Reich.

The tactical plan called for infantry and engineers to punch holes in the thinly held American lines; then hundreds of panzers would be unleashed to race northwest to the key Allied port of Antwerp. The American and British armies would be split and never recover from the unexpected debacle, Hitler declared. *O-Tag* (D day) for Wacht am Rhein was only seventy-two hours away—December 16. H hour was 5:30 A.M., just before dawn.

Planning for the offensive had been conducted in Berlin under the most intense security precautions. Those involved had to take pledges of silence, with the death penalty to be imposed for violations. Each planning officer had been assigned a code name, which was changed every two weeks. Cities, rivers, and topographic landmarks all had code names. Even when two planning officers were alone in a room, they had never spoken of the true names of places (the room might be bugged).

Four days prior to O-Tag, the airwaves on the German side had gone "dead"—a customary clue that an attack was imminent. Allied monitors were aware of the radio blackout, but no one seemed to be unduly concerned. Nor did anyone in the Allied camp read anything sinister into the fact that Ultra had failed to pick up Enigma signals in recent days—for the first time since war had broken out five years earlier. (All German communications were by land wires or couriers. Hitler had begun to suspect that the Allies were intercepting Enigma traffic.)

Before the German radio traffic was shut down, Field

Marshal Model had sent out to all generals on the Western Front a directive, in a simple code that the Allies could easily break, that stated offensive plans should be abandoned, for all forces were needed to defend the Third Reich. To further confuse the Allies, the Germans set up a radio network north of the Ardennes that simulated the presence of a phantom Twenty-fifth Army.

In another ploy, code-named Operation Heinrich, panzers and large numbers of infantry units began shuffling about frantically behind German lines opposite Aachen, some thirty to forty miles north of where the offensive would strike. This was to convey to the Allies the impression that the Germans were preparing to oppose a threatened American attack from the Aachen region. Just prior to O-Tag many of these decoy forces would suddenly be shifted southward and join in the Ardennes operation.

Meanwhile, the citizens of Bastogne, a quiet little Belgian town in the Ardennes, had been fearful for days. They had seen subtle signs that a calamity was about to strike the town. In Bastogne's marketplace and in the countryside, frightened neighbors whispered to each other that the dreaded Hun was coming back. They told of seeing "strange lights" in the fields around Bastogne in the stillness of the night and of sinister-looking strangers in civilian clothes moving around the area: German spies, they were convinced.

In desperation a delegation of Bastogne citizens called at the U.S. VIII Corps headquarters inside the town, where they relayed their fears to a pair of polite but bored staff captains. Assured that the situation would be investigated, the partially relieved Belgians departed. As they closed the door behind them, one American captain pointed to his head, grinned, and told his comrade: "Spy mania!" The two men went back to playing cards.

Far from the Ardennes, in Allied prisoner-of-war camps in France, Belgium, and England, leaders among the captured Germans were drawing up clandestine plans for mass breakouts to support the impending Ardennes offensive. (The POWs had established contact with Wacht am Rhein planning headquarters, probably through coded messages in routine-appearing letters from "family members.") In the breakouts the German POWs were to secure weapons by seizing lightly guarded arsenals, steal tanks, and create confusion far to the rear of Allied lines. (The scheme would be thwarted when agents, planted among the German POWs, tipped off the Allies.)

During the first two weeks of December, Wehrmacht assault units began stealing into the Ardennes under scrupulously rigid security procedures. All vehicle movements into the Ghost Front (and for one hundred miles behind it) were made only at night. Orders had been given to shoot out the tires of any vehicle moving in daylight. Supplied with prime movers, winches, and sand, a special road service was organized to assist tanks and trucks in distress and to get them off the roads before daylight.

Straw was spread over the roads to muffle the sound of tank treads and artillery pieces, and the big guns were pulled by horses shod with specially padded shoes. Officers were designated to be road commanders, and their word was law. They were to enforce camouflage measures stringently and to keep vehicles off the roads during the day; in flagrant cases of violation, the road commanders were empowered to arrest or even to shoot the offenders—no matter what their rank.

As troops, panzers, and guns edged closer to jump-off positions on successive nights, Luftwaffe planes flying low up and down the front lines helped to mute the noise. Assault units were forbidden to send out reconnaissance patrols, which might be captured. General of Panzer Troops Hasso von Manteuffel, the leader of the Fifth Panzer Army, disguised himself in the uniform of an infantry colonel to go forward to discuss the front line situation with his regimental commanders; ostensibly "Colonel" Manteuffel was reconnoitering routes for the routine relief of a division.

Charcoal was issued to field kitchens so that smoke from wood cooking fires would not betray the presence of large formations behind the Ghost Front. Marketing roads and routes to various headquarters, a routine procedure, was strictly forbidden; an Allied spy would recognize from the signs that there had been large-scale troop movements into the Ardennes. Potential deserters who might tip off the Americans were the targets of an edict issued by SS Reichsfuehrer Heinrich Himmler: the family of any deserter would be sent to a concentration camp—or shot.

German generals along the Western Front, who were drawing up orders for their units in the attack, had to do so themselves in longhand. Gestapo agents were assigned to each major headquarters to guard against treachery by the generals.

Two months prior to O-Tag, SS Colonel Otto Skorzeny, a folk hero in the Reich, a villain in the Allied world, had been summoned by Adolf Hitler: "Skorzeny, I have a mission for you that may well decide whether Germany lives or dies!" Thus, on the eve of the Ardennes offensive, the hulking giant was ready to spring into action with one of the war's strangest hoaxes.

At the Gräfenwohr Training Ground in Bavaria, Skorzeny had collected and trained a force of English-speaking German soldiers, who were equipped with authentic American weapons, trucks, armored cars, jeeps, and two Sherman tanks—all of which had been captured earlier. Wearing genuine American uniforms, some seventy-five *Skorzeny-Leute* (Skorzeny people) would join the spearheads, fan out behind disorganized American lines, create fear and confusion, and engage in sabotage. The subterfuge was code-named Operation *Greif* (Griffin).[1]

Some two thousand German soldiers and sailors, claiming that they spoke fluent English, had reported to Gräfenwohr. Tests showed that only a small percentage were competent in the English language. Much of the short time Colonel Skorzeny had to prepare for his crucial mission was devoted to turning German men into "genuine GIs." The volunteers watched American films and were smuggled into POW camps to mingle with unsuspecting GIs and to try to pick up their idiom, slang, and curse words. Skorzeny's men even practiced chewing gum American style (Germans believed that all American soldiers chewed gum).

By December 13 (O-Tag minus 3) Skorzeny's infiltration teams had slipped into the Ardennes and hidden in a forest. There they were taken into a large tent, where a crate was opened. Eyes of the Greif men bugged out. The crate was crammed with huge numbers of American greenbacks and

British pound notes (all counterfeit, probably printed in Major Bernhard Krüger's concentration-camp plant). The money was distributed. Then other crates were opened, and their contents were also allocated—genuine American cigarettes, tins of coffee, matches, and canned rations.

Skorzeny's men did not know that the currency was phony, but it was obviously brand-new, and they spent considerable time soiling and crumpling it to give it the appearance of having been used. The money was for bribing Belgian officials or perhaps GI guards if the German imposters were captured.

Yet another crate held hundreds of American cigarette lighters. The lighters were authentic, but the cotton in each one held a vial of cyanide. If about to be captured, the Greif man could bite the cyanide container, guaranteeing a quick death.[2]

From a large pile of GI dog tags and documents (taken from dead or captured Americans), each German infiltrator had been furnished with the genuine identity of a U.S. soldier—presto, a Sergeant Fritz Ohlendorf would become a Private John Brown.

While Otto Skorzeny's men had been practicing GI slang and the art of chewing gum, 37-year-old parachute Colonel Friedrich August Baron von der Heydte was trying to whip into shape a force of twelve hundred *Fallshirmjaeger* (paratroopers). Under a heavy veil of secrecy, von der Heydte's men had been collected from scattered units and told that they were to jump behind Russian lines, surrounding a hard-pressed German bridgehead on the Vistula River in Poland. Only on December 13—three days before O-Tag—was Colonel von der Heydte informed that he and his paratroopers were not to jump behind Russian lines, but instead would be attached to Generaloberst SS Josef "Sepp" Dietrich's Sixth Panzer Army on the Western Front.

Secretly, von der Heydte was depressed. He had been promised crack, combat-experienced paratroopers, but had been saddled with a ragtag collection of misfits. Few had seen battle, many had never jumped from a flying airplane. Only twenty-four hours before jump-off in the Ardennes, the colonel learned that his objective was a crossroads south of Liège, Belgium, to block American reinforcements that would be heading down to the Ardennes from the north. He was jolted by another surprise: he and his men were to bail out wearing captured triangular-shaped Russian parachutes—which might or might not open.

Only hours before lifting off for the Ardennes, von der Heydte received a shipment of three hundred straw dummies. Taking a page out of the Allied hoax playbook, a ploy used in the Normandy D day parachute operations, German airborne planners had decided to drop these dummies (in worn-out parachutes) over a wide expanse of the Ardennes to confuse the Americans about the true German drop zone and the size of von der Heydte's unit.

At dawn on December 15, two American jeeps, carrying Skorzeny's people wearing American uniforms, slipped through the Ghost Front lines to launch Operation Während, a scheme to disrupt Allied supply lines. With them were more than twenty-five million French and Belgian francs (all of them phony). Their mission was to contact German agents in Belgium and Holland and divide the money between them. The agents in turn were to contact dockworkers in Antwerp and railroad workers at key yards and to bribe them with a week's wages not to report to their work for a week (while the German offensive was taking place). This, according to plan, would result in a drastic slowdown in the unloading of Allied supplies. The harebrained stratagem fizzled, and only about half of the Operation Während men would eventually manage to slip back to German lines.

It was 5:28 A.M. on December 16. Silence continued to reign along the Ghost Front. Except for a few going through the motions of outpost and guard duty, American soldiers were sleeping peacefully in warm and comfortable lodgings. Suddenly the hush was shattered by an ear-splitting roar, as nineteen hundred German guns began pouring death and destruction on American positions, headquarters, and installations. When the terrifying bombardment lifted after forty minutes, tens of thousands of German assault infantrymen, supported by nearly one thousand panzers, plunged into the thinly held chaotic American lines and began the dash for Antwerp. Operation *Herbstnebel* (Autumn Mist), as the assault phase was code-named, had gained the crucial ingredient for success—total surprise.

Now Colonel Skorzeny's seventy-five English-speaking commandos were ready to go into action. Riding three or four to a jeep in fourteen vehicles, they would have to crisscross Belgium several times, so there was always the possibility that the various teams would interfere with each other's activities. Foreseeing this, Skorzeny had established recognition signals. Each German infiltrator wore a blue or pink scarf, a neck adornment many GIs had affected. The second button from the top of each imposter's field jacket was left undone, and painted on the American jeeps were the inconspicuous letters CD, X, Y, or Z. A Greif man was to identify himself to a suspected GI imposter with two taps on the helmet, and after dark by two flashes from a blue light, which was to be answered with a series of red flashes.

On the heels of the German spearheads, Skorzeny's people, wearing American uniforms and driving American vehicles, spread out behind American "lines." They ambushed vehicles carrying officers and shot couriers; planted signs along roads, marking nonexistent minefields; cut telephone lines; blew up isolated vehicles; and created panic among excited, confused, and largely green Americans.

In the meantime Colonel Friedrich von der Heydte's twelve hundred paratroopers had jumped behind American lines in the Ardennes. The colonel, who had bailed out with a broken arm received in a training mishap, crashed to the frozen earth and blacked out. When he regained consciousness, von der Heydte was alone in the darkness. By dawn he had collected six men—five frightened teenagers seeking their first action and a sergeant with an injured ankle. At daybreak another twenty or so men joined their commander.

The tiny band struggled to the task force's objective, the key Belle-Croix crossroads, and lay in a roadside ditch and watched helplessly as a long convoy of trucks packed with men of the American 1st Infantry Division (the Big Red One) rolled past to confront the German spearheads. Von der Heydte knew that his mission had failed—militarily.[3]

Psychologically, however, the bungled parachute operation was a bonanza, helping to trigger mass panic among civilians

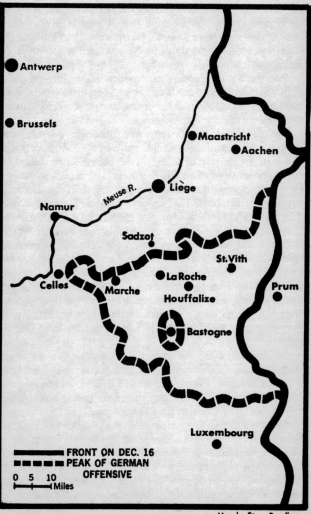

Antwerp

Brussels

Maastricht
Aachen

Meuse R.   Liège

Namur

Sadzot

St.Vith

Celles   La Roche   Prum

Marche   Houffalize

Bastogne

Luxembourg

FRONT ON DEC. 16
PEAK OF GERMAN
OFFENSIVE
0 5 10
Miles

Map by Steve Brodhage

and Allied soldiers over much of Europe. Flying in darkness, the inexperienced Luftwaffe pilots had dropped their cargoes all over Belgium and beyond. Far to the north German paratroopers came down behind British lines in Holland, and other parachutists were reported far to the south in France. The three hundred straw dummies were scattered wildly over the Ardennes—only partly by design.

Wild rumors of German paratroopers hiding behind every bush began to flood the Allied camp. Soon there were reports that ten to fifteen thousand enemy parachutists, armed to the teeth, were roaming the Ardennes.

Two days after the German breakthrough, an American military policeman at Aywaille, eleven miles south of a key Wehrmacht objective of Liège on the Meuse River, asked for the password from three GIs in a jeep. The occupants did not know the password, not an unusual event in the chaos in American ranks, but the MP grew suspicious. The men showed their GI dog tags, which identified them as Privates Charles W. Lawrence, George Sensenbach, and Clarence van der Werth.

Clearly the halted men were nervous. The MP pointed his rifle at them and yelled, "Hands up!" Other MPs rushed up and took the three soldiers into custody. Concealed in the jeep was a German revolver, two American Colt .45s, two English submachine guns, and six American grenades. On their persons were German military paybooks (an incredible security lapse), one thousand American dollars, and one thousand English pounds.

On December 22 the three Skorzeny men were court-martialed under their real German names and ranks—Sergeant Wilhelm Schmidt, Corporal Guenther Billing, and naval cadet Manfred Pernass. The next day they were tied to poles, blindfolded, and shot to death by a firing squad.

As the result of the apprehension at Aywaille, word quickly spread through the U.S. Army that "thousands" of cutthroat Germans dressed as American officers and soldiers, fluent in English and well armed, were stalking around behind American "lines," which by now had collapsed. Tensions bordering on paranoia permeated some American units. No one trusted another unless he recognized his face.

An American colonel, commanding an infantry regiment,

inadvertently strayed into the area of another GI unit while wearing a pair of fleece-lined German boots. He was disarmed and locked in a barn for eight hours, until officers arrived to vouch for his true identity.

Military police roadblocks were set up at hundreds of places in Belgium. Not even generals were beyond suspicion. Omar Bradley, commander of Twelfth Army Group, one morning was halted ten times in three miles while calling on combat-unit headquarters. MPs were taking to heart the stern admonition: "Take no one at face value." Some long-suffering military policemen no doubt relished their new authority to halt and quiz generals before "permitting" the brass to proceed.

German spies and saboteurs and killers were spotted everywhere, and hundreds of genuine Americans were arrested because they did not know the password or because they "looked suspicious." Hulking Brigadier General Bruce Clarke of the 7th Armored Division, whose remnants were making a last-ditch stand at the key road junction of Saint Vith, was halted by a pair of MPs.

"I'm General Bruce Clarke of CCB [Combat Command B]," the angry armored leader protested repeatedly.

"The hell you are," an MP shouted. "You're one of Skorzeny's bastards. We were told to be on the lookout for a Kraut posing as a one-star general!"

While Clarke ranted and raved, his captors kept him locked up for five hours. All over the Ardennes a half million Americans played a cat-and-mouse game with each other—all because of seventy-five Skorzeny men.

Aided incalculably by a SHAEF-imposed news blackout on what was taking place in the Ardennes, the Skorzeny "killers on the loose" hysteria spread rapidly to the civilian population far from the turmoil in Belgium. No longer was the swashbuckling and notorious (in Allied eyes) SS colonel searching merely for military victims, he was dedicated to murdering any man, woman, or child he could get in his bloody clutches—or so the civilian populations in Belgium, France, Luxembourg, and Holland had started to believe. The mass hysteria among civilians heightened when headlines in European newspapers tagged Skorzeny with the sinister sobriquet: The Most Dangerous Man in Europe.

* * *

On December 20 Paris police distributed tens of thousands of pictures of "The Most Dangerous Man in Europe." Hard on the heels of the mass distribution of the photos, Paris police compounded the hysteria. They announced that German paratroopers had landed near SHAEF headquarters in the Trianon Palace in Versailles, outside Paris. SHAEF was turned into an armed fortress. The guard was doubled, then quadrupled, as reports arrived that Skorzeny and his men were bearing down on Paris to murder General Eisenhower. At the same time, the SS colonel was reliably reported to be in Bordeaux, Cherbourg, Marseilles, Lyons, Brussels, Brest, and scores of other towns large and small, in France and Belgium.

Wild rumors were not limited to the sophisticated capital of France. At Valenciennes, a nervous police official informed the citizens that Otto Skorzeny and his "murderers," dressed as priests and nuns, had parachuted to earth just outside the town. For several days doors and windows were kept shut and tightly locked. Few civilians dared to venture into the streets. Genuine priests and nuns remained inside for more than a week, fearful that mayhem might be committed on their persons by a frightened and panicky populace that might mistake them for Skorzeny's killers.

At Meaux, east of Paris, a man in civilian clothes was collared by gendarmes and hustled off to jail, where he was vigorously grilled despite his protests that he was a longtime resident of the city. Only later would the man learn that he had been fingered by a woman as being Otto Skorzeny. He even had the telltale facial scar, the excited woman had told police over the telephone. Eventually the man was released. He stood five feet five (a full twelve inches shorter than Skorzeny), and his "facial scar" was a small nick received when he had been shaving that morning.

In the meantime SHAEF panic grew more intense. General Eisenhower was one of the few in his headquarters who refused to succumb to Skorzeny mania. Ike railed against the elaborate security precautions taken to protect him from "The Most Dangerous Man in Europe." Then Colonel Gordon Sheen, SHAEF security officer, briefed the supreme commander on details of the Skorzeny plot to murder Eisenhower. Sheen said that the SS colonel and fifty of his assassins were to rendezvous in Paris at the Café de la Paix on the Place de l'Opéra and proceed from there to Versailles. Actually, his cloak-and-dagger murder scenario had been concocted on the spur of the moment by Lieutenant Guenther Schulz, who, along with three other Skorzeny men in American uniforms, had been apprehended the day before near Namur, Belgium, on the Meuse River. The glib Guenther Schulz had spoken freely (and falsely) of Skorzeny's objectives, the principal one of which, so said Schulz, was murdering Eisenhower. The doomed German had even invented details of the nonexistent assassination plot.

Now the alarmed Colonel Sheen was proposing a ploy to foil the plot. Reluctantly, Eisenhower agreed to it, "but only so you people will let me get back to running the war."

The supreme commander moved from his villa in Saint-Germain-en-Laye to a house close to SHAEF headquarters. Then an officer who bore a remarkable resemblance to Eisenhower, Lieutenant Colonel Baldwin B. Smith, was instantly "promoted" to five-star general. He moved into the Saint-Germain-en-Laye villa and twice each day, in Eisenhower's Packard with its five-star flag, drove to headquarters and back.

American counterintelligence officers established an ambush (including the use of two tanks) around the Café de la Paix, but neither Skorzeny nor any of his men showed up. Scarface Otto, in fact, had never gotten within two hundred miles of the French capital, nor had any of his men. Throughout what became known as the Battle of the Bulge, Skorzeny would wear only his regular SS colonel's uniform.

In the meantime the hysteria pot in the Allied camp was kept boiling. The German-language "black radio" in England broadcast that 250 of Skorzeny's men in American uniforms had been captured (only 3 had been apprehended at that time). A newspaper in Nice, on the French Riviera hundreds of miles from the Ardennes, reported that Scarface Otto's cutthroats had landed by parachute and robbed a Nice bank (which no doubt took the heat off the real perpetrators of the heist). And an otherwise staid London newspaper solemnly published a story that beautiful, English-speaking German women, armed with sharp knives, had been recruited by Skorzeny to parachute behind American lines. Their mission was to seduce GIs and stab them in the back while a torrid romantic interlude was in progress. Seven of these Teutonic Mata Haris had already been arrested, the London paper reported.

Taken within the context of the mass hysteria, these preposterous rumors were accepted as gospel truth by millions in the Allied camp—civilian and military. The panic and confusion generated by only seventy-five Skorzeny people (augmented by von der Heydte's bungled paratroop operation) no doubt exceeded even the wildest dreams of the architect of this *ruse de guerre*—Adolf Hitler.[4]

In the meantime more than a million American and German soldiers clashed in a savage, no-holds-barred, no-quarter-asked-and-none-given fight to the death in brutal, freezing weather. Thirty days later remnants of the Wehrmacht, who had burst into American positions with the battle cry "On to Antwerp!" ringing in their ears, limped back behind the Siegfried Line. The fuehrer's final hope for victory in the West had been smashed.

Bloody fighting lay ahead, but in March 1945 Allied armies poured over the Rhine River and began racing into the Reich's heartland. On April 28, with the Russian Army only a few blocks away in pulverized Berlin, Adolf Hitler put the muzzle of a Lüger to his head and pulled the trigger. The fuehrer had lost the shooting war as well as the secret war with the Western Allies.

EPILOGUE

Peace in Europe brought with it the annihilation of Adolf Hitler's Third Reich. Victory may have come none too soon. Shortly after hostilities ceased, Allied air barons found that their fears of the awesome potential of the Germans' revolutionary jet fighter planes were fully justified. U.S. Air Corps Generals Carl Spaatz and Hoyt Vandenberg asked Reich Marshal Hermann Goering if the jets could have altered the outcome of the conflict.

The rotund Luftwaffe chief replied that if Hitler had had only four months' more time, the jets could have won the war by eventually driving the Allied propeller-driven armadas from the skies. He pointed out that one underground factory (in the Harz Mountains of central Germany), ready for full production when it was overrun by the Americans in April 1945, would have produced twelve hundred Messerschmitt jets each month. "With five or six thousand jets, the outcome [of the war] would have been quite different," Goering declared. He added that there was a surplus of jet pilots and that underground factories had been set up for fuel.

In the final months of the war, SS Colonel Otto Skorzeny had been the driving force behind top-secret Operation Suicide, a project undertaken out of desperation and patterned after the Japanese kamikazes who wreaked havoc on American warships in the Pacific. At a secret airfield at Larz, German scientists had built a modified buzzbomb (V-1), which carried a pilot, and attached it to the underside of a Heinkel bomber. The bomber-buzzbomb combination took off, and at a designated point the V-1 and its pilot dropped free of the mother craft, and the manned flying bomb was steered toward its objective (in real action the V-1 and its pilot would crash into the target).[1]

Skorzeny was ecstatic over the successful test, and he began recruiting volunteer pilots who would knowingly bring about their own deaths. But by late 1944 the Third Reich was at bay, and the SS colonel was sidetracked from his kamikaze project into Operation Greif, the infiltrating of German commandos in American uniforms during the Battle of the Bulge.

At war's end Colonel Skorzeny surrendered peacefully to American soldiers. Military policemen, no doubt awed by Skorzeny's reputation as "The Most Dangerous Man in Europe," promptly handcuffed him with his arms behind his back and kept their weapons pointed at the unarmed colonel. The Allies tried Skorzeny for "war crimes" in the Operation Greif affair, but the case took a curious twist. RAF Wing Commander Forrest Yeo-Thomas, one of Britain's most gallant and daring secret agents, who had been captured and tortured by the Gestapo, took the stand as a surprise witness for the defense. Code-named White Rabbit, Yeo-Thomas told the trial court of nine American officers that, when he had been an Allied agent in German-held France, he had dressed some of his partisans in Wehrmacht uniforms and supplied them with fake German papers. He had then stolen a German vehicle and rigged it to resemble a prison van and sent the underground men into a Gestapo-run prison in Brittany to hoodwink the Germans into releasing a prisoner.

"If the Gestapo had not released the prisoner," Yeo-Thomas testified, "we would have disposed of the guards quickly and silently."

"How did you obtain German uniforms?" Skorzeny's American attorney asked.

"I cannot give you the details," White Rabbit replied. "I had merely ordered that they be obtained by hook or by crook."

That remark was not lost on the court; in wartime France there would have been only one way to obtain German uniforms. The case against Colonel Skorzeny collapsed.

In another curious postwar turn of events, Abwehr Major Hermann Giskes, the mastermind of Operation North Pole, which had wiped out the Dutch underground, was arrested by the Allies. After months of interrogation, Giskes was released and eventually went to work for an old boss, General Reinhard Gehlen, Hitler's shadowy spy master for Russian intelligence. Gehlen was later recommended to Washington by an American wartime intelligence officer, for the German had vast knowledge of the Soviet spy apparatus. By early 1948 both Gehlen and Giskes were said to be working for the CIA.

With the final huge Allied offensive in March 1945, Holland was overrun along with the V-1 and V-2 launching sites. The last missile exploded on London on March 27 (killing 127 civilians), and the final buzzbomb struck the British capital two days later. But the missiles chief, SS General Hans Kammler, acting under Hitler's orders, collected as many V-2's as he could from Holland and hurried into the Harz Mountains.[2]

For several months the Allied high command had fretted about a so-called Nazi redoubt in the Alps of southern Germany, into which the fuehrer, his top honchos, and two hundred thousand crack SS troops would withdraw and defy efforts to dig them out of the rugged mountain terrain. After storming across the Rhine, American spearheads began racing for the alpine redoubt to seize it before the SS troops could become entrenched. But the Allies had been hoodwinked. The redoubt had been but a hoax, one created by the cunning genius of Nazi propaganda minister Josef Goebbels.

Now General Kammler, in accordance with the fuehrer's orders, began preparing a last-ditch redoubt, not in the Alps, but in the Harz Mountains, where an underground factory was still turning out missiles and buzzbombs. A site for launching missiles toward London was set up on a plateau, and underground lodging was being rapidly established for technicians and firing crews.[3]

On April 1, 1945, the SS general received a final order from Hitler: the Harz Mountains redoubt was to be defended to the last man. A few days later American spearheads overran Kammler's stronghold; he had not been able to fire a single missile from that locale.[4]

For the most part, Allied undercover machinations were cloaked in impenetrable secrecy for thirty years after the war. Even the existence of Ultra and Colonel John Bevan's London Controlling Section remained secret until 1974; they might have to be employed in another major war—this one against Russia.

When SOE and its subordinate XX-Committee went out of business, most of their guiding lights disappeared from public view. Many were bitter. Strident voices demanded "public explanations" for the deaths of scores of SOE agents and hundreds of those who had helped them in Nazi-occupied countries. General Sir Colin Gubbins, SOE chief during the last two war years, remained silent, his lips sealed by the Official Secrets Act. But he received a postwar letter from General Eisenhower that stated: "I express my great admiration for the brave and often spectacular exploits of the agents and special groups under [your] control."[5]

There was an especially persistent uproar in The Netherlands over the peculiar circumstances surrounding Operation North Pole. Although Major Hermann Giskes had promised the fifty-four Dutch-British agents he had seized that their lives would be spared if they "cooperated" in his *Englandspiel*, matters were taken out of his hands. Reichsfuehrer Heinrich Himmler's Gestapo shot forty-seven of the agents late in 1944 at Mauthausen concentration camp.[6]

In 1945 the Dutch Parliament formed a Commission of Enquiry headed by Dr. L. A. Donker, a judge. Donker requested the British government to allow SOE leaders to give testimony before his panel. Twice Donker's request was rejected, but in early 1948 two Foreign Office men were dispatched to The Hague. The confrontation turned into a series of strong accusations against the British—including one that there was a Nazi spy high up in the SOE. The Foreign Office officials heatedly denied all charges, and they were incensed over the suggestion that there had been a British traitor in The Firm.

Dr. Donker asked permission to conduct further probing in England, and approval was granted. Among the high SOE officials questioned was General Gubbins, who briefed the Dutch delegation on the inner workings of The Firm. But the records of the Dutch Section of SOE had been destroyed in a fire at the Baker Street headquarters in February 1946, Gubbins is said to have told Donker and his colleagues.[7] As time went by the investigation into North Pole drifted into misty oblivion.

Whatever may have been the true facts behind SOE operations in The Netherlands, there was nothing indefinite about the fate of Schwarze Kapelle leaders. In the wake of a July 20, 1944, bomb plot that had nearly succeeded in killing Adolf Hitler, a wave of executions decimated the conspiratorial group. Among those who were hanged by piano wires were Abwehr chief Wilhelm Canaris; his aide, Colonel Hans Oster; and Colonel Alexis Baron von Roenne, who had furnished the fuehrer grossly inflated figures on pre-D-day Allied strength in England.

What was the true role played by Admiral Canaris in the myriad plots and counterplots between the adversaries? After the war a colonel in the British secret service brushed off the Abwehr chief as "a lisping, traitorous queer." De Gaulle's espionage chief labeled Canaris a "trapeze artist," and SS Colonel Skorzeny excoriated Canaris for "traitorously betraying his country's military secrets to Britain."[8]

General Stewart Menzies, the British MI-6 chief, had a different point of view, calling the German "damned brave and damned unlucky."[9] The Abwehr spy master's widow, Erika, lived for many years in Spain in a villa reputedly provided by Francisco Franco. It was said that Frau Canaris was sustained by a pension supplied covertly by the U.S. Central Intelligence Agency.

Rudolf Hess, the Number 3 Nazi, who had parachuted into Scotland on a peace mission, was still a prisoner in late 1986. Now ninety-one years of age, Hess is the only inmate of Berlin's Spandau prison. Despite constant appeals by the United States and British governments for the elderly man's release, the Russians have insisted on keeping him behind bars.

Shortly before his death in 1965, Winston Churchill declared, "Reflecting upon the whole of this story, I am glad not to be responsible for the way in which Hess had been and is being treated. Whatever may be the moral guilt of a German who stood near to Hitler, Hess had atoned for this by his completely devoted and fanatic deed of lunatic benevolence."

Hardly had Europe's rubble settled and the stench of death evaporated than Churchill came under fire from some sources. His alleged role in the Dieppe raid and reputed involvement in the manipulation of secret agents and the European underground were challenged. But the British Bulldog, who had been a beacon of hope for England and the free world when there seemed to be no hope, weathered the storm. Among other achievements, he would always be remembered as the visionary who had conceived the massive campaign of fraud, deceit, and deception that had played a major role in the Allies' winning the war.

BIBLIOGRAPHY

Adams, Henry H. *Harry Hopkins*. New York: Putnam, 1977.
————. *Years of Deadly Peril*. New York: McKay, 1969.
Air Ministry, The. *By Air to Battle*. London: His Majesty's Stationery Office, 1945.
Alcorn, Robert H. *No Banners, No Bugles*. New York: McKay, 1965.
————. *No Bugles for Spies*. New York: McKay, 1962.
Ambrose, Stephen E. *The Supreme Commander*. New York: Doubleday, 1970.
Arct, Bohdan. *Poles Against the "V" Weapons*. Warsaw: Interpress, 1972.
Babington-Smith, Constance. *Air Spy*. New York: Harper, 1957.
Bank, Aaron. *From OSS to Green Berets*. Novato, CA: Presidio Press, 1986.
Barkus, Geoffrey. *The Camouflage Story*. London: Cassell, 1952.
Bauer, Eddy. *Encyclopedia of World War II*. New York: Cavendish, 1970.
Beesly, Patrick. *Very Special Intelligence*. Garden City, N.Y.: Doubleday, 1972.
Bekker, Cajus. *The Luftwaffe War Diaries*. New York: Doubleday, 1968.
Best, Steven P. *The Venlo Incident*. London: Hutchinson, 1950.
Braun, Wernher von. *History of Rocketry*. London: Nelson, 1966.
Brome, Vincent. *The Spy*. New York: Norton, 1957.
Brown, Anthony C. *Bodyguard of Lies*. New York: Harper & Row, 1975.
Buckmaster, Maurice. *They Fought Alone*. New York: Norton, 1958.
Bullock, Alan. *Hitler—A Study in Tyranny*. New York: Harper & Row, 1963.
Butcher, Harry C. *My Three Years with Eisenhower*. New York: Simon & Schuster, 1946.
Carse, Robert. *Dunkirk 1940*. Englewood Cliffs, N.J.: Prentice-Hall, 1970.
Cavendish, Marshall. *Illustrated History of World War II*. London: Cavendish, 1972.
Churchill, Winston S. *The Second World War*. 5 vols. Boston: Houghton Mifflin, 1948–1953.
Collier, Basil. *The Battle of Britain*. New York: Berkley, 1969.

————. *The Battle of the V-Weapons*. London: Hodder & Stoughton, 1964.

Collier, Richard. *Ten Thousand Eyes*. New York: Dutton, 1958.

Colvin, Ian. *Master Spy*. New York: McGraw-Hill, 1951.

Cookridge, E. H. *Inside SOE*. London: Barker, 1966.

Deacon, Richard. *History of the British Secret Service*. New York: Taplinger, 1969.

De Guingand, Francis W. *Operation Victory*. New York: Scribners, 1947.

Delmer, Sefton. *Black Boomerang*. New York: Viking, 1962.

————. *The Counterfeit Spy*. New York: Harper & Row, 1971.

Dewavrin, André. *Souvenirs*. Monte Carlo: Solar, 1947.

Divine, David. *Dunkirk*. New York: Dutton, 1948.

Dornberger, Gen. Walter. *V-2*. New York: Viking, 1958.

Dourlein, Peter. *Inside North Pole*. London: Kimber, 1953.

Dulles, Allen W. *The Craft of Intelligence*. New York: Harper & Row, 1963.

————. *Germany's Underground*. New York: Macmillan, 1947.

Ehrlich, Blake. *The Resistance: France*. Boston: Little, Brown, 1965.

Eisenhower, Dwight D. *Crusade in Europe*. New York: Doubleday, 1948.

Farago, Ladislas. *The Game of the Foxes*. New York: McKay, 1971.

Ferguson, Bernard. *The Watery Maze*. New York: Holt, Rinehart & Winston, 1961.

Fine, Lenore, and Remington, Jesse A. *The Corps of Engineers*. Washington, D.C.: Office of the Army Chief of Military History, 1972.

Fleming, Peter. *Invasion 1940*. New York: Simon & Schuster, 1957.

Foot, M. R. D. *SOE in France*. London: Her Majesty's Stationery Office, 1966.

Foote, Alexander (pseud.). *Handbook for Spies*. New York: Doubleday, 1949.

Ford, Corey. *Donovan of OSS*. Boston: Little, Brown, 1970.

Fuller, Jean O. *Double Webs*. New York: Putnam, 1958.

Gaevernitz, Gero V. *They Almost Killed Hitler*. New York: Macmillan, 1947.

Ganier-Raymond, Philippe. *The Tangled Web*. New York: Pantheon, 1968.

Garlinski, Jozef. *Hitler's Last Weapons*. New York: Times Books, 1978.

Gehlen, Reinhard. *The Service*. New York: World, 1972.

Gisevius, Hans B. *To the Bitter End*. Boston: Riverside Press, 1947.

Gulbenkian, Nubar. *Pantaraxia*. London: Hutchinson, 1965.

Hart, B. H. Lidell. *The German Generals Talk*. New York: Morrow, 1948.

Hitler, Adolf. *Hitler's Secret Conversations*. New York: Farrar, Straus & Young, 1953.

Hoettl, Wilhelm. *The Secret Front*. New York: Praeger, 1954.

Hogg, Ian V., and King, J. B. *German and Allied Secret Weapons*. New Jersey: Chartwell, 1976.

Hutton, J. Bernard. *Hess*. New York: Macmillan, 1970.

Infield, Glenn B. *Skorzeny*. New York: St. Martin's, 1981.

Ingersoll, Ralph. *Top Secret*. New York: Harcourt, Brace, 1946.

Irving, David. *The Mare's Nest*. London: Kimber, 1964.

Ismay, Lord Hastings. *Memoirs*. New York: Viking, 1960.

James, M. E. Clifton. *I Was Monty's Double*. New York: McGraw-Hill, 1954.

Jones, Reginald V. *The Wizard War*. New York: Coward, McCann & Geoghegan, 1978.

Kahn, David. *The Code-Breakers*. New York: Macmillan, 1978.

Ladd, James. *Commandos and Rangers*. New York: St. Martin's Press, 1978.

Leasor, James. *Green Beach*. New York: Morrow, 1975.

Lewin, Ronald. *Ultra Goes to War*. New York: McGraw-Hill, 1978.

Littlejohn, David. *The Patriotic Traitors*. Garden City, N.Y.: Doubleday, 1972.

Longmate, Norman. *If Britain Had Failed*. New York: Stein & Day, 1974.

Lovell, Stanley. *Of Spies and Stratagems*. New York: Prentice-Hall, 1962.

Martelli, George. *The Man Who Saved London*. New York: Doubleday, 1961.

Masterman, John C. *The Double-Cross System*. New Haven: Yale University Press, 1972.

McLachlan, Donald. *Room 39*. New York: Atheneum, 1963.

Millar, George. *The Bruneval Raid*. Garden City, N.Y.: Doubleday, 1975.

Montagu, Ewen. *The Man Who Never Was*. New York: Lippincott, 1954.

Moran, Lord. *Churchill: Taken from the Diaries of Lord Moran*. Boston: Houghton Mifflin, 1966.

Morgan, Frederick. *Overture to Overlord*. New York: Doubleday, 1950.

Morgan, William. *The OSS and I*. New York: Norton, 1957.

Mosley, Leonard. *The Cat and the Mouse*. New York: Harper & Row, 1959.

Neave, Airey. *Room 900*. Garden City, N.Y.: Doubleday, 1970.

Ordway, Frederick I., III, and Sharpe, Mitchell R. *The Rocket Team*. New York: Crowell, 1979.

Page, Bruce. *The Philby Conspiracy*. New York: Doubleday, 1969.

Patton, Gen. George S., Jr. *War As I Knew It*. Boston: Houghton Mifflin, 1947.

Pawle, Gerald. *The Secret War*. New York: Sloane, 1957.

Payne, Robert. *The Life and Death of Adolf Hitler*. New York: Popular Lib., 1974.

Perrault, Giles. *The Red Orchestra*. New York: Simon & Schuster, 1969.

Piekalkiewicz, Janusz. *Secret Agents, Spies, and Saboteurs*. New York: Morrow, 1973.

Pinto, Oreste. *Friend or Foe?* New York: Putnam, 1953.

Popov, Dusko. *Spy-Counterspy*. New York: Grosset & Dunlap, 1974.

Reader's Digest Association. *History of World War II*. Pleasantville, N.Y., 1969.

————. *Secrets and Spies*. Pleasantville, N.Y., 1964.

Reiss, Curt. *They Were There*. New York: Putnam, 1944.

Reit, Seymour. *Masquerade*. New York: Hawthorne, 1978.

Rémy, Colonel (Gilbert Renault). *Bruneval*. Paris: France-Empire, 1968.

Reynolds, Quentin. *The Man Who Wouldn't Talk*. New York: Random House, 1953.

————. *Raid at Dieppe*. New York: Random House, 1943.

Root, Waverly. *Secret History of the War*. New York: Scribners, 1946.

Rothfels, Hans. *The German Opposition to Hitler*. New York: Regnery, 1948.

Saunders, Hilary St. George. *Combined Operations*. New York: Macmillan, 1943.

————. *The Red Beret*. London: Joseph, 1950.

Schellenberg, Walter. *The Labyrinth*. New York: Harper, 1956.

Schlabrendorff, Fabian von. *The Secret War Against Hitler*. New York: Putnam, 1965.

Schwarzwalder, John. *We Caught Spies*. New York: Duell, Sloan & Pearce, 1946.

Shirer, William. *The Rise and Fall of the Third Reich*. New York: Simon & Schuster, 1981.

Smith, R. Harris. *OSS*. Berkeley: University of California Press, 1972.

Speer, Albert. *Inside the Third Reich*. New York: Macmillan, 1962.

Stanford, Alfred B. *Force Mulberry*. New York: Morrow, 1951.

Tickel, Jerrard. *Moon Squadron*. Garden City, N.Y.: Doubleday, 1958.

Trevor-Roper, Hugh R. *Blitzkrieg to Defeat*. New York: Rinehart & Winston, 1971.

Tully, Andrew. *The Inside Story*. New York: Morrow, 1962.

Warlimont, Walter. *Inside Hitler's Headquarters*. New York: Praeger, 1966.

Watson-Watt, Robert. *The Pulse of Radar*. New York: Dial, 1959.

Wheatley, Ronald. *Operation Sea Lion*. London: Cassell, 1958.

Wheeler-Bennett, John. *Nemesis of Power*. New York: Macmillan, 1964.

Whitehead, Don. *The FBI Story*. New York: Random House, 1956.

Whitehouse, Arch. *Espionage and Counterespionage*. Garden City, N.Y.: Doubleday, 1964.

Winterbotham, F. W. *The Ultra Secret*. New York: Harper & Row, 1974.

Young, Desmond. *The Desert Fox*. New York: Harper, 1950.

Zacharias, Ellis M. *Secret Missions*. New York: Putnam, 1946.

NOTES

Chapter 1: Operation Himmler
1. William L. Shirer, *Rise and Fall of the Third Reich*, p. 41.
2. John Wheeler-Bennett, *Nemesis of Power*, p. 446.
3. Alan Bullock, *Hitler: A Study in Tyranny*, p. 526.
4. Ibid., p. 527.
5. Reader's Digest Association, *History of World War II*, p. 66.
6. Ibid., p. 67.
7. Affidavit signed by Alfred Naujocks at Nuremberg, November 10, 1945.
8. Robert Payne, *The Life and Death of Adolf Hitler*, p. 365.

Chapter 2: Rounding Up the Spies
1. Wilhelm Hoettl, *The Secret Front*, p. 75.
2. After the war the ardent anti-Nazi German Pastor Martin Niemoeller declared that Hitler had cooked up the bomb plot to strengthen his own popularity. This was personal conjecture. The enigma of who was responsible for the bombing had never been untangled.
3. Henry Stevens and Payne Best spent five years in German concentration camps, but survived the war.

Chapter 3: A Ghost Army Arises
1. Allen W. Dulles, *Germany's Underground*, pp. 58–61.
2. Winston Churchill revealed in the House of Commons later in the month that the Allies had been taken by surprise.
3. Despite the British debacle in France, Lord Gort, commanding the B.E.F., was called to Buckingham Palace and decorated by King George.
4. Marshall Cavendish, *Pictorial History of World War II*, p. 316.
5. Robert Payne, *Hitler*, p. 394.
6. Ibid., p. 400.
7. Janusz Piekalkiewicz, *Secret Agents, Spies, and Saboteurs*, p. 27.
8. SS Colonel Six later "distinguished" himself in Russia, where he was active in Einsatzgruppen wholesale massacres of the population.
9. Anthony C. Brown, *Bodyguard of Lies*, p. 22. Alfred Dilwyn Knox,

one of the saviors of England, did not live to see the full exploitation of Ultra. He died at age sixty in 1943.

Chapter 4: Propaganda and Rumor
1. Documents of German Foreign Policy (DGFP) captured by Allies, pp. 550–51. Such an advertisement appeared in the *New York Times* on June 25, 1940.
2. Ibid., pp. 558–59.
3. William L. Shirer, *Third Reich*, p. 748.
4. Ladislas Farago, *The Game of the Foxes*, pp. 235–36.
5. Ibid., p. 236.
6. Wilhelm Hoettl, *The Secret Front*, p. 71.
7. Sefton Delmer, *Black Boomerang*, pp. 15–16.

Chapter 5: Sparring Across the Channel
1. Walter Schellenberg's memoirs, *The Labyrinth*, Chapter 2. Also in DGFP, Vol. X.
2. Ibid.
3. Ibid.
4. Alan Bullock, *Hitler*, pp. 543–44.
5. William Shirer, *Third Reich*, p. 684.
6. Robert Payne, *Hitler*, p. 401.
7. When the British underground was eventually dissolved, there were more than one thousand hidden bunkers scattered throughout the British Isles. On September 7, 1940, when a false alarm sounded that the invasion was taking place, much of the male population of Scotland disappeared underground for a week, leaving other civilians wondering what had become of them.

Chapter 6: Radar Duel of Wits
1. The term *radar* was coined by Americans. Germany and England had their own names for the device. For clarity's sake, the word *radar* is generally used in this story.
2. George Millar, *The Bruneval Raid*, p. 23.
3. The mystery man in the Oslo report will probably remain unidentified forever. Dr. Robert Cockburn, then chief of radar countermeasures of the Telecommunications Research Establishment, said years later: "It seemed quite possible that the report was [Admiral] Canaris's doings. But we never found out for sure." The distinguished British scientist, Reginald V. Jones, who examined the data in the Oslo parcel, said in 1978 that he believes he knows the identity of the mystery man, but that "revealing his name must wait until a later period."
4. Ronald Lewin, *Ultra Goes to War*, p. 76.
5. George Millar, *Bruneval*, p. 57.
6. Reginald V. Jones, *The Wizard War*, p. 101.
7. Ibid., p. 35.

Chapter 7: Decoys to Confound the Luftwaffe

1. George Millar, *Bruneval*, p. 46.
2. Seymour Reit, *Masquerade*, pp. 52–53.
3. German scientists were indeed working on an "air torpedo." It was later used with telling effect during the Allied invasion at Salerno, Italy, in September 1943. It became known as a glide bomb.
4. Ronald Wheatley, *Operation Sea Lion*, pp. 161–62.
5. Peter Fleming, *Invasion 1940*, p. 293.
6. Diary of General Franz Halder, German army chief of staff.
7. William L. Shirer, *Third Reich*, p. 771.
8. In a bizarre twist, Admiral Dowding was relieved of his post shortly after he had won the Battle of Britain. He was removed abruptly, partially because of the enormous strain he had been under constantly, but also because his tactics had been questioned by a subordinate, General Trafford Leigh-Mallory.

Chapter 8: Camouflage and Hoax

1. Ladislas Farago, *The Game of the Foxes*, p. 245.
2. Ibid., p. 259.
3. Long after the war a former MI-5 official hinted that The Countess had provided valuable information to the British, presumably on Abwehr matters, and was quietly released at the close of hostilities.
4. Reader's Digest Association, *Secrets and Spies*, p. 137.

Chapter 9: SOE and Double-X

1. By D day in Europe (June 6, 1944) the Moon Squadrons would make 2,562 sorties into enemy-held territory, flying in more than 1,000 agents and bringing out some 2,000 British spies, as well as delivering 40,000 containers of supplies to assorted underground groups.
2. Gerald Pawle, *The Secret War*, p. 103.
3. Ibid., pp. 102–12.
4. Dusko Popov, *Spy-Counterspy*, p. 66.
5. Ibid., p. 67.

Chapter 10: Measure and Countermeasure

1. Reginald V. Jones, *The Wizard War*, p. 125.
2. Ibid., p. 126.
3. George Millar, *The Bruneval Raid*, p. 70.
4. Dr. Cockburn, Professor Jones, and several key officials at Ultra all declared long after the war that it was not known in advance that Coventry was the target for certain, that it was only one of many possible targets.
5. The Luftwaffe's pathfinder technique was quickly adopted by the RAF and was later used by the U.S. bomber forces.
6. Details of Major Grant Taylor's one-man raid on the Far Shore were

told the author (at his request) by Maj. G. G. Norton (Ret.), World War II British paratroop officer and in 1986 curator at the Airborne Forces Museum at Aldershot, England. Also providing details were British Major K. H. M. O'Kelly (Ret.), who knew Grant Taylor well. Lieutenant Colonel Taylor died in 1957 at age fifty-seven from typhoid fever contracted in the Far East.

7. Gerald Pawle, *The Secret War*, pp. 188–89.
8. Sefton Delmer, *Black Boomerang*, p. 28.
9. Ibid., p. 29.
10. Even the existence of the London Controlling Section long remained a secret in London and in Washington. The LCS came to light only in 1975 when a memo referring to it was found by a historian in yellowed files in the National Archives.

Chapter 11: "Peace Proposal" Mission

1. Reader's Digest Association, *Secrets and Spies*, p. 146.
2. Rudolf Hess demanded to be returned to Germany, claiming his role was that of a peace emissary. But the British government kept him under house arrest until the end of the war. He was convicted of vague crimes at the Nuremberg trials and sentenced to life imprisonment. In 1986 he was still in Spandau Prison in Berlin, the only living top Nazi.
3. Alan Bullock, *Hitler*, p. 593.
4. Robert Payne, *Hitler*, p. 428.
5. J. Bernard Hutton, *Hess*, p. 107. (Arguments have continued for forty-five years as to whether Rudolf Hess was and is insane.)
6. Sefton Delmer, *Black Boomerang*, p. 41.

Chapter 12: Underground Escape Lines

1. Later Churchill remarked, "Stalin and his commissars showed themselves at this moment the most completely outwitted bunglers of the Second World War."
2. Winston S. Churchill, *The Second World War*, Vol. 3, p. 331.
3. Ibid., p. 1,392.
4. After the war, Alfred Owens (Snow/Johnny) was released quietly by the British and vanished.
5. Jerrard Tickel, *Moon Squadron*, p. 45.
6. Nebur Gulbenkian, *Pantaraxia*, pp. 97–99.
7. Ibid., p. 105.
8. Ian Garrow survived the war and was decorated for his work in establishing escape routes.

Chapter 13: Escape of German Warships

1. Indeed Gilbert Renault's (Rémy's) family did suffer. His mother and three sisters spent a long period in prison, and two other sisters were sent to a German concentration camp at Ravensbrük. His brother

Philippe was also deported to Germany and was killed at Lübeck only hours before the British army arrived there in 1945.

2. Patrick Beesly, *Very Special Intelligence*, p. 124.
3. Cavendish, *History of World War II*, Vol. 6, p. 833.
4. Ibid.
5. Ibid.
6. Janusz Piekalkiewicz, *Secret Agents, Spies, and Saboteurs*, p. 83.
7. In the fall of 1942, Squadron Leader Tony Hill was killed on a mission over German-held France.

Chapter 14: Raid to Steal a Würzburg
1. Janusz Piekalkiewicz, *Secret Agents, Spies, and Saboteurs*, p. 85.
2. George Millar, *The Bruneval Raid*, p. 80.
3. Roger Dumont (Pol) took one too many chances. He was captured and executed by the Gestapo in 1943.
4. James Ladd, *Commandos and Rangers*, p. 40.
5. Two years later Wing Commander Charles Pickard, who had been highly decorated, was killed over Amiens, France.
6. Hilary St. George Saunders, *The Red Beret*, p. 63.
7. Ibid., p. 64.
8. Sergeant Major G. Strachan made a near-miraculous recovery and went back on duty a few weeks later.
9. Major John Frost would become world renowned as the officer who led the gallant Red Devil parachute battalion that was surrounded at the Arnhem Bridge in Holland in September 1944.
10. Curiously, perhaps, decorations were sparse for those in the Bruneval raid. Major Frost and Lieutenant Charteris received the Military Cross, Flight-Sergeant Cox the lesser Military Medal, and several others relatively minor awards.
11. The author is indebted to Major General John D. Frost (Ret.) for furnishing many of the details in the raid he led at Bruneval.

Chapter 15: Hitler's Eavesdroppers
1. In his postmortem, SS Brigadefuehrer Walter Schellenberg declared that the transatlantic cable tapping yielded precious data about Allied armament production and military plans and produced valuable information to U-boats for attacks on shipping.
2. Ladislas Farago, *The Game of the Foxes*, p. 588.
3. *Time* magazine, April 6, 1942, p. 32.
4. Jerrard Tickel, *Moon Squadron*, p. 121.
5. Ibid., p. 122.

Chapter 16: Trojan Horse of Saint-Nazaire
1. Janusz Piekalkiewicz, *Secret Agents, Spies, and Saboteurs*, p. 107.
2. Ibid., p. 108.
3. Hilary St. George Saunders, *Combined Operations*, p. 94.

4. Janusz Piekalkiewicz, *Secret Agents, Spies, and Saboteurs*, p. 112.
5. Hilary St. George Saunders, *Combined Operations*, p. 98.
6. Ibid., p. 99.

Chapter 17: *Englandspiel*
1. Dutch Army Lieutenant Teller was sent to a concentration camp in Germany and later executed.
2. Reader's Digest Association, *Secrets and Spies*, p. 208.
3. Janusz Piekalkiewicz, *Secret Agents, Spies, and Saboteurs*, p. 282.
4. Philippe Ganier-Raymond, *The Tangled Web*, p. 72.
5. Janusz Piekalkiewicz, *Secret Agents, Spies, and Saboteurs*, p. 187.
6. Abwehr Major Hermann Giskes was never decorated for his feat of wiping out the Dutch spy network. His immediate superior, a Colonel Harter, who knew nothing of North Pole for more than a year, had written directly to Heinrich Himmler and taken credit for the counter-espionage operation.

Chapter 18: French Underground
1. Anthony C. Brown, *Bodyguard of Lies*, p. 95.
2. Ibid., p. 94.

Chapter 19: Dieppe: Sacrificial Ploy?
1. Copies of these intercepted conversations were found in Heinrich Himmler's files long after the war.
2. No recorded proof has been found that Churchill knew that the Dieppe raid would result in disaster.
3. Anthony C. Brown, *Bodyguard of Lies*, p. 90.
4. James Leasor, *Green Beach* (James Leasor's postwar interview of Colonel Merritt), p. 39.
5. Two years later this German 302d Division would drive the Americans almost into the sea at Omaha Beach in Normandy, on June 6, 1944.
6. In his memoirs Winston Churchill said that "from available intelligence, Dieppe was held only by low-category troops . . . 1,400 men in all."
7. After the war Jack Nissenthall shortened his name to Nissen. In 1986 he was living in Toronto, Canada. The author is indebted to him for furnishing many details on his role at Dieppe.
8. Files of Canadian General Staff Historical Section, Ottawa.
9. Winston S. Churchill, *The Second World War*, Vol. 4, p. 467.
10. Lord Moran, *Churchill: Taken from the Diaries of Lord Moran*, p. 73.
11. Anthony C. Brown, *Bodyguard of Lies*, p. 90.

Chapter 20: Atlantic Wall
1. Quentin Reynolds, *The Man Who Wouldn't Talk*, p. 57.
2. Ibid., p. 59.
3. James Ladd, *Commandos and Rangers*, p. 55.

4. Anthony C. Brown, *Bodyguard of Lies*, pp. 258–59.
5. It was said after the war that Captain Herbert Wichmann, the Abwehr station chief at Hamburg, had obtained from a high-grade source information that North Africa was the Allied target. Apparently his urgent report was brushed aside by the German high command.

Chapter 21: Spies and Spy Masters
1. Ladislas Farago, *The Game of the Foxes*, p. 282.
2. Ibid., p. 283.
3. Eddie Chapman (Zigzag) was sent back to England by the Germans in June 1944, just after the Allied invasion. But he became suspect, and the XX-Committee jailed him for the rest of the war.
4. Airey Neave, *Room 900*, p. 152.
5. Teenager Elsie Maréchal and her parents survived the war and were decorated by the Belgian government.
6. R. Harris Smith, *OSS*, p. 165.
7. David K. E. Bruce later became ambassador to Great Britain, France, Germany, and China.
8. Before the year (1943) ended, Jean Moulin, one of the more daring and effective underground organizers, was caught and executed by the Gestapo.

Chapter 22: Operation Bernhard
1. Reader's Digest Association, *Secrets and Spies*, pp. 507–509. In the postwar chaos Major Bernhard Krüger vanished.
2. The parents of "Major Martin" approved the use of their son's body for an unspecified "patriotic purpose."
3. Lieutenant General James M. Gavin (Ret.) told the author in 1985 that it was two decades before he learned that the high command had withheld crucial intelligence in order to protect the secret of Ultra.
4. Gen. Walter Dornberger, *V-2*, p. 131.
5. Albert Speer, *Inside the Third Reich*, p. 368.
6. David Irving, *The Mare's Nest*, p. 117.

Chapter 23: Battles on the Airwaves
1. Anthony C. Brown, *Bodyguard of Lies*, pp. 352–57.
2. Ibid.
3. B. H. Lidell-Hart, *The German Generals Talk*, p. 231.
4. George Martelli, *The Man Who Saved London*, p. 214.
5. In his memoirs General Eisenhower gave credit to the European underground for playing a major role in limiting the carnage inflicted by the V-1 and V-2 weapons. Instead of the 50,000 buzzbombs that were to plaster England, "only" 10,611 landed.
6. Author interviews with Kenneth R. Shaker, Stanley Gerk, and Dolphus "Doc" Walker, who participated in the raid.
7. Reader's Digest Association, *Secrets and Spies*, pp. 392–93.

Chapter 24: Invasion Deceptions

1. B. H. Lidell-Hart, *The German Generals Talk*, p. 233.
2. Lieutenant General James M. Gavin (Ret.) to author.
3. Anthony C. Brown, *Bodyguard of Lies*, pp. 558–59.
4. Ibid., p. 560.
5. Before his death in 1984, General Mark Clark told the author that he had been aware of the Gestapo "hit squad" that was out to murder him, but, he added, "I was so busy trying to keep us from getting kicked off the Anzio beachhead that I had no time to dwell on who may have been trying to personally do me in."

Chapter 25: Buzzbombs

1. Aaron Bank, *From OSS to Green Berets*.
2. Dwight D. Eisenhower, *Crusade in Europe*, p. 302.

Chapter 26: Specter of the V-2

1. Jozef Garlinski, *Hitler's Last Weapons*, p. 156. Also Arct, *Poles Against the "V" Weapons*.
2. Jozef Garlinksi, *Hitler's Last Weapons*, p. 173. Also background from Dornberger, *V-2*.
3. After the war General Eisenhower wrote: "Had the pious, teetotaling Monty staggered into SHAEF with a hangover," he could not have been more astonished than he was by the boldness of the field marshal's Operation Market-Garden plan.
4. Marshall Cavendish, *Encyclopedia of World War II*, p. 1973. In late 1986 Major General John D. Frost (Ret.) was hale and hearty and living the good life of a gentleman farmer.

Chapter 27: Cowboys and Choirboys

1. Allen Dulles later became director of the CIA, successor to the OSS. Kolbe escaped from Germany to Switzerland early in 1945 and survived the war.
2. From *Official History of the Office of Strategic Services*.
3. The Natter manned rocket may have been the forerunner of the manned space flights by Russia and the United States beginning some fifteen years later.

Chapter 28: "The Most Dangerous Man in Europe"

1. Allied monitors had recorded the German order to form the English-speaking unit, but in the heady optimism of the day, the revelation had gotten pigeonholed.
2. There was no evidence that any Skorzeny people had killed themselves by taking the cyanide capsules.
3. Frozen, hungry, thirsty, in pain from a broken arm, dispirited, Baron von der Heydte stumbled into a Belgian village and gave himself up to the Americans.

4. Altogether eighteen Skorzeny people were captured; eighteen were court-martialed and shot.

Epilogue

1. An American historian, Glenn Infield, told of the German "Kamikaze plan" in his book *Skorzeny*. He had learned details in an interview with a woman test pilot, Hanna Reitsch.

2. Some one thousand V-2 missiles had struck England, killing 8,588 people and injuring 46,836 others.

3. Josef Garlinski, *Hitler's Last Weapons*, pp. 187–89.

4. Frederick I. Ordway III and Mitchell R. Sharpe, *The Rocket Team*, p. 114.

5. M.R.D. Foot, *SOE in France*, p. 442.

6. In his memoirs Abwehr Major Hermann Giskes wrote: "Their [the forty-seven Allied spies] liquidation was one of the many crimes typical of [Reich Fuehrer Heinrich] Himmler's system which cannot be justified by any necessities of war. I can remember [their deaths] only with shame and bitterness."

7. Philippe Ganier-Raymond, *The Tangled Web*, pp. 187–88.

8. John Wheeler-Bennett, *Nemesis of Power*, p. 589.

9. Anthony C. Brown, *Bodyguard of Lies*, p. 157.

Index